Contents

LIBRARIES NI
WITHDRAWN FROM STOCK

D1388481

How to use this book

This book covers the content requirements of the Edexcel GCSE Religious Studies in Religion and Life Based on a Study of Roman Catholic Christianity (Unit 3) and Religion and Society Based on a Study of Christianity and at Least One Other Religion (Unit 8) and the provisions of the RE Curriculum Directory for Catholic Schools (2012).

Each section of the book is one of the four sections of the units in the GCSE specification (3.1, 3.2, 3.3, 3.4 and 8.1, 8.2, 8.3, 8.4), and every sub-topic within the sections of the specification (11 for each section) is covered as a separate topic in the book. The main body of the text gives you all the information you need for each topic. The sources in the margin give you extra information for greater understanding of the topic.

For Unit 3 you only need to study Catholic Christianity, but for Unit 8 you will have to study another religion as well as Christianity. This book covers Islam, Judaism, Hinduism and Sikhism. Your teacher will no doubt decide which of these you will study.

In each examination (one for Unit 3 and one for Unit 8), you will have to answer four questions: one question on Section 1, one question on Section 2, one question on Section 3 and one question on Section 4. Each question is divided into sub-questions: a) for 2 marks, b) for 4 marks, c) for 8 marks and d) for 6 marks. Examples of b), c) and d) sub-questions are given for each topic, and an exam tip is given on how to answer one of them to give you hints as to the approach which will gain you full marks. The other questions are to help you see what other types of question can be asked on the topic.

Before you begin Unit 3, you should work through the Introduction to Unit 3 to help you to understand the relationship between the Catholic Church and the other Christian Churches.

Before you begin Unit 8, you should work through the Introduction to Unit 8 for your chosen religion to help you understand how it approaches issues.

For each Unit you should work through each topic. Words that you might not understand are in bold type so that you can look up their meanings in the glossary at the end of the book.

Quotations from the Catechism of the Catholic Church are identified by their paragraph numbers in the Eighth Edition. Scriptures quoted are from the New International Version.

Introduction

Before starting the course, it may be useful to have an overview of the non-Catholic Christian Churches and the four non-Christian religions featured in this book.

The key features of non-Catholic Churches

The Orthodox Churches

These are national Churches led by a chief bishop called a Patriarch. Most of them are based in Eastern Europe (Greece, Russia, Romania, Serbia). They have **priests** who may marry, but their bishops must be celibate. Their worship is very elaborate and they revere icons and use incense.

The Church of England

This is the established Church in England. The Queen is the head of the Church and appoints **bishops**. The Church of England has branches in all the English-speaking parts of the world. These Churches are known as either **Anglican** or Episcopalian. Some are very Protestant and are called Low Church; others are very **Catholic** and are called High Church.

Nonconformist Churches

These are Protestant Churches which thought the Church of England was not Protestant enough. Instead of bishops or priests, they have ministers who are regarded as no different from lay people. They are governed by democratically elected bodies and their services are Bible-based rather than communion-based. The main **Nonconformist Churches** are the Methodist, the United Reformed (URC), the Baptist, the Society of Friends (Quakers), **Pentecostals** and a variety of Black Churches.

How Christians make moral decisions

All Christians believe that moral decisions should be based on the teachings of Jesus in the **New Testament** and the Ten Commandments in the **Old Testament**.

▶ Roman Catholics believe that these teachings are best interpreted by the Church, especially the head of the Church, the **Pope**, and the bishops. Therefore, to guide and direct their moral decisions, they refer to the teachings of the Church contained in the *Catechism of the Catholic Church* (1999) or the teachings of the Pope together with the bishops in the Encyclical letters. They would also ask their local priest.

▶ Orthodox Christians would base their decisions on how the Bible has been interpreted by councils of bishops, or simply ask advice from their priest.

▶ **Protestants** believe that each individual should make their own decisions on the basis of what the Bible says, but most would also be guided by decisions made by democratically elected bodies of Church leaders (for example, the General Synod of the Church of England or the Conference of the Methodist Church).

Islam

Islam was founded by Muhammad (570CE–632CE). He was born in Makkah, Arabia, into the Arab religion of Makkah (though he had a lot of contact with Jews and Christians). Muhammad claimed that, although Judaism and Christianity had had the truth, their ideas had become confused.

Islam is the majority religion in North Africa, all of the Middle East (except Israel), Indonesia, Bangladesh, Pakistan, Malaysia, Turkey, Kazakhstan, Azerbaijan Turkmenistan, Uzbekistan, Kyrgyzstan, Tajikistan, Brunei and Albania.

Basic Muslim beliefs

- The word 'Islam' means giving yourself to God and a Muslim is one who has submitted to God.
- There is only one God ('Allah' is the Arabic word for 'God').
- Islam is the first religion which God gave to Adam and renewed with the later prophets. Jesus (Isa in Arabic) was a prophet, not God's son.
- Muhammad was God's last prophet who was given God's actual words in the **Qur'an**. As the final prophet, Muhammad was the last and perfect example for people to follow.
- There will be a **Last Day** when the dead will be raised and everyone will have a final judgement from God when the good will go to heaven and the bad to hell.
- The way to heaven is to follow God's laws and the five pillars (witness, prayer, fasting, charity, pilgrimage) all of which are based on the Qur'an.

How Muslims make moral decisions

- To make moral decisions, Muslims follow the holy law of Islam called the **Shari'ah**. They often need the advice of a Muslim lawyer to understand this.
- Everything a Muslim is allowed to do is called 'halal'. Everything they are banned from doing is called 'haram'.

Judaism

Judaism was founded by Abraham in Israel around 2000BCE. There are substantial numbers of Jews in some cities of the USA and Europe, but the only country in which it is the majority religion is Israel.

Basic Jewish beliefs

- There is only one God who created the universe and all that is in it.
- God made special agreements (**covenants**) with the Jewish people through the prophets Abraham and Moses.
- The covenant means that the Jews are the people of God, called to bear witness to God by following the Law they were given by God through Moses. This law is the **Torah**.
- The Torah is the first part of the Jewish holy book, the **Tenakh** (which is the Old Testament of the Christian Bible).

- Some Jews believe that if a person loves and obeys God, their soul will go straight to heaven when they die. Other people believe that God will send his Messiah to end evil in the world. When he comes, anyone who has loved and obeyed God whilst they were alive will be resurrected and live in heaven.

How Jews make moral decisions

- Jews base their moral decisions on God's commands in the Torah which they call **mitzvot**.
- The **Talmud** and the **Responsa** are records of explanations of the mitzvot by rabbis which help in making decisions.

Hinduism

Hinduism began with various **swamis** and **gurus** in India around 3000BCE. It is the majority religion in India and Nepal.

Basic Hindu beliefs

- There are different Hindu beliefs about God. Many Hindus believe that Brahman is the creative force behind the universe and is part of the universe. People have come from Brahman and a part of Brahman is in each person. Other Hindus believe in many forms of Brahman, such as Vishnu and Shiva, who have come to Earth as **avatars**, such as Krishna.
- Hindus believe in reincarnation: life is a process of being born, living, dying and being reborn (**samsara**).
- The purpose of life is to live such a good life that your soul is not reborn but joins with Brahman.
- Escape from rebirth is called **moksha** and life after moksha is **nirvana**.
- There are different ideas about how to achieve moksha, some think it is by doing your duty as a Hindu (**dharma**) others that it is through meditation and yoga.
- The Hindu holy books are the **Vedas**, the Upanishads and the Bhagavad Gita.

How Hindus make moral decisions

- Hindus look at the Hindu dharma as shown in the **Laws of Manu**.
- Many Hindus would seek advice from a holy person (swami or guru) or a Brahmin priest.

Sikhism

Sikhism was founded by Guru Nanak in the Punjab area of North India in about 1500CE. It developed from Hinduism and Islam. There are substantial numbers of Sikhs in some cities of the UK, the USA, Canada, Australia and New Zealand, but it is only the majority religion in the Punjab area of India.

Basic Sikh beliefs

- There is only one God (Waheguru).
- God can be found by anyone anywhere, and there is no need for pilgrimage.

- Sikhs believe in reincarnation: life is a process of being born, living dying and being reborn (samsara).
- The purpose of life is to move from being human centred (**manmukh**) to being God centred (**gurmukh**), allowing you to escape from rebirth (**mukti**).
- If people live the Sikh way as shown by the Ten **Gurus** (from Guru Nanak to Guru Gobind Singh) they will not be reborn.
- The way to achieve mukti is to meditate upon the One and to serve other people (Sikhs believe this is shown in their holy book the **Guru Granth Sahib**).
- Many Sikhs believe that they must join the **khalsa** to reach heaven.
- Sikhs who join the khalsa follow what are known as the Five Ks – Kesh (uncut hair hence wearing a turban), kangha (comb to keep hair under control), kara (steel bangle), kirpan (symbolic sword), kachera (under-shorts symbolising good living).

How Sikhs make moral decisions

- Sikhs use the **Rahit Maryada**, a book of rules for Sikhs.
- Sikhs follow guidance given by the Akal Takht at the Golden Temple in Amritsar.

Section 3.1

Believing in God

Introduction

This section of the examination specification requires you to look at the issues surrounding belief in God.

Reasons why some people believe in God

You will need to understand the effects of, and give reasons for your own opinion about:

- the main features of a Catholic upbringing
- religious experience
- the argument from design
- the argument from causation.

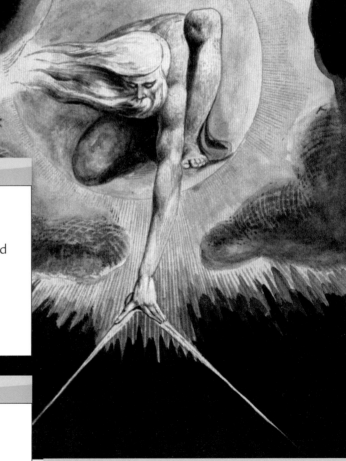

Reasons why some people do not believe in God

You will need to understand the effects of, and give reasons for your own opinion about:

- scientific explanations of the origins of the world
- unanswered prayers
- evil and suffering.

How Catholics respond to the reasons why some people do not believe in God

You will need to understand the effects of, and give reasons for your own opinion about how Catholics respond to:

- scientific explanations of the world
- the problem of unanswered prayers
- the problem of evil and suffering.

The media and belief in God

You will need to understand the effects of, and give reasons for your own opinion about how two television or radio programmes about religion may affect attitudes to belief in God.

Topic 3.1.1 The main features of a Catholic upbringing and how it may lead to belief in God

> The ceremony of baptism assumes ... that you will bring your child up in the practice of the faith. This means:
>
> you teach your child to pray
>
> you teach your child to live a good Christian life
>
> you come to Mass on Sundays
>
> you teach your child the Catholic faith.
>
> *Guidance for parents on Catholic baptism*

There are many reasons for believing in God. Some people are led to believe in God by one reason only, others find that a number of reasons taken together make it difficult not to believe in God. The next four topics investigate the following reasons for believing in God:

▶ Religious upbringing
▶ **Religious experience**
▶ The argument from design
▶ The argument from causation.

The main features of a Catholic upbringing

Children of Catholic parents will often be baptised when they are babies or young children. **Baptism** is the 'basis of the whole Christian life ... the door which gives access to the other **sacraments**' (**Catechism** 1213). As part of this sacrament, the parents will promise to bring up their children as Catholics and provide them with a Christian home of love and faithfulness. To bring their children up as Catholics, the parents are likely to:

▶ teach their children prayers
▶ teach their children about Jesus, the saints and the Church
▶ take their children to church – in many **parishes** the children would go to the **children's liturgy** during Sunday **Mass** and on other special days where worship would be child friendly and help them to understand about God
▶ send their children to a Catholic school where the National Curriculum and RE are taught in a Catholic Christian environment.

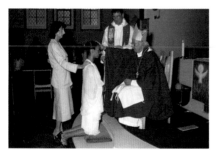

A bishop laying on hands at a Catholic confirmation ceremony. Why might being confirmed lead to, or support, belief in God?

As part of fulfilling their **vows** at baptism, Catholic parents will encourage their children to make their first **confession** and Holy Communion and later be confirmed as full members of the Church. During the liturgies of these sacraments children may feel the presence of God.

How a Catholic upbringing may lead to, or support, belief in God

A Catholic religious upbringing helps make belief in God seem natural because:

▶ A child's parents will have told them about God as part of their promises to bring them up as a Catholic and young children believe what their parents tell them.

> I am a Catholic Christian because I was born to Catholic parents, and I was educated in a Catholic school. All my upbringing made me believe in God, and I have never really thought that God might not exist. God is a part of my life just as my parents and friends are.

- Catholic parents teach their children how to pray to God and about the lives of Jesus' **disciples** and other saints of the Church. This shows that prayer is a natural and important part of their lives and encourages children to believe in God.
- Going to church and seeing so many people praying to and worshipping God is likely to make children think that God must exist.
- Going to children's liturgy would support belief in God because children would learn why Catholics believe in God and what they believe about him.
- Going to a Catholic school would have a similar effect, as God and Christianity would be a normal feature of school life. The school children have RE lessons which teach them that God exists and the children are likely to believe it because their teachers tell them it is true.
- Being confirmed would be likely to support their belief, as they learn more about God in the **confirmation** lessons, and possibly have a religious experience when the bishop lays his hands on them.

Why might attending a Catholic school lead to, or support, belief in God?

Questions

b) Do you think children should follow the same religion as their parents? Give two reasons for your point of view. **(4)**

c) Explain how a Catholic upbringing can lead to, or support, belief in God. **(8)**

d) 'A Catholic upbringing leads children to believe in God.'

    (i) Do you agree? Give reasons for your opinion. **(3)**

    (ii) Give reasons why some people may disagree with you. **(3)**

Exam Tip

c) 'Explain how' means give ways. One way to answer this question would be to name four features of a Catholic upbringing and explain, in two or three sentences for each, how they might lead to belief in God. Remember you have four marks for spelling, punctuation and grammar in this section so try to use some specialist vocabulary such as baptism, sacrament, prayer, worship, confirmation, priest, bishop.

Exam Focus

Spelling, punctuation and grammar

Up to four marks will be awarded for your spelling, punctuation and grammar in your answer to Section 1 of both exam papers. This means you should take extra care with your spelling and make sure you use full stops and capital letters. You should use a wide range of specialist vocabulary, but don't let your use of specialist words confuse the meaning of your answer.

Summary

Having a Catholic upbringing is likely to lead to belief in God because children are taught that God exists and they spend most of their time with people who believe that God exists.

Topic 3.1.2 How religious experience may lead to belief in God

KEY WORDS

Conversion – when your life is changed by giving yourself to God

Miracle – something which seems to break a law of science and makes you think only God could have done it

Numinous – the feeling of the presence of something greater than you

Prayer – an attempt to contact God, usually through words

Religious experience is an event that people feel gives them direct contact with God. You need to know four types of religious experience: numinous, conversion, miracle and prayer.

1. The numinous and belief in God

The numinous is a feeling of the presence of God. When people are in a religious building, in a beautiful place or looking up at the stars on a clear night, they may be filled with the awareness that there is something greater than them, which they feel to be God. It is often described as an experience of the transcendent (something going beyond human experience and existing outside the material world).

If someone has a numinous experience, it may lead them to believe in God because the experience will make them feel that God is real. If you become aware of a presence greater than you, you are likely to believe that that presence is God and so you will believe in him.

Example of the numinous

Father Yves Dubois has had numinous experiences while praying before a statue of Our Lady.

'Twice I have experienced the certainty of the presence of the Mother of God, which was an awareness of purity, holiness and love unlike anything I have ever known. Her holiness would have been frightening, but for the strong feeling of love and compassion.'

Source: Quoted in Christians in Britain Today, *Hodder, 1991*

Do you think Father Yves Dubois could doubt the existence of God after these numinous experiences?

---

2. Conversion and belief in God

Conversion is the word used to describe an experience of God, which is so great that the person experiencing it wants to change their life and commit themselves to God in a special way. It can also be used to describe an experience, which causes someone to change their religion or change from agnosticism or atheism to belief in God. It is sometimes called a regenerative experience because it gives a feeling of being '**born again**'. If someone has a conversion experience, that will lead them to believe in God because they will feel that God is calling them to do something for him. When **St Paul** was on the road to Damascus (Acts 9:1–19) and Jesus spoke to him from a bright light in the sky, telling him to become a Christian, the experience was so powerful that Paul decided to convert to Christianity.

Example of a conversion

During the Civil War in the Lebanon, Raymond Nader was a commander in the Christian militia who led the fighting against Muslim militias. On a cold November night in 1994, he went to pray at the shrine of St Charbel. Suddenly the night got warmer and he felt surrounded by a great light. He reached out to touch the light and his arm was burned by what he, and the Church authorities, believed was the presence of St Charbel. The vision made him give up his work in the militia to work for Tele Lumiere, the only Christian television station in the Middle East. Tele Lumiere and Nader are dedicated to spiritual peace, the defence of human rights and dignity as a way of challenging the violence and horror of the Middle East.

Do you think that Raymond Nader would have been able to be an atheist after this conversion experience?

3. Miracles and belief in God

A miracle is an event which seems to break a law of science and the only explanation for which seems to be God. Miracles are recorded in most religions and usually involve a religious experience.

Example of a miracle

On Thursday 11 February 1858, fourteen-year-old Bernadette Soubirous saw a beautiful young girl in a niche at a rocky outcrop called Massabielle near Lourdes. The apparition beckoned to her, but Bernadette did not move and the girl smiled at her before disappearing. Bernadette later described how she had seen a young girl of about her own age and height, clothed in a brilliant and unearthly white robe, with a blue girdle round her waist and a white veil on her head. This was the beginning of eighteen apparitions during the spring and early summer of 1858. During one of these, Bernadette asked the lady her name and she said, 'I am the **Immaculate Conception**.' During another, the lady led Bernadette to a grotto where a miraculous spring appeared. Since these miraculous appearances of the Virgin Mary, Lourdes has become a great place of pilgrimage for Catholics and many healing miracles have taken place there which have been verified by an independent bureau of scientists and doctors. Many people say that while not all people who go to Lourdes are cured through their religious experience, they receive great inner strength to cope with their illnesses and other problems of life.

'The Blinding of St Paul' by Augustin Cranach in 1586, shows St Paul on the Road to Damascus. Saul was a persecutor of Christians and was on his way to Damascus to arrest the Christians there, when he had a vision of Jesus which blinded him. After this conversion experience, his sight recovered and he became a great Christian missionary and changed his name to Paul.

The shrine at Lourdes.

Miracles can lead to belief in God because, if a miracle has really happened, it means that God has acted on the Earth and that the people witnessing it have had direct contact with God. If an atheist or agnostic witnesses a miracle, their first reaction will be to look for a natural explanation. However, if they cannot find one, it might lead them to believe in God.

Miracles are a major part of Catholic belief. The process of declaring someone a new saint (canonisation) depends on being able to establish two miracles connected with the proposed saint. In the Bible, miracles are linked to people's faith and help faith to grow.

4. Prayer

All Catholics believe they can communicate with God through prayer. The Catechism teaches that human beings are born searching for God and that prayer is a way to complete the search. Prayer is the way to encounter God; it is a gift from God because God is waiting to hear human prayers. Although people may not always know how to pray properly, the Church teaches that if prayers come from the heart they are acceptable to God and allow communion with God. The importance of prayer for Catholics can be seen in the fact that one quarter of the Catechism is about Christian prayer.

There are many different types of prayer, from the formal prayers offered in worship, such as the prayers said during Mass, to the very informal prayers where a believer makes their own prayer to God in their own private place or as they go about their daily activities.

How religious prayer may lead to belief in God

If the person praying to God feels that God is listening to the prayer, then they have a religious experience through prayer and are sure that God exists. Perhaps the biggest religious experience anyone can have is when their private prayer is answered, for example, when someone prays for a sick loved one to recover and they do. During prayer, a person may experience a sense of joy and peace, the closeness of God, or not feel anything in particular. The desire to pray is in itself a religious experience. Christians believe no prayer is ever wasted, though prayer is answered in God's time and on God's terms. As Jesus prayed 'thy will be done'.

> 'If you knew the gift of God!' The wonder of prayer is revealed beside the well where we come seeking water: there, **Christ** comes to meet every human being. It is he who first seeks us and asks us for a drink. Jesus thirsts; his asking arises from the depths of God's desire for us. Whether we realise it or not, prayer is the encounter of God's thirst with ours. God thirsts that we may thirst for him.
>
> *Catechism of the Catholic Church 2560*

> In the New Covenant, prayer is the living relationship of the children of God with their Father who is good beyond measure, with His Son Jesus Christ and with the **Holy Spirit**;... Thus the life of prayer is the habit of being in the presence of the thrice-holy God and in communion with him.
>
> *Catechism of the Catholic Church 2565*

Example of prayer leading to belief

... I began to pray for my children's safety, and this became a habit which I have never lost, and often the answer to such prayer is spectacular. I find it best to live as if the soul of man were in communion with a superhuman force which makes for righteousness. May I add that since this belief grew in me, I feel that I had grown, as if my mind had stretched to take in the vast universe and be part of it.

Source: Alister Hardy Trust, Oxford

Any religious believer who has any form of religious experience will find that the experience supports their belief in God and makes it stronger because they now have more direct evidence for God's existence.

Remember that NOT getting what you want is sometimes a wonderful stroke of luck.

What do you think the Dalai Lama meant when he said this?

Why do you think children are taught to pray in all religions?

Questions

b) Do you think miracles prove that God exists? Give two reasons for your point of view. **(4)**

c) Explain how religious experience can lead to, or support, belief in God. **(8)**

d) 'Religious experiences prove that God exists.'
   (i) Do you agree? Give reasons for your opinion. **(3)**
   (ii) Give reasons why some people may disagree with you. **(3)**

Exam Tip

b) You should already have thought about this, and you just have to give two reasons for your opinion. For example, if you think miracles prove God's existence, you could use these two reasons:
   - if a miracle happens there is no explanation for it except that God caused it to happen
   - Christians believe that Jesus rising from the dead proves he was God's Son because only God could rise from the dead.

Exam focus

What do you think?

In these questions (part b) in the examination) you must decide what you think about the issues and ideas you study. For this topic you need to think about whether:

- there is such a thing as the numinous and whether it means God exists
- conversions really happen and whether they prove God exists
- you believe in miracles and whether a miracle would prove that God exists
- prayer is valuable.

The questions are meant to be quite easy and to get full marks you just need to give two reasons.

Summary

People experience God in the numinous, conversion, miracles and answered prayers. Religious experience makes people feel that God is real.

Topic 3.1.3 The argument from design and belief in God

Could this car have been made without a design?

What is design?

Any complex mechanism is designed for a purpose. Design involves things working together according to a plan to produce something that was intended. If you look at a car you can see that the fuel powers an engine which turns a shaft which turns the wheels and so makes a self-propelled vehicle to allow people to travel further and more easily. A look at any part of the car makes you think that the car has been designed.

Evidence of design in the world

Laws of science

A main reason why some people think the universe has been designed is because the universe works according to laws. The laws of gravity, electricity, magnetism, motion, bonding, gases, and so on, all involve complex things working together.

DNA

DNA seems to be another piece of evidence of design in the world. DNA is a nucleic acid which forms the material of all living organisms.

▶ DNA is made up of two strands that form a ladder-like structure, which forms a right-hand spiral called a double helix.
▶ The DNA molecule replicates by unzipping and using each strand as a template to form a new strand.
▶ These new DNA strands are then passed on to daughter cells during cell division.

The structure of DNA and its formation of templates seem to indicate a design or blueprint for the structure of organisms.

Evolution

Some scientists also see evidence of design in the process of evolution where complex life forms develop from simple ones.

Beauty of nature

Artists see evidence of design in the beauties of nature where sunsets, mountains and oceans appear to have beauty which an artist would have to spend a long time designing.

How the appearance of design may lead to, or support, belief in God

Using the appearance of design to lead to belief in God is often called the argument from design (the most famous version is Paley's Watch). It goes like this:

Paley's Watch

If you came across a watch in an uninhabited place, you could not say it had been put there by chance. The complexity of its mechanism would make you say it had a designer. The universe is a far more complex mechanism than a watch, and so, if a watch needs a watchmaker, the universe needs a universe maker. As the only being that could design the universe would be God, it follows that God must exist.

Paley's Watch Argument for the Existence of God

- Anything that has been designed needs a designer.
- There is plenty of evidence that the world has been designed (laws of science, DNA, evolution, beauties of nature).
- If the world has been designed, the world must have a designer.
- The only possible designer of something as beautiful and complex as the world would be God.
- Therefore the appearance of design in the world proves that God exists.

This argument shows how the appearance of design in the world can lead people who are not sure to believe that God exists; and how it will give extra reasons for believing in God to those who already believe.

How the appearance of design may not lead to belief in God

Many people think the argument from design does not lead to belief in God because:

- The argument ignores the evidence of lack of design in the universe, for example, volcanoes, earthquakes, hurricanes and diseases.
- All the evidence for design can be explained by science without needing even to think of God (see Topic 3.1.5).
- The argument does not refer to the existence of dinosaurs, which must have been a part of design, but no one thinks they could have been part of a design plan for the world.
- The argument only proves that the universe has a designer, not God. The designer could be many gods, an evil creator, a god who used this universe as a trial run so that he could create a better one.

Exam focus

Evaluation questions
- Decide what you think about the statement.
- Give at least three brief reasons, or two longer reasons, or a paragraph reason, supporting your point of view.
- Look at the opposite point of view and give at least three brief reasons, or two longer reasons, or a paragraph reason, why people have this view.

The evaluation questions mean that you must always be aware not only of your own point of view about a topic, but also about the opposite point of view.

Remember

In Unit 3, either your point of view, or the reasons for disagreeing with your point of view, should always be a Catholic one but you do not have to agree with the Catholic view, just be able to give reasons for it.

Questions

b) Do you think God designed the world? Give two reasons for your point of view. **(4)**

c) Explain why the design argument leads some people to believe in God. **(8)**

d) 'The design argument proves that God exists.'
   (i) Do you agree? Give reasons for your opinion. **(3)**
   (ii) Give reasons why some people may disagree with you. **(3)**

Exam Tip

d) Use the evaluation technique from this page. Arguments for design would be the argument itself. Arguments against would come from why some people disagree with the design argument.

Summary

The universe seems to be designed. Anything that is designed must have a designer. Therefore God must exist because only God could have designed the universe. Some people disagree because things like volcanoes and earthquakes show a lack of design, and the argument does not prove God, only a designer who could be evil.

Topic 3.1.4 The argument from causation and belief in God

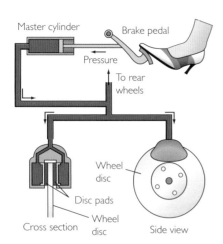

Putting your foot on the brake when driving a car causes hydraulic pressure in the brake pipes, which causes the brake pads to put pressure on the discs, which causes the wheels to stop turning, which causes the car to slow down.

What is causation?

Causation is the process whereby one thing causes another. It is often known as cause and effect; in the example in the diagram, the cause would be pressing the brake pedal and the effect would be the car slowing down.

Evidence of causation in the world

Cause and effect seem to be a basic feature of the world. Whatever we do has an effect. If I do my homework, I will please my parents and/or teachers. If I do not do my homework, I will annoy my parents and/or teachers. Modern science has developed through looking at causes and effects and in particular looking for single causes of an effect. Just as my parents' happiness may be caused by other things than my doing my homework, so the increase in someone's heart rate may be caused by other things than exercise. So when a scientist tries to discover the cause of increase in heart rate, he/she tries to reduce all the variables (for example, the arrival of girl/boyfriend) so that a single cause can be identified. Science seems to show that, when investigated sufficiently, any effect has a cause and any cause has an effect.

The argument from causation

The argument for God's existence based on the appearance of causation in the world is based on the First Cause Argument as put forward by the Catholic philosopher St Thomas Aquinas. The argument goes like this:

> If we look at things in the world, we see that they have a cause; for example, ice is caused by the temperature falling and water becoming solid at below 0°C.

> Anything caused to exist must be caused to exist by something else because to cause your own existence, you would have to exist before you exist, which is nonsense.

> You cannot keep going back with causes because in any causal chain you have to have a beginning; for example, you have to have water to produce ice. So if the universe has no First Cause, then there would be no universe, but as there is a universe, there must be a First Cause.

> The only possible First Cause of the universe is God, therefore God must exist.

This argument makes people think that the universe, the world and humans must have come from somewhere, they must have had a cause. As God is the only logical cause of the universe, it makes them think that God must exist, or it supports their belief in God if they already believe.

People who believe that causation proves that God exists often use the example of a goods train. Each wagon is caused to move by the wagon that is pulling it. But although each wagon is caused to move by another wagon, which is caused to move by another wagon, and so on, the whole process can only be explained if there is an engine that is not moved by something in front but is 'an unmoved mover'. In the same way, the process seen in the world – of things being caused or moved by something else – can only be explained if there is an Unmoved Mover causing it all to happen and this could only be God.

Does the universe need a First Cause? If so, and that First Cause is God, does God need a cause?

People who believe in the First Cause often use the example of a line of railway wagons, claiming that just as the wagons need an engine to explain how they are moving, so the universe needs God to explain how it is working.

Why some people disagree with the argument

Some people may think the argument from causation does not prove that God exists because:

▶ Why should the causes stop at God? If everything needs a cause then God must need a cause.
▶ A better explanation may be that the matter of the universe itself is eternal and so the process of causes goes on for ever.
▶ Even if the First Cause were to exist it would not have to be God, it could be any sort of creator.

> Whatever is moved must be moved by another. If that by which it is moved, be itself moved, then this also must needs be moved by another, and that by another again. But this cannot go on to infinity, because then there would be no first mover, and consequently no other mover … Therefore it is necessary to arrive at a first mover, moved by no other; and this everyone understands to be God.
>
> *From* Summa Theologica *by St Thomas Aquinas*

Questions

b) Do you think God is the cause of the universe? Give two reasons for your point of view. **(4)**

c) Explain how the argument from causation may lead to belief in God. **(8)**

d) 'The argument from causation proves that God exists.'

   (i) Do you agree? Give reasons for your opinion. **(3)**

   (ii) Give reasons why some people may disagree with you. **(3)**

Exam Tip

c) One way to answer this question would be to outline the argument and make sure you emphasise the conclusion (the last step in the flowchart and the first paragraph after the flowchart) so that you show exactly how it might lead to belief in God. Remember to take care with spelling, punctuation and grammar. Use some specialist terms such as St Thomas Aquinas, First Cause, logical cause, Unmoved Mover.

Summary

The way everything seems to have a cause makes people think the universe must have a cause, and the only possible cause of the universe is God, so God must exist.

Topic 3.1.5 Scientific explanations of the world and agnosticism and atheism

KEY WORDS

Agnosticism – not being sure whether God exists

Atheism – believing that God does not exist

Science explains how the world came into being in this way:

- Matter is eternal, it can neither be created nor destroyed, it can only be changed (scientists call this the law of thermo-dynamics).
- About 14 billion years ago, the matter of the universe became so compressed that it produced a huge explosion (the Big Bang).
- As the matter of the universe flew away from the explosion, the forces of gravity and other laws of science joined some of the matter into stars and, about 5 billion years ago, the solar system was formed.
- The combination of gases on the Earth's surface produced primitive life forms, like amoeba.
- The genetic structure of these life forms produces changes (mutations).
- Any change that is better suited to living in the environment will survive and reproduce.
- Over millions of years new life forms were produced leading to vegetation, then invertebrate animals, then vertebrates and finally, about 2.5 million years ago, humans evolved.

The Large Hadron Collider

The Higgs boson

For many years, scientists knew that without something to give mass to the basic building blocks of matter, everything would behave as light does and so matter, as we know it, would not exist. Then, 50 years ago Peter Higgs and five other theoretical physicists suggested that there must be an invisible field (the Higgs field) lying across the universe giving particles their mass and allowing them to form stars and planets. Higgs predicted that the field would have a signature particle, a massive boson. Scientists have been looking for the Higgs since the 1960s, but it was only discovered when conditions present a billionth of a second after the Big Bang were recreated in the Large Hadron Collider particle accelerator near Geneva in July 2012. About 13.7 billion years ago, the Big Bang gave birth to the universe and caused an outburst of massless particles and radiation energy. Scientists think that fractions of a second later, part of the radiation energy congealed into the Higgs field. When the universe began to cool, particles acquired mass from the Higgs field, slowed down and began to bunch up to form composite particles and, eventually, atoms.

Compiled from newspaper reports

Evidence for the Big Bang

The main evidence for the Big Bang theory is called the Red Shift Effect where the red shift in light from other galaxies is evidence that the universe is expanding. In March 2014, scientists announced that they had detected the ripples in deep space triggered by the rapid expansion of the universe using a special telescope at the South Pole. The gravitational waves are claimed to be direct evidence for the Big Bang as the origin of the universe.

Evidence for evolution

The evidence for the theory of evolution is the fossil record (the evidence from fossils of life developing from simple to complex), and the similarities between life forms being discovered through genetic research (about 50 per cent of human DNA is the same as that of a cabbage).

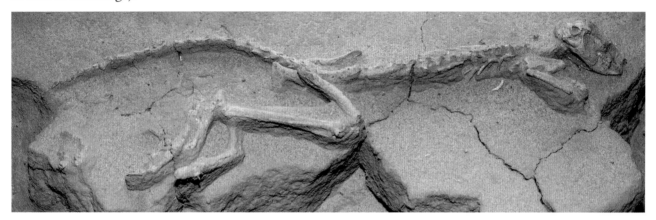

A fossil of a Tasmanian tiger, believed to be thousands of years old

How the scientific explanation of the world may lead to agnosticism or atheism

Science can explain where the world came from and where humans came from without any reference to God. This may lead some people to be agnostic, that is they are unsure whether there is a God or not. The argument that you need God to explain why we are here is no longer valid for them.

Other people may be led to become atheists and be sure there is no God because they believe that, if God exists, he must have made the world and he must be the only explanation of the world. The scientific explanation of the world and humans without any reference to God is proof to such people that God does not exist.

Exam Tip

d) Use the answering evaluation questions advice from page 9. The arguments for the statement are in this topic, the arguments against are in Topic 3.1.6.

Questions

b) Do you think science shows that God did not design the world? Give two reasons for your point of view. **(4)**

c) Explain why the scientific explanation of the world leads some people to become atheists or agnostics. **(8)**

d) 'Science proves that God did not create the universe.'

    (i) Do you agree? Give reasons for your opinion. **(3)**

    (ii) Give reasons why some people may disagree with you. **(3)**

Summary

Science says that matter is eternal and that the universe began when this matter exploded. The solar system came out of the explosion, and the nature of the Earth allowed life to develop through evolution.

Topic 3.1.6 How Catholics respond to scientific explanations of the world

> What is revealed of the divine in the human life of Jesus is also to be discerned in the cosmic story of creation.
>
> *J. Polkinghorne in* Science and Creation

> The point is that, for the existence of any forms of life that we may conceive, the necessary environment, whatever its nature, must be complex and dependent on a multiplicity of coincident conditions, such as are not reasonably attributable to blind forces or to pure mechanism.
>
> *F. R. Tennant in* The Existence of God

There are two main Catholic responses to scientific explanations of the world.

Response 1

Many Catholics believe that the scientific explanations are true. However, they believe that the scientific explanation does not mean that everyone should be agnostic or atheist. They believe that the scientific explanation proves that God created the universe because of such reasons as:

▶ The Big Bang had to be at exactly the right micro second. If it had been too soon, it would have been too small to form stars; if it had been too late, everything would have flown away too fast for stars to form.
▶ There had to be scientific laws such as gravity for the matter of the universe to form solar systems, and only God could have made the laws on which the universe is based.
▶ Life on Earth requires carbon to be able to bond with four other atoms and water molecules. This could not have happened by chance, so God must have ensured it happened.

Can you explain how the solar system works without using the laws of gravity and motion created by God?

Response 2

Some Catholics believe that both the scientific explanations and the Bible are correct. They claim that the main points of the Bible story fit with science. One of God's days could be millions or billions of years. They claim that Genesis 1:3 'God said, "Let there be light"', is a direct reference to the Big Bang and that the order in which God creates life as described in Genesis – plants, trees, fish, birds, animals, humans – is the same order as described in the theory of evolution for the development of species.

Can we know how God created the world?

Questions

b) Do you think the scientific explanation of the universe shows that God exists? Give two reasons for your point of view. **(4)**

c) Explain how Catholics respond to scientific explanations of the world. **(8)**

d) 'Science needs God to explain the universe.'
   (i) Do you agree? Give reasons for your opinion. **(3)**
   (ii) Give reasons why some people may disagree with you. **(3)**

Exam Tip

c) 'Explain how' means explaining the responses of Catholics to the scientific explanations. To answer this question you should give four responses of Catholics to scientific explanations of the world. Remember you have four marks for spelling, punctuation and grammar in this section so try to use some specialist vocabulary such as agnostic, atheist, Big Bang, microsecond, scientific laws, matter, solar system, carbon, bonding, molecules, Genesis.

The **Vatican** observatory is one of the most specialised in the world and the Pontifical Academy of Science conducts leading international research projects. As part of a renewed commitment to the dialogue between faith and science, there has been a recognition that the truth of faith and the truth of science must be respected. As a result, the work of Galileo, previously condemned by the Church, has been recognised.

The question about the origins of the world and of man has been the object of many scientific studies that have splendidly enriched our knowledge of the age and dimensions of the cosmos, the development of life forms and the appearance of man. These discoveries invite us to even greater admiration for the greatness of the Creator.

Catechism of the Catholic Church 283

Summary

Many Catholics accept the scientific explanations but believe they show that God created the universe through the Big Bang.

Some Catholics believe that both science and the Bible are true because one of God's days could be billions of years.

Topic 3.1.7 Why unanswered prayers may lead to agnosticism or atheism

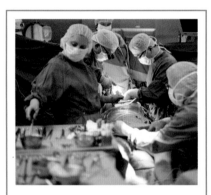

There have been at least ten studies of the effects of prayer on patients' health, the most extensive of which monitored 1,802 patients at six hospitals who received coronary bypass surgery and appeared in *The American Health Journal* in 2006. The patients were broken into three groups. Two were prayed for; the third was not. Half the patients who received the prayers were told that they were being prayed for; half were told that they might or might not receive prayers. The researchers found no differences between those patients who were prayed for and those who were not, but slightly more of the patients who knew they were being prayed for suffered complications – perhaps because knowing you are being prayed for makes you worried!

Compiled from news reports.

Are atheists correct in thinking that those who are prayed for should have better outcomes?

As can be seen in Topic 3.1.2 How religious experience may lead to belief in God (pages 4–7), one reason for people believing in God is that when they pray, they feel the presence of God and/or their prayers seem to be answered by God. However, prayer can also lead people to become agnostics or atheists.

Not feeling God's presence when praying

Prayer can be defined as 'an attempt to contact God, usually through words'. So when people pray, they are attempting to contact God. Many religious people claim that when they pray, they feel that God is there listening to their prayers.

However, other people say their prayers in church and at home, but never feel the presence of God when they pray. This is likely to make them feel that something is wrong: either they are not praying correctly, or there is no God listening to them. They may ask for advice from people they respect within the religion and try even harder in their praying. But if, despite all their efforts, they still have no feeling of the presence of God when they pray, then they may begin to question whether God is there at all. In other words, the feeling that no one is listening to their prayers may lead them to agnosticism, or even atheism.

Prayers not being answered

Even more likely to make people reject belief in God are unanswered prayers. Christians believe that God is their loving heavenly father who will answer their prayers. In some churches, they are likely to be told of people whose prayers have been answered by God. For example, many Catholic Christians believe that St Jude is the patron saint for those who have no other hope of help and many Catholics believe that St Jude has helped them after they prayed to him. This is one example from a Catholic Christian.

> **Example of an answered prayer**
>
> I spent five years with a boyfriend who would not commit himself to marriage. I was severely depressed and prayed to St Jude for help. With St Jude's intervention, my prayers were finally answered, and at last I am happily married.
>
> Thank you St Jude, I promise to let your good deeds be known to all.

However, if another person prays, and their prayer is not answered, they may begin to wonder about a god who answers some people's prayers, but not others.

If parents have a child suffering from leukaemia, for example, and they pray to God for help, yet the child still dies, this may make them question or reject the existence of God. If there was a God who helped Jesus to raise Jairus' daughter from death by curing her life-threatening disease, why wouldn't he help the parents of this child? As their child did not recover, they may begin to think that God does not exist.

If prayers continue to be unanswered, especially if the person believes they are praying for good things like the end of wars, or the end of a terrible drought in a developing country, then the unanswered prayers become evidence that God does not exist. In this way, unanswered prayers can lead a person to become an agnostic or an atheist.

In September 1992, a young Baptist missionary couple and their family asked the members of their church in Peterborough to pray that they would have a safe journey to their new posting in Nepal where they were to establish a Christian church. However, the plane crashed killing them and their three young children.

Why might this event have caused some people to question God's existence?

Why do you think the church's prayers were unanswered?

Questions

b) Do you think unanswered prayers prove that God does not exist? Give two reasons for your point of view. **(4)**

c) Explain why unanswered prayers may lead some people to become atheists. **(8)**

d) 'God always answers prayers.'

    (i) Do you agree? Give reasons for your opinion. **(3)**

    (ii) Give reasons why some people may disagree with you. **(3)**

Exam Tip

d) Use the answering evaluation questions advice from page 9. Evidence for God answering prayers is in Topic 3.1.8. Evidence against God answering prayers is in this topic.

Summary

If people do not feel God's presence when they pray, or if people pray for good things, but their prayers are not answered, this might make some people doubt God's existence. If God does not answer prayers, how do you know he exists?

Topic 3.1.8 How Catholics respond to unanswered prayers

Do not be troubled if you do not immediately receive from God what you ask him; for he desires to do something even greater for you, while you cling to him in prayer.

Catechism of the Catholic Church 2737

Gracious Lord, oh bomb the Germans

Spare their women for Thy Sake,

And if that is not too easy

We will pardon Thy Mistake,

But, gracious Lord, whate'er shall be,

Don't let anyone bomb me.

From In Westminster Abbey, *By John Betjeman*

Why do you think God might not have answered this prayer supposedly made by an Englishwoman during the Second World War?

Some even stop praying because they think their petition is not heard. Here two questions should be asked: Why do we think our petition has not been heard? How is our prayer heard, how is it efficacious?

Catechism of the Catholic Church 2734

Most Catholics believe that God answers all prayers and that what seem to be unanswered prayers can be explained in many different ways.

▶ If what you pray for is selfish, for example, 'Please God, help me to pass this exam', it would be wrong of God to allow you to pass the exam if you had not revised for it. So God is answering your prayer by encouraging you to work hard for what you want to achieve.

▶ If what you pray for is personal, for example, 'Please cure my grandad from his cancer', your prayer may not be answered in the way you expect because God has different plans and may be wanting your grandad to enter heaven.

▶ Human parents do not always give their children what they ask for, but they do give them what they need. In the same way, God may be answering our prayers by giving us what we need rather than what we have asked for.

▶ Catholics believe that God loves people and they trust God's love to do what is best for them. They believe that God's omnipotence and benevolence mean that he knows them better than they know themselves, therefore they trust God to answer their prayers in the best possible way, even though it does not look like a direct answer.

▶ Jesus said that his followers must have faith to have their prayers answered. Modern Catholics have faith that God will answer all prayers in a way designed for the long-term good of the person praying, or the people prayed for, even though God's way might be a different way from the expected one.

Two girls stand in the rubble after a tornado hit Oklahoma in 2013.

Don't you just hate it when you pray for something and things don't seem to work out the way that you had hoped they would? You might find yourself thinking, 'God, why are you doing this,' when you don't get the answer you wanted. You might become angry, not understanding why God has ignored your requests. I've got news for you: the reason your prayer hasn't been answered isn't God's fault; it's yours! Allow me to explain. Often times the things we pray for are not necessarily what we need or will do more harm than good. Often we pray for them because we think we need them. Sometimes what we think we desire, we desire for the wrong reasons. For example, a man may pray for more money, explaining to God that he will use this extra money to help people in need. He doesn't get the money and just can't understand why God would deny him these funds – after all, he wants to help others with it. If he were to search deeper, he'd see that really he's praying for more money because he has a fear of not having enough money. He doesn't feel like he can ask God to give him more money just to have more – that's greed after all. He masks his desire for more money with a desire to help others. He can now ask God for more money because he's turned it into an admirable request. But 'Our father in heaven knows what we want before we ask for it'. God knows what we really desire, even when we don't. Rather than ignore it or get angry with us, he answers our prayer by helping us see more clearly.

Article in St Louis Catholic Examiner *by Robby Francis, 3 July 2009*

Why do you think people pray in times of stress and danger?

Questions

b) Do you think prayer is a waste of time? Give two reasons for your point of view. **(4)**

c) Explain how Catholics respond to unanswered prayers. **(8)**

d) 'Unanswered prayers prove that God does not exist.'

(i) Do you agree? Give reasons for your opinion. **(3)**

(ii) Give reasons why some people may disagree with you. **(3)**

Exam Tip

b) You should already have thought about this, and you just have to give two reasons for your opinion. For example, if you think prayer is not a waste of time, you could use these two reasons:

- For people who believe in God, prayer is the best way to improve their relationship with God.
- If God answers your prayers, for example, by helping you pass an exam, you are not going to think prayer is waste of time.

Summary

Catholics believe that God cannot answer selfish prayers. But, he answers all other prayers, though not always in the way people expect, because his answers have to fit in with his overall plans.

Topic 3.1.9 Evil and suffering

KEY WORDS

Free will – the idea that human beings are free to make their own choices

Moral evil – actions done by humans which cause suffering

Natural evil – things which cause suffering but have nothing to do with humans

Omni-benevolent – the belief that God is all-good

Omnipotent – the belief that God is all-powerful

Omniscient – the belief that God knows everything that has happened and everything that is going to happen

You shall not murder.

You shall not commit adultery.

You shall not steal.

You shall not give false testimony ...

You shall not covet ...

The last five of the Ten Commandments, Exodus 20:13–17

Would breaking these lead to moral evil?

Evil and suffering can take two forms:

1. Moral evil

This is evil that is caused by humans misusing their free will (the human faculty of making choices). It is always possible to choose to do something good or something evil. Humans choosing to do evil makes a moral evil.

War is a good example of moral evil. Wars cause large amounts of suffering. Not only are military personnel on both sides made to suffer, but modern warfare also involves the use of weapons that kill and maim large numbers of innocent civilians. All wars are caused by the actions of humans who could have chosen to act differently. Suicide bombers actively choose to cause suffering to innocent people, who are likely to include babies and children, in order to draw attention to their cause.

Rape, murder and burglary are clear examples of moral evil. Less clear would be such suffering as famines where humans making wrong choices may have caused the suffering, for example, landowners growing **cash crops** like cotton instead of food in order to make more money. However, the famine could have been caused by something out of the control of humans, such as a lack of rain.

Christians often call acts of moral evil 'sins' because they are against what God wants humans to do (as revealed to them, for example, in the Ten Commandments).

Burglaries cause much suffering by the actions of humans.

2. Natural evil

Natural evil is suffering that has not been caused by humans. Earthquakes, floods, volcanoes, drought, tsunamis, hurricanes, tornadoes, cancers and so on are not actually caused by humans, but they result in massive amounts of human suffering. However, the destruction of the natural environment by humans does lead to the balance of nature being upset and more disasters happening.

Debris is strewn over an area affected by an earthquake and tsunami in Miyako, Iwate Prefecture, March 14, 2011.

Workmen risk being swept away by violent waves hitting the sea wall as they work to repair the railway line and breached sea defences at Dawlish, Devon, Britain, February 8, 2014.

> It is evident again that all evil is essentially negative and not positive; i.e. it consists not in the acquisition of anything, but in the loss or deprivation of something necessary for perfection. Pain, which is the test or criterion of physical evil, has indeed a positive, though purely subjective existence as a sensation or emotion; but its evil quality lies in its disturbing effect on the sufferer. In like manner, the perverse action of the will, upon which moral evil depends, is more than a mere negation of right action, implying as it does the positive element of choice; but the morally evil character of wrong action is constituted not by the element of choice, but by its rejection of what right reason requires.
>
> *Catholic Encyclopedia*

How evil and suffering cause people to question or reject belief in God

I cannot imagine any omnipotent sentient being sufficiently cruel to create the world we inhabit.

The Severed Head, *Iris Murdoch*

Some people cannot believe that a good God would have designed a world with natural evils in it. If they had been God, they would not have created a world with floods, earthquakes, volcanoes, cancers, and so on; and, as they believe God must be better than them, they cannot believe that God would have done so. They find it easier to believe that these features are a result of the Earth evolving by accident from the Big Bang and so they question or reject God's existence.

When British and American troops liberated concentration camps in 1945 it made many of the soldiers doubt God's existence. Why do you think this was?

How are atheists produced? In probably nine cases out of ten, what happens is something like this:

A beloved husband, or wife, or child, or sweetheart is gnawed to death by cancer, stultified by epilepsy, struck dumb and helpless by apoplexy, or strangled by diphtheria; and the looker-on, after praying vainly to God to refrain from such horrible and wanton cruelty, indignantly repudiates faith in the divine monster.

Saint Joan, *George Bernard Shaw (1856–1950)*

Some people cannot believe in a God who allows humans to cause so much evil and suffering when he could stop it if he wanted to. If God exists, he must have known what Adolf Hitler would do, so why did he not give Hitler a heart attack before all the suffering caused by the Second World War and the **Holocaust**? As the suffering was not stopped, this may mean that God does not exist.

Philosophers express the problem in this way:

- If God is **omnipotent** (all-powerful), he must be able to remove evil and suffering from the world.
- If God is **omni-benevolent** (all-good), he must want to remove evil and suffering from the world because they cause so much unhappiness.
- It follows that, if God exists, there should be no evil or suffering in the world.
- As there is evil and suffering in the world, either God is not omnipotent, or God is not omni-benevolent, or God does not exist.

This is often connected with God's omniscience, because if God knows everything that is going to happen, he must have known all the evil and suffering that would come from creating the universe in the way he did. Therefore he should have created the universe in a different way to avoid evil and suffering.

Most religious believers (especially Christians, Jews and Muslims) believe that God is omnipotent, omni-benevolent and omniscient. So the existence of evil and suffering challenges their beliefs about God, and as these beliefs come from their holy books, it challenges the whole of their religion.

For many religious believers evil and suffering become a problem when they come into contact with it. So, if they experience the suffering caused by a natural disaster like an earthquake, or if their child dies from a disease, the problem can sometimes change them into an atheist or agnostic.

Rescue workers in northeastern Japan two days after a powerful tsunami triggered by an earthquake hit the country's east coast in March 2011.

Questions

b) Do you think evil and suffering show that God does not exist? Give two reasons for your point of view. **(4)**

c) Explain how the existence of evil and suffering may lead some people to deny God's existence. **(8)**

d) 'A loving God would not let us suffer.'

    (i) Do you agree? Give reasons for your opinion. **(3)**

    (ii) Give reasons why some people may disagree with you. **(3)**

Exam Tip

c) One way to answer this question would be to identify the nature of natural evil and then explain why it causes problems by outlining the four bullet points at the bottom of the previous page, and the first paragraph on this page. Remember to take care with spelling, punctuation and grammar, and use some specialist terms such as natural evil, omnipotent, omni-benevolent, omniscient, universe.

Summary

Some people do not believe in God because they think that there would be no evil and suffering in a world created by a good and powerful God. A good God should not want such things to happen, and a powerful God ought to be able to get rid of them, but does not.

23

Topic 3.1.10 How Catholics respond to the problem of evil and suffering

> Then the righteous will answer him, 'Lord, when did we see you hungry and feed you, or thirsty and give you something to drink? When did we see you a stranger and invite you in, or needing clothes and clothe you? When did we see you sick or in prison and go to visit you?' The King will reply, 'I tell you the truth, whatever you did for one of the least of these brothers of mine, you did for me.'
>
> *Matthew 25:37–40*

Organisations like CAFOD work with armed child soldiers such as the one seen here in the uniform of the South Sudan Democratic Movement. Do you think Christian workers feel compelled to do this kind of work by the words of Jesus in Matthew 25?

There are several Catholic responses to the problem of evil and suffering, and most Catholics would combine at least two to explain why evil and suffering is compatible with God's omni-benevolence and omnipotence. However, almost all Catholics would begin with response one.

Response 1

Catholics believe that God wants them to help those who suffer. The New Testament teaches Catholics that Jesus regarded evil and suffering as something to be fought against. Jesus healed the sick, fed the hungry, challenged those who were evil, and even raised the dead.

Catholics feel that they should follow the example of Jesus and fight against evil and suffering by:

▶ praying for those who suffer. This is called intercessionary prayer and all Christian services include prayers of intercession, asking God to help those who suffer from poverty, sickness, famine, war, and so on. Catholics believe that prayer is a powerful way of dealing with a problem.

▶ helping those who suffer. Many Catholics become doctors, nurses, social workers, for example, so that they can help to reduce the amount of suffering in the world. Catholics have also founded charities to help to eliminate suffering, such as the St Vincent de Paul Society to help the poor and homeless, and CAFOD (Catholic Agency for Overseas Development) to help to ease the suffering of those in less economically developed countries (LEDCs).

Christ's actions were focused on those who were suffering. Four of his beatitudes are addressed to people who are afflicted. He suffered fatigue, homelessness, misunderstanding, hostility, torture and death on the cross. Catholics also pray to Mary as the mother of those in sorrow because she saw her own son suffer.

Response 2

Many Catholics respond by claiming that evil and suffering are not God's fault. According to Genesis 1, God created humans in his image, which means he created them with free will. They claim that God wanted people to be free to decide whether to believe in God or not. To be free means to be free to do either good or evil, and so God could not have created people who always did good. So evil and suffering are a problem caused by humans, and are not God's fault.

Response 3

Often connected with the free will response is the Christian belief that the evil and suffering in this life are not a problem because they are part of a plan in which those who suffer will be rewarded by eternal paradise after they die.

Most Catholics claim that this life is a preparation for paradise. If people are to improve their souls they need to face evil and suffering in order to become good, kind and loving. They claim that the evil and suffering of this life is something God cannot remove if he is going to give people the chance to become good people. But, in the end, he will show his omni-benevolence and omnipotence by rewarding them in heaven.

Catholics often connect this to the belief that good can come out of evil. For example, in the evil of the Holocaust, Maximilian Kolbe, a Franciscan friar, was arrested and sent to Auschwitz. Here he continued his priestly ministry discreetly, hearing many confessions and smuggling in bread and wine for Mass. When a married man with children was to be executed, Maximilian offered to take his place. He was canonised in 1982, when the man whose life he saved was still living, and able to attend the ceremony in Rome.

Response 4

Many Catholics believe that there is no point in worrying about the problem because humans cannot understand God's reasons for doing things. God must have a reason for allowing evil and suffering, but humans cannot know what it is because they are not God. However, Catholics know from the life of Jesus that even God's own son had to suffer, and that Jesus commanded his followers to respond to suffering by helping those who suffer. They believe that Catholics should respond to the problem by helping those who suffer and trusting in God for the answer to the problem.

Exam focus

A 'response' is a way of answering a problem. Exam questions are likely to use the words 'The response of one religion' or 'How do the followers of one religion respond to'. They mean the same thing.

Questions

b) Do you think God allows us to suffer? Give two reasons for your point of view. **(4)**

c) Explain how Catholics respond to the problem of evil and suffering. **(8)**

d) 'Evil and suffering in the world prove that God does not exist.'

    (i) Do you agree? Give reasons for your opinion. **(3)**

    (ii) Give reasons why some people may disagree with you. **(3)**

Exam Tip

d) Use the answering evaluation questions advice from page 9. Evidence for evil and suffering proving God does not exist is in Topic 3.1.9. Evidence against evil and suffering proving God does not exist is in this topic.

Summary

Catholics respond to the problem of evil and suffering by:

- praying for and helping those who suffer
- claiming that evil and suffering are the fault of humans misusing their free will
- claiming that evil and suffering are part of a test to prepare people for heaven.

Some Catholics believe that God has a reason for allowing evil and suffering, but humans are too limited to understand it.

Topic 3.1.11 How two programmes about religion may affect a person's attitude to belief in God

You have to study two programmes or films about religion in depth and assess how they could affect a person's attitude to belief in God.

Your programmes could be from what the television companies call their 'religious broadcasts' which tend to be factual programmes about religion. The BBC's religious output includes worship programmes like *Songs of Praise*, reality shows like *An Island Parish*, documentaries like *The Making of the King James Bible* and discussion programmes like *The Big Questions*. However, your programmes do not have to be obviously religious, the crucial thing is that they should be about belief in God, so programmes like *The Simpsons* could be used as long as they have sufficient content about belief in God. Also your programmes do not have to be on television, they can be radio programmes or films too.

When you have chosen your two programmes, you need to make notes on the following for each of them:

1. An outline of the programme's contents.
2. Decide which parts of the programme might have encouraged belief in God in some people and write down four reasons (using evidence from the programme) for this.
3. Decide which parts of the programme might have encouraged some people not to believe in God and write down four reasons (using evidence from the programme) for this.
4. Decide what effect the programme had on your own attitude to belief in God and write down four reasons for this.

Sample programme – *Songs of Praise*, St David's Day 2014

Programme Outline

The programme from Llandaff Cathedral looked forward to St David's Day 2014 and aimed to show the positive effects of Christian faith through the singing of hymns and interviewing people about their faith.

There were four interviews, the first with Kate Woolveridge, an opera singer, about her work with Forget-me-not, a choir for dementia sufferers which gained her a nomination as 'Inspirational Woman of the Year'. The second with Steve Hamnett, a singer with Only Men Aloud, looked at how his music and work as a gardener affected his faith. The third

Llandaff Cathedral in Wales where the St David's Day edition of *Songs of Praise* was filmed.

was with organist David Geoffrey Thomas about the new organ which had to be installed after lightning struck the cathedral in 2007. The final interview was with Toby Faletau, the Welsh rugby forward, about the influence of his faith on his life and the effects of his father bringing the family over from Tonga when he was hired to play rugby in Wales.

How the programme might have encouraged some people to believe in God

- People who used to go to church, but had either stopped going or stopped believing, might have been encouraged to believe in God again by joyous hymns like 'How Great Thou Art' and 'Love Divine' and the singing of 'Ave Maria'.
- Others might have been encouraged to believe by the way in which Kate Woolveridge's faith in God both inspired her and gave her the strength to do such difficult work with dementia sufferers.
- Anyone who likes the music of Only Men Aloud, might have been encouraged by Steve Hamnett's words about his faith and especially by his work in the garden where the new spring flowers might have reminded them of God's power to bring about new life from what appears dead.

How the programme might have encouraged some people not to believe in God

- Some people might have been encouraged not to believe in God by the interview with the wife and daughter of a man suffering from Alzheimer's disease. They may have thought that if God existed, he would not have allowed someone to lose their memory and personality and become such a burden to their family.
- In the same way they might have thought that God can't exist when he allowed the organ to be destroyed by lightning. After all, lightning is part of the natural world and therefore must be under God's control if God exists, so lightning striking a church (God's 'house') must be a sign that God does not exist.
- The hymn singing, the dressed-up priests and choir, the congregation looking so fervent and religious might all have reminded some people of why they rejected God before.

Questions

b) Do you think programmes about religion can affect your belief in God? Give two reasons for your point of view. **(4)**

c) Choose one programme about religion and explain how it might affect someone's belief about God. **(8)**

d) 'Religious programmes on television or the radio encourage you to believe in God.'
   (i) Do you agree? Give reasons for your opinion. **(3)**
   (ii) Give reasons why some people may disagree with you. **(3)**

Exam Focus

Questions may ask about the media and belief in God. The media is a plural word and refers to television, radio, newspapers, magazines and film. You should use both your programmes to answer questions on belief in God and the media.

Exam Tip

c) It would be a good idea to begin with a brief outline of the programme, then give two reasons why the programme might have encouraged some people to believe in God and two reasons why it might have encouraged some people not to believe in God. Remember you have four marks for spelling, punctuation and grammar in this section so try to use some specialist vocabulary such as Llandaff Cathedral, St David's Day, dementia, faith, agnosticism, atheism.

Summary

You need to study two programmes or films about religion. For each of them, you will need to know:

- an outline of its contents
- how it might have encouraged some people to believe in God
- how it might have encouraged some people not to believe in God
- whether it affected your beliefs about God.

How to answer exam questions

a) What is meant by 'moral evil'? (2)

Moral evil means actions which are done by humans which cause suffering.

b) Do you think miracles have happened? Give two reasons for your point of view. (4)

Yes I do because in 1858 St Bernadette saw visions of the Blessed Virgin Mary in a grotto in Lourdes, and since those visions many people have been cured by the holy waters in the grotto and their cures have been verified by scientists and doctors. Also miracles are a major part of Catholic belief. People can only be canonised if the Church can authenticate two miracles linked to them. Mother Teresa has had one miracle proven and so was beatified by Pope John Paul II.

c) Explain why scientific explanations of how the world began may lead some people not to believe in God. (8)

Science can explain where the world came from and where humans came from without any reference to God. Science says that matter is eternal and that the universe began when this matter exploded. The solar system came out of the explosion, and the nature of the Earth allowed life to develop through evolution. This may lead some people to be agnostic, that is they are unsure whether there is a God or not.

Other people may be led to become atheists and be sure there is no God because they believe that, if God exists, he must have made the world and he must be the only explanation of the world. They might think that the scientific explanation of the world and humans without any reference to God has much more proof (for example the Red Shift Effect as proof of the Big Bang, the evidence from fossils of life developing from simple to complex, and the similarities between life forms being discovered through genetic research as proof of evolution) than religious arguments, therefore convincing them that God does not exist.

d) 'The media help people to believe in God.'
In your answer you should refer to Roman Catholic Christianity.
   (i)   Do you agree? Give reasons for your opinion. (3)
   (ii) Give reasons why some people may disagree with you. (3)

(i) I do agree because there are Catholic newspapers and magazines like the 'Catholic Herald' and 'The Tablet' which have articles about religion and belief in God, so they would certainly help people to believe in God. Then there are television programmes like 'Songs of Praise' which help people to believe in God because they visit churches and have interviews with people about their faith in God. There are other programmes on TV such as 'Island Parish' whose visits to the Catholic island of Barra following the work of the parish priest there certainly helped me believe.

(ii) Some people might disagree with me because they find programmes like 'Songs of Praise' turn them off belief in God because they do not like hymn singing or religious people. They might also have watched programmes such as 'Horizon' which put forward the idea that scientific discoveries have made it difficult to believe in God. There are also some newspapers such as 'The Morning Star' which always report religion in a bad way and so would not help people to believe in God.

Question a

High marks because it is a correct definition.

Question b

A high mark answer because an opinion is backed up by two developed reasons.

Question c

A high mark answer because it explains how the scientific explanation leads some people to become agnostic with a good, well-developed reason. It then explains how science may lead some people to become atheists with a good, well-developed reason. There is good use of specialist vocabulary such as matter, solar system, evolution, Red Shift Effect, Big Bang, fossils, genetic research.

Question d

A high mark answer because it states the candidate's own opinion and backs it up with three clear reasons for thinking that the media help people to believe in God, two of which refer to Catholicism. It then gives three reasons for people disagreeing and believing that the media do not help people.

SPaG

A high mark answer because the answer spells, punctuates and uses the rules of grammar with consistent accuracy and effective control of meaning. A wide range of specialist terms is used adeptly and with precision.

Section

3.2

Matters of life and death

Introduction

This section of the examination specification requires you to look at issues surrounding life after death, abortion, euthanasia, the media and matters of life and death, and Catholicism and world poverty.

Life after death

You will need to understand the effects of, and give reasons for your own opinion about:

▶ why Catholics believe in life after death and how this belief affects their lives
▶ non-religious reasons for believing in life after death (near-death experiences, ghosts, mediums and evidence of reincarnation)
▶ why some people do not believe in life after death.

Abortion

You will need to understand the effects of, and give reasons for your own opinion about:

▶ the nature of abortion, including current British legislation, and why abortion is a controversial issue
▶ different Christian attitudes to abortion and the reasons for them.

Euthanasia

You will need to understand the effects of, and give reasons for your own opinion about:

▶ the nature of euthanasia including current British legislation, and why euthanasia is a controversial issue
▶ different Christian attitudes to euthanasia and the reasons for them.

The media and matters of life and death

You will need to understand the effects of, and give reasons for your own opinion about:

▶ arguments over whether the media should or should not be free to criticise religious attitudes to matters of life and death
▶ how an issue from matters of life and death has been presented in one form of the media, including whether the treatment was fair to religious beliefs and religious people.

World poverty

You will need to understand the effects of, and give reasons for your own opinion about:

▶ the causes of world poverty
▶ how and why CAFOD is trying to end world poverty.

Topic 3.2.1 Why Catholics believe in life after death and how this affects their lives

KEY WORDS

Immortality of the soul – the idea that the soul lives on after the death of the body

Resurrection – the belief that, after death, the body stays in the grave until the end of the world, when it is raised

For what I received I passed on to you as of first importance: that Christ died for our sins according to the Scriptures, that he was buried, that he was raised on the third day according to the Scriptures, and that he appeared to Peter, and then to the Twelve ... But if it is preached that Christ has been raised from the dead, how can some of you say that there is no resurrection of the dead ... For as in Adam all die, so in Christ all will be made alive.

1 Corinthians 15: 3–5, 12, 22

I believe in ... the resurrection of the body and the life everlasting.

Apostles' Creed

Why Catholics believe in life after death

Catholics believe that this life is not all there is. They believe God will reward the good and punish the bad in some form of life after death. Catholics believe in life after death because:

▶ The main Catholic belief is that Jesus rose from the dead. All four Gospels record that Jesus was crucified and buried in a stone tomb. They also record that, on the Sunday morning, some of his women disciples went to the tomb and found it empty. Different Gospels then record different 'resurrection appearances' of Jesus. The rest of the New Testament is full of references to the resurrection of Jesus. Clearly, if Jesus rose from the dead, then there is life after death.

▶ St Paul teaches in 1 Corinthians 15 that people will have a resurrection like that of Jesus, and will have a spiritual resurrection body given to them by God.

▶ The major **creeds** of the Church teach that Jesus rose from the dead and that there will be life after death. Catholics follow the teaching in the creeds about life after death.

▶ Most Catholics believe in the immortality of the soul. They believe that when the body dies, the soul leaves the body to live with God.

▶ The Catholic Church teaches that there is life after death. The Catechism is very clear there is life after death. The Catechism represents the teaching of the **Magisterium**, which all Catholics should believe, and so Catholics should believe in life after death.

▶ Many Catholics believe in life after death because it gives their lives meaning and purpose. They feel that for life to end at death does not make sense. A life after death, in which people will be judged on how they live this life with the good rewarded and the evil punished, makes sense of this life.

How beliefs about life after death affect the lives of Catholics

1. Many Catholics believe that they will be judged by God after death and that only if they have lived a good Catholic life will they be allowed into heaven. This means that Catholics will try to live a good Catholic life following the teachings of the Bible and the Church so that they go to heaven and not **purgatory** or hell when they die.

2. Living a good Catholic life means following scripture, tradition and the teaching authority of the Church. The teachings of Jesus taught that the two greatest commandments are to love God and to love your neighbour as yourself. So Catholics' lives will be

affected as they try to love God by praying and by worshipping God as well as attending Mass every Sunday.

3. Trying to love your neighbour as yourself is bound to affect a Catholic's life. In the Parable of the Sheep and Goats, Jesus said that only those who fed the hungry, clothed the naked, befriended strangers, visited the sick and those in prison, would be allowed into heaven. This is a similar teaching to the Good Samaritan where Jesus taught that loving your neighbour means helping anyone in need. These teachings are bound to affect Catholics' lives and this explains why Catholic charities like CAFOD are so involved in helping those in need.

4. Catholics believe that sin prevents people from going to heaven. The Catholic Church teaches that those who die with unforgiven sins will go to purgatory to be purified before they can reach heaven. Clearly these teachings mean that Catholics will try to avoid committing sins in their lives so that they will go straight to heaven.

5. Catholic beliefs about life after death give their lives meaning and purpose. Living your life with a purpose and believing that this life has meaning, both affect the way you live. It may be why in surveys Christians suffer less from depression and are less likely to commit suicide than atheists and agnostics.

> Jesus links faith in the resurrection to his own person: 'I am the Resurrection and the life'. It is Jesus himself who on the Last Day will raise up those who have believed in him.
>
> *Catechism of the Catholic Church 994*

> Every action of yours, every thought, should be those of one who expects to die before the day is out. Death would have no terrors for you if you had a quiet conscience.
>
> *The Imitation of Christ by Thomas à Kempis (a medieval saint)*

Questions

b) Do you think Catholics are right to believe in life after death? Give two reasons for your point of view. **(4)**

c) Explain why Catholics believe in life after death. **(8)**

d) 'Catholics only believe in life after death because they're scared of dying.'

  (i) Do you agree? Give reasons for your opinion. **(3)**

  (ii) Give reasons why some people may disagree with you. **(3)**

Exam Tip

c) 'Explain why' means give reasons. One way to answer this question would be to give four of the reasons on these pages. Make sure you use some specialist vocabulary such as: Jesus, Gospels, resurrection appearances, New Testament, St Paul, 1 Corinthians, creeds, Church, immortality of the soul.

Summary

Catholics believe in life after death because:

- Jesus rose from the dead.
- The Bible and the creeds say there is life after death.
- The Church teaches that there is life after death.
- The soul is something that can never die.

Their beliefs about life after death affect their lives because Catholics will try to love God and love their neighbour so that they go to heaven and not purgatory or hell.

Topic 3.2.2 Non-religious reasons for believing in life after death

KEY WORDS

Near-death experience – when someone about to die has an out-of-body or religious experience

Paranormal – unexplained things which are thought to have spiritual causes, for example, ghosts, mediums

Reincarnation – the belief that, after death, souls are reborn in a new body

Non-religious reasons for believing in life after death are connected to evidence for the paranormal. This can refer to a wide range of things from ghosts to telekinesis (moving objects without touching them). However, there are three main parts of the paranormal that provide reasons for believing in life after death:

1. Near-death experiences

This is a fairly recent phenomenon and happens when people are clinically dead for a period of time and then come back to life. In his research, Dr Sam Parnia of Southampton General Hospital found that four out of 63 patients who had survived a heart attack had near-death experiences. Similar research in Holland by Dr Pim van Lommel, in the USA by Dr Raymond Moody and elsewhere in Britain by Dr Peter Fenwick and Dr Sue Blackmore produced similar results.

Frequently quoted in near-death experiences are: feelings of peace and joy; feelings of floating above the body; seeing a bright light; entering another world; meeting dead relatives; and coming to a point of no return.

Some people have near-death experiences during heart surgery.

Example of evidence of a near-death experience

Jeanette Mitchell-Meadows had such an experience when she was undergoing major spinal surgery. She felt herself leaving her body and following a bright light to what she thought was heaven. It was very peaceful, she heard music more clear and tuneful than anything on Earth and then she felt she met Jesus. She met her grandparents and her daughter, who had been killed in an accident about six months earlier. She did not want to leave, but was told God had things for her to do on Earth. When she returned to her body she felt great pain.

Clearly, if near-death experiences are true then there is a heaven and there is life after death, but this is not the same as resurrection, as described in the Gospels.

2. Evidence for a spirit world

Ghosts and ouija boards appear to give evidence of the spirits or souls of the dead surviving death, but the clearest evidence seems to come from mediums.

A medium is a person who claims to have the gift of communicating between the material world in which we live and the spirit world inhabited by those who have died. They are sometimes called psychics, clairvoyants or spirit guides.

This research is very good work, which is needed to understand the near-death experience, but it proves absolutely nothing about the soul. All claims about this being evidence for consciousness existing without a brain are unfounded, baseless rubbish.

Dr Sue Blackmore

Mediums have always existed, but they have become more well-known in the twenty-first century thanks to cable television programmes such as *Psychic Witness*, *Psychic Investigations* and *Medium*.

Example of evidence for the spirit world

The medium Stephen O'Brien told Marion Jones that he could see a peasant grandmother figure sitting on a rickety chair outside a wooden shack. She was nodding and looking very happy. Then she told Stephen that she was thanking Marion for helping her grandson and she was speaking the word Cruz. Stephen thought perhaps there was a South American connection. Marion realised that Cruz was the surname of a 10-year-old Mexican boy whose education and health she was sponsoring. She was sure that Stephen O'Brien had contacted the boy's grandmother in the spirit world and had information he could not possibly have known otherwise.

If mediums can contact the dead in a spirit world, then there must be a life after death.

3. The evidence of reincarnation

Hindus, Sikhs and Buddhists believe that life after death involves souls being reborn into another body (reincarnation). There are many stories of this in India, one of the most famous being reported in July 2002 at the National Conference of Forensic Science in India.

Example of reincarnation

In 1996, Taranjit Singh was born to a poor peasant family and received no education. From the age of two he claimed he had a previous life and had been killed by a motor scooter on 10 September 1992. His present parents took him to the village he said he came from and the village teacher confirmed the accident had happened and introduced him to his original parents whom he recognised. The forensic scientist, Vikram Chauhan, checked the first boy's education and asked Taranjit to write the English and Punjabi alphabets (even though Taranjit had never been taught them). Not only could he write them, but when Vikram tested his handwriting against that of the dead boy, he found they were identical.

Example of reincarnation

Crowds are flocking to Indian temples to see a Muslim baby with a tail who is believed to be the reincarnation of a Hindu god. The 11-month-old boy has been named Balaji, another name for monkey-faced Lord Hanuman. He is reported to have a four-inch tail caused by genetic mutations during the development of the foetus. Iqbal Qureshi, the child's maternal grandfather, is taking Balaji from temple to temple where people offer money to see the boy. Mr Qureshi says the baby has nine spots on his body like Lord Hanuman and has shown them to journalists.

Source: The Tribune *of India, 2003*

We know that memories are extremely fallible. We are quite good at knowing that something happened, but we are very poor at knowing when it happened. It is quite possible that these experiences happened during the recovery or just before the cardiac arrest. To say that they happened when the brain was shut down, I think there is little evidence for that at all.

Dr Chris Freeman, Consultant Psychiatrist

Two of the most famous mediums in America are Terry and Linda Jamison who are known as the Psychic Twins. They claim to have foretold the 9/11 disaster at the World Trade Center.

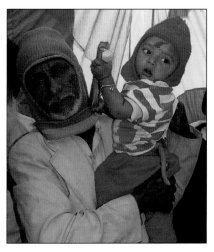

Baby with tail who some Hindus believe to be a reincarnation of a Hindu god.

Robert Thouless (President of the Society for Psychical Research) made an encrypted message before he died that would allow mediums to prove that they had contacted him after his death. At least 100 mediums submitted keys to the cypher, but none were correct, whereas a computer program solved it easily. A simple explanation is that Thouless had not survived death and so could not be contacted by mediums.

Adapted from The Case Against Immortality *by Keith Augustine*

The theory that mediums communicate with discarnate intelligences becomes even more suspect in the light of experiments in which mediumistic contact has been made with living or demonstrably fictional characters.

From Paranormal Experiences and Survival of Death *by C. Becker*

In only eleven of the approximately 1,111 rebirth cases had there been no contact between the two families before an investigation was begun. Of these, seven were seriously flawed in some respect ... The rebirth cases are anecdotal evidence of the weakest sort.

From Immortality *by Paul Edwards*

If these examples are true, then it would be evidence for reincarnation, and so life after death.

The Catholic Response

The Catholic Church teaches that there is no reliable evidence for the claims of mediums, and that such things as fortune-telling, astrology and ghosts are simply superstitions. The official teaching of the Church is that: 'All forms of divination are to be rejected ... Consulting horoscopes, astrology, palm reading ... the phenomena of clairvoyance and recourse to mediums all ... contradict the honour, respect and loving fear that we owe to God alone' (Catechism of the Catholic Church 2116). All Christian Churches (and Muslims and Jews) reject reincarnation. The Catholic Church teaches that, 'It is appointed for men to die once. There is no reincarnation after death' (Catechism of the Catholic Church 1013).

Questions

b) Do you think that some people see ghosts? Give two reasons for your point of view. **(4)**

c) Explain why some people believe that the paranormal proves there is life after death. **(8)**

d) 'The paranormal proves that there is life after death.'

  (i) Do you agree? Give reasons for your opinion. **(3)**

  (ii) Give reasons why some people may disagree with you. **(3)**

Exam Tip

d) Use the answering evaluation questions advice from page 9. The arguments for can be found in this topic. The arguments against could be the quotes in the margin from Sue Blackmore, Chris Freeman, Keith Augustine and Paul Edwards. You could also use some of the arguments from Topic 3.2.3.

Summary

Some people believe in life after death for non-religious reasons such as:

- near-death experiences when people see things during heart attacks, operations, etc.
- evidence of the spirit world, ghosts, mediums, etc.
- evidence of reincarnation, such as people remembering previous lives.

Topic 3.2.3 Why some people do not believe in life after death

Not all people believe in life after death. Many people who do not believe in God believe this life is all there is, and, just like animals and plants, humans cease to exist when they die.

They believe this because:

- If there is no God, there is nothing non-material. There is no heaven to go to after death.
- The different religions have different ideas about life after death, whereas, if it were true, they would all say the same things about it. This is especially true of the difference between the reincarnation ideas of Hinduism, Buddhism and Sikhism and the one life leading to judgement and heaven and hell of Judaism, Christianity and Islam.
- The evidence for life after death is either based on holy books, and there is no way for a non-believer to decide which holy book should be believed, or the paranormal, which has been criticised by scientists.
- Most beliefs in life after death assume that the mind or soul can survive without the body. But the evidence of science is that the human mind developed as the brain grew more complex, and so the mind cannot exist without the brain (for example, people who are brain-dead on a life-support machine).
- There is nowhere for life after death to take place. Space exploration has shown there is no heaven above the sky and physics has shown there is no non-material world on Earth. Where, then, could life after death take place?
- We can only recognise people by their bodies, so how would we recognise souls without bodies? If souls survive death, then they would be alone with no way of contacting other souls, which would not really be life after death.
- Some people have been brought up not to believe in life after death either because their parents are not religious, or because their parents' experience of the death of loved ones is that there is nothing after death.

Some people who do not believe in life after death have an eco-funeral. What might be the benefits of an eco-funeral?

Exam Tip

c) 'Explain why' means to give reasons and so one way to answer this question would be to give four of the reasons on this page. Make sure to use some specialist vocabulary such as: non-material, heaven, hell, judgement, reincarnation, holy books, non-believer, paranormal.

Questions

b) Do you believe there can be a life after death? Give two reasons for your point of view. **(4)**

c) Explain why some people do not believe in life after death. **(8)**

d) 'When you're dead, you're dead and that's the end of you.'

    (i) Do you agree? Give reasons for your opinion. **(3)**

    (ii) Give reasons why some people may disagree with you. **(3)**

Summary

Some people do not believe in life after death because:

- they do not believe in God
- there is no scientific evidence
- they do not see where life after death could take place.

Topic 3.2.4 The nature of abortion

KEY WORD

Abortion – the removal of a foetus from the womb before it can survive

Statistics
Number of abortions carried out in England and Wales

1971	94,570 (78% carried out at under 13 weeks gestation)
1991	190,000
2001	176,364
2011	189,931
2012	185,122 (91% at under 13 weeks gestation)

Source: Office of National Statistics

United Kingdom law on abortion

The 1967 Abortion Act states that an abortion can only be carried out in a medically registered facility, and only if two doctors agree that:

▶ the mother's life is at risk
▶ there is a risk of injury to the mother's physical or mental health
▶ there is a risk that another child would put at risk the mental or physical health of existing children
▶ there is a substantial risk that the baby might be born seriously handicapped.

The 1990 Human Fertilisation and Embryology Act states that abortions cannot take place after 24 weeks of pregnancy, unless the mother's life is gravely at risk or the foetus is likely to be born with severe mental or physical abnormalities, because advances in medical techniques mean that such foetuses have a chance of survival.

Pro-choice is the name given to those who support a woman's right to abortion. They do not want women to risk their lives by having operations carried out by non-doctors in bad conditions.

Why abortion is a controversial issue

Abortion is a controversial issue because there are so many different issues about abortion itself:

▶ Many religions, and anti-abortion groups (many of which are religious), believe that life begins at the moment of conception when the male sperm and the female ovum combine. Therefore abortion is wrong because it is taking a human life.
▶ Many people believe that a baby cannot be considered as a separate life until it is capable of living outside the mother. Therefore abortions before a certain length of pregnancy are not taking life.
▶ Many non-religious people believe that a woman should have the right to do what she wants with her own body in the same way that men do. They would argue that an unwanted pregnancy is no different

from an unwanted tumour. The problems caused to a woman by having an unwanted baby justify her having an abortion.

▶ Many religious people believe that the unborn child's rights are equivalent to those of the mother and that both the father and the child have claims on the mother's body.

▶ Some people argue that because foetuses born at 22–24 weeks can now survive, the time limit for abortions should be reduced to 18 or 20 weeks.

▶ There are also arguments about whether medical staff should have to carry out abortions. Some people argue that they should not be made to act against their conscience; others argue that abortion is just a medical procedure like any other.

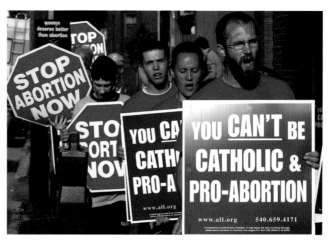

Pro-life is the name given to those who support the foetus' right to life and want abortion banned because it denies the foetus' right to life.

If carrying out a particular procedure or giving advice about it conflicts with your religious or moral beliefs, and this conflict might affect the treatment or advice you provide, you must explain this to the patient and tell them they have the right to see another doctor. You must be satisfied that the patient has sufficient information to enable them to exercise that right. If it is not practical for a patient to arrange to see another doctor, you must ensure that arrangements are made for another suitably qualified colleague to take over your role. You must not express to your patients your personal beliefs, including political, religious or moral beliefs, in ways that exploit their vulnerability or that are likely to cause them distress.

Advice to doctors from Personal Beliefs and Medical Practice *published by the General Medical Council 2008*

Questions

b) Do you agree with abortion? Give two reasons for your point of view. **(3)**

c) Explain why abortion is a controversial issue. **(3)**

d) 'Abortion is always wrong.'

    (i) Do you agree? Give reasons for your opinion. **(3)**

    (ii) Give reasons why some people may disagree with you. **(3)**

Exam Tip

b) You should already have thought about this, and you simply have to give two reasons for your opinion. For example, if you do not agree with abortion you could use the first and fourth bullet points from 'Why abortion is a controversial issue' or two Catholic reasons against abortion from Topic 3.2.5. If you agree with abortion you could use the arguments such as the woman's rights over her body and the foetus not being a human life until it can survive outside the womb from this topic.

Summary

Abortion is allowed in the United Kingdom if two doctors agree that there is a medical reason for it.

Abortion is a controversial issue because:

● people disagree about when life begins
● people disagree about whether abortion is murder
● people disagree about whether a woman has the right to choose.

Topic 3.2.5 Different Christian attitudes to abortion

KEY WORD

Sanctity of life – the belief that life is holy and belongs to God

Human life must be respected and protected absolutely from the moment of conception. From the first moment of his existence, a human being must be recognised as having the rights of a person – among which is the inviolable right of every innocent being to life … Abortion and infanticide are abominable crimes … The law must provide appropriate penal sanctions for every deliberate violation of the child's rights.

Catechism of the Catholic Church 2270–71, 2273

Before I formed you in the womb I knew you, before you were born I set you apart; I appointed you as a prophet to the nations.

Jeremiah 1:5

Christians have two differing attitudes to abortion:

1. The Catholic attitude

The Catholic Church teaches that all direct abortion is wrong whatever the circumstances and so can never be permitted. This teaching is based on scripture, Apostolic Tradition and the **Magisterium**. The Church teaches that life begins at the moment of conception. This means that a woman does not have the right to do what she wants with her body after she has become pregnant because the new life has rights. The Church also teaches that because abortion is wrong, all medical staff should have the right to refuse to be involved in abortions. Catholics believe abortion is wrong because:

▶ Life is holy and belongs to God, therefore only God has the right to end a pregnancy.
▶ Life begins at conception. Human life begins when an ovum is fertilised and, as there is no break from conception to birth, abortion is therefore taking life.
▶ The Ten Commandments teach that it is wrong to take life, therefore abortion is wrong.
▶ Every person has a natural 'right to life'. A foetus is a human being and abortion destroys its right to life, so it follows that abortion is wrong.
▶ The Church points to evidence that women who have abortions can suffer from traumas leading to guilt complexes and sometimes mental illness.
▶ They also believe that adoption is always a better solution to unwanted pregnancy than abortion as it preserves life and brings joy to a new family.

Catholics accept there are difficult issues surrounding abortion, for example, if doctors discover that a pregnant mother has cancer and chemotherapy would kill the foetus. In this situation Catholic moral philosophers use the doctrine of double effect – the first effect is to save the mother's life, the second (double) effect is to end the life of the foetus. As the death of the foetus is secondary, and so not intended, an abortion has not occurred.

Another difficult situation is if a woman becomes pregnant as a result of rape. The Church teaches that one sinful act should not provoke another. With counselling, help and adoption, good can come out of evil in the form of a new life. The **Bishops** of England and Wales issued a statement saying that a rape victim may be given contraception to prevent implantation of the rapist's sperm as long as it could be established that conception had not taken place.

The Catholic Church recognises that the decision to have an abortion is often complex and painful: the mother can be under severe psychological pressure from family and friends. Efforts should be made by individuals and politicians to come to the help of families, mothers and children so as to prevent abortion occurring for socio-economic reasons such as poverty.

Evangelical Protestant Christians have exactly the same attitude to abortion as Catholics.

2. The Liberal Protestant attitude

Other Christians (mainly **Liberal Protestants**) believe that abortion is wrong, but it must be permitted in certain circumstances such as if the mother has been raped, if the mother's life is at risk or if the foetus is so disabled that it would have no quality of life. Some of these Christians would also allow abortion for social reasons such as poverty and the effects on the rest of the family. These Christians believe that abortion can be permitted in certain circumstances because:

> Jesus told Christians to love their neighbour as themselves, and abortion may be the most loving thing to do.
> They believe life does not begin at conception.
> The sanctity of life can be broken in such things as a just war, so why not in a just abortion (for example, when the mother's life is at risk)?
> Christians should accept technological advances in medicine, therefore if doctors have developed amniocentesis tests to detect disease and suffering in a foetus, parents should be allowed abortions on the basis of the results of such tests.
> Christianity is concerned with justice and if abortions were banned, an unjust situation would arise. Rich women would pay for abortions in another country, but the poor would use 'back-street' abortionists.

Methodists would strongly prefer that through advances in medical science and social welfare, all abortions should become unnecessary. But termination as early as possible in the course of pregnancy may be the lesser of evils. If abortion were made a criminal offence again, the result would be 'one law for the rich and another for the poor', with increased risks of ill-health and death as a result of botched 'back-street' abortions.

Statement by the Methodist Church of England and Wales in What the Churches Say

Questions

b) Do you think abortion is murder? Give two reasons for your point of view. **(4)**

c) Explain why some Christians allow abortion, but some do not. **(8)**

d) 'No Christian should ever have an abortion.'

    (i) Do you agree? Give reasons for your opinion. **(3)**

    (ii) Give reasons why some people may disagree with you. **(3)**

Exam Tip

c) One way to answer this question would be to give two reasons why some Christians do not allow abortion (Catholics and Evangelical Protestants), and two reasons why some Christians allow abortion in certain circumstances (Liberal Protestants). Make sure to use some specialist vocabulary such as: Magisterium, sanctity of life, Ten Commandments, quality of life, love of neighbour.

Summary

Christians have different attitudes to abortion:

- Some Christians believe that abortion is always wrong because it is murder and against God's will.
- Some Christians believe that abortion is wrong but must be allowed in some circumstances as the lesser of two evils.

Topic 3.2.6 The nature of euthanasia

KEY WORDS

Assisted suicide – providing a seriously ill person with the means to commit suicide

Euthanasia – the painless killing of someone dying from a painful disease

Non-voluntary euthanasia – ending someone's life painlessly when they are unable to ask, but you have good reason for thinking they would want you to do so

Quality of life – the idea that life must have some benefits for it to be worth living

Voluntary euthanasia – ending life painlessly when someone in great pain asks for death

Nancy Crick was assisted to commit suicide by right-to-die campaigners because she had terminal cancer. After her death it was discovered that she was in remission. Her relatives and the campaigners still believe her euthanasia was right. Her son said, 'It makes little difference whether she had cancer or not. Our main concern is that our mother is at peace.'

A dictionary definition of euthanasia is that it provides a gentle and easy death to someone suffering from a painful, terminal disease who has little quality of life. This can be done by: assisted suicide, voluntary euthanasia, or non-voluntary euthanasia.

British law says that all these methods of euthanasia can lead to a charge of murder. However, the law now agrees that withdrawing artificial nutrition and hydration is not murder. In the same way, withholding treatment from patients with little or no chance of survival and ensuring a peaceful death for them is not murder. These two types of euthanasia (the withdrawal or withholding of treatment) are often called passive euthanasia, in contrast to positive euthanasia which is actually bringing someone's life to an end.

Why euthanasia is a controversial issue

1. Many people want euthanasia to remain illegal because:
    ▶ There is always likely to be doubt as to whether it is what the person really wants. If there is money involved, unscrupulous relatives might request euthanasia for a rich relative to gain from their will.
    ▶ There is also the problem as to whether the disease is terminal. A cure might be found for the disease, or the patient may go into remission. Also people thought to be in irreversible comas have recovered after many years.
    ▶ Doctors would also face a big problem if they started to kill patients, even though the patient requested it. It is the role of doctors to save lives, not end them. Would patients trust their doctors if they weren't sure about their dedication to saving life?
    ▶ People might change their mind about wanting euthanasia, but then it would be too late.
    ▶ Who would decide to allow the euthanasia to take place? What safeguards could there be that they were only killing people who really wanted and needed euthanasia?

2. Many people want euthanasia to be made legal because they argue that:
    ▶ Advances in medicine have led to people being kept alive who would previously have died, but they judge their quality of life as poor. It is claimed that doctors and relatives should have the right to give such patients a painless death.
    ▶ The development of life-support machines has already brought in a form of euthanasia as doctors and relatives can agree to switch off such machines if there is no chance of the patient regaining consciousness because they are said to be brain-stem dead. It is claimed that the National Health

Service cannot afford to keep people alive for years on a life-support machine that could be used to save the life of someone who has a chance of recovery.

- Just as doctors can now switch off life-support machines, so judges have said that doctors can stop treatment.
- Many people feel that it is a basic human right to have control about ending your life. If people have the right to commit suicide, then they have the right to ask a doctor to assist their suicide if they are too weak to do it themselves.

This is the Dignitas House in Switzerland which provides assisted suicide facilities for those who feel their illnesses are unbearable. Do you think it is right for people to be helped to end their lives when they have terminal illnesses?

Questions

b) Do you agree with euthanasia? Give two reasons for your point of view. **(4)**

c) Explain why euthanasia is a controversial issue. **(8)**

d) 'The law on euthanasia should be changed.'

    (i) Do you agree? Give reasons for your opinion. **(3)**

    (ii) Give reasons why some people may disagree with you. **(3)**

Exam Tip

b) You should already have thought about this, and you just have to give two reasons for your opinion. For example, if you don't agree with euthanasia, you could use the reasons of unscrupulous relatives, and doctors having a duty to save lives, not kill.

Summary

There are various types of euthanasia that are all aimed at giving an easy death to those suffering intolerably. British law says that euthanasia is a crime, but withholding treatment from dying patients is not.

Euthanasia is a controversial issue because:

- Medicine can keep people alive with little quality of life.
- Suicide is no longer a crime.
- We give euthanasia to suffering animals.
- The role of doctors is to save life, not kill.
- Can you ever be sure that euthanasia is what someone wants?

Topic 3.2.7 Christian attitudes to euthanasia

> The use of painkillers to alleviate the suffering of the dying, even at the risk of shortening their days, can be morally in conformity with human dignity if death is not willed either as an end or a means, but only foreseen and tolerated as inevitable.
>
> *Catechism of the Catholic Church 2279*

> If we live, we live to the Lord; and if we die, we die to the Lord. So, whether we live or die, we belong to the Lord.
>
> *Romans 14:8*

> Discontinuing medical procedures that are burdensome, dangerous, extraordinary, or disproportionate to the expected outcome can be legitimate; it is the refusal of 'over-zealous' treatment.
>
> *Catechism of the Catholic Church 2278*

Although all Christians believe that euthanasia is basically wrong, there are slightly different attitudes to the complex issues involved.

1. Catholics believe that assisted suicide, voluntary euthanasia and non-voluntary euthanasia are all wrong. However, they accept that modern medicine has introduced new issues. The Catechism defines euthanasia as 'an act or omission which, of itself or by intention, causes death' (Catechism of the Catholic Church 2277). They believe that the switching off of life-support machines is not euthanasia if brain death has been established by medical experts. They also believe that it is not wrong to allow death to occur by not giving extraordinary treatment (treatment that could cause distress to the patient and family, and is only likely to put off death for a short time), nor is it wrong to give dying people painkillers which may shorten their life. They have this attitude because:

   ▸ They believe in the sanctity of life. Life is created by God and so it is sacred to God. It is up to God, not humans, when people die. Euthanasia is to put oneself on a par with God, which is condemned in the Bible.

   ▸ They regard any form of euthanasia as a form of murder, and murder is forbidden in the Ten Commandments.

   ▸ They believe that it is up to medical experts to determine when death has occurred. If doctors say someone is brain-dead, then they have already died, so switching off the machine is accepting what God has already decided and it is not euthanasia.

   ▸ They believe painkillers may be given to a dying person in great pain. This might shorten the person's life but the painkillers are given to remove the pain. That is the intention, rather than to hasten the person's death. This is called the doctrine of double effect. There must not be a direct link between painkillers and the death of the patient.

   ▸ Not giving extraordinary treatment is permitted by the Catechism – see the Catechism 2278 quote on the left.

   Most non-Catholic Christians have very similar attitudes to euthanasia as Catholics.

2. Some Christians believe any form of euthanasia is wrong and they do not allow the switching off of life-support machines, the refusal of extraordinary treatment, or the giving of large doses of painkillers. They have this attitude because:

   ▸ They take the Bible teachings literally and the Bible bans suicide. Both assisted suicide and voluntary euthanasia are forms of suicide, so they are wrong.

- They regard switching off a life-support machine, the refusal of extraordinary treatment, or giving a large dose of painkillers, as euthanasia. Life is being ended by humans, not God, and this is wrong.
- They regard any form of euthanasia as murder, and murder is banned by God in the Ten Commandments.
- They believe in the sanctity of life. Life is created by God and so it is sacred to God. It is up to God, not humans, when people die. Euthanasia is to put oneself on a par with God, which is condemned in the Bible.

3. A few Christians accept a limited use of euthanasia. They agree with living wills in which people state what sort of treatment they wish to receive and how they want to die if they have a terminal illness. They believe this because:
   - Modern medical science means that we can no longer be sure what God's wishes about someone's death actually are.
   - The teaching of Jesus on loving your neighbour and helping people in trouble could be used to justify assisting suicide.
   - Living wills give people a chance to be in control of what doctors are doing to them, which is a basic human right.

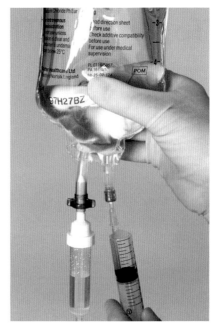

Does the right to end someone's life rest with doctors or God?

Questions

b) Do you think switching off a life-support machine is euthanasia? Give two reasons for your point of view. **(4)**

c) Explain two different Christian attitudes to euthanasia. **(8)**

d) 'Life belongs to God and should only be taken by God.'

   (i) Do you agree? Give reasons for your opinion. **(3)**

   (ii) Give reasons why some people may disagree with you. **(3)**

Exam Tip

d) Use the answering evaluation questions advice from page 9. The arguments for could come from the Christian arguments against euthanasia. The arguments against could be from Topic 3.2.6 on reasons for allowing euthanasia.

Summary

All Christians are against euthanasia because they believe life is sacred and belongs to God.

However, there are some different attitudes among Christians about switching off life-support machines, withdrawing treatment, and so on, because some think these are not euthanasia.

The common experience of Christians throughout the ages has been that the grace of God sustains heart and mind to the end. To many, the end of life is clouded by pain and impaired judgement, and whilst we believe that it is right to use all and any medical treatment to control pain, experience denies the rightness of legalising the termination of life by a doctor, authorised by a statement signed by the patient whilst in health. Such euthanasia threatens to debase the function of doctors and impairs the confidence of their patients.

Statement by the Salvation Army in What the Churches Say on Moral Issues

Topic 3.2.8 The media and matters of life and death

Different forms of communication.

The media are all forms of communication, whether written, spoken or printed. In the examination specification, it refers to newspapers, television, radio, films and the internet. Note that the word is plural, in the singular it would be 'medium'.

Religion makes many statements in the media about such matters of life and death as abortion and euthanasia. What you need to know to answer questions on this topic are:

1. arguments which say that the media should not be free to criticise what religion says about these issues
2. arguments which say that the media must be allowed to criticise what religion says about these issues.

1. Arguments that the media should not be free to criticise what religions say about matters of life and death

▶ Some people would argue that criticising what religions say about issues like abortion and euthanasia is a way of stirring up religious hatred, which is banned by the Racial and Religious Hatred Act of 2007. For example, the Catholic Church told Catholics to withdraw their support from Amnesty International because Amnesty had decided in 2007 to back abortion as a human right for women who had been raped. When the media reported this, they quoted examples that were bound to show the Catholic position in a bad light. One of the examples used related to the Christian women of Darfur who were gang-raped by Sudanese soldiers and were expected to have the babies and bring them up, even though their husbands and families rejected them.

▶ Many religious believers would argue that there should be some restrictions on the freedom of the media because criticism of religious attitudes can cause serious offence to believers. For example, when the media condemned leaders of the Catholic Church for bringing a court case to stop the separation of conjoined twins, Mary and Jodie, because it meant euthanising the life of Mary, Catholics around the world were offended.

▶ Some religious believers, but not the Catholic Church itself, would argue that criticising what religious leaders such as the Pope or the Archbishop of Canterbury say about matters of life and death is close to the crime of blasphemy. Essentially, if the media criticise the Pope's teachings on a topic like abortion or euthanasia, they are condemning the Catholic Church. At the last blasphemy trial in the UK (1977) the judge said blasphemous libel was committed if

Amnesty International is a global movement dedicated to ending serious abuses of human rights. It had always been supported by the Catholic Church, but in April 2007, Amnesty decided to support women's rights to terminate their pregnancies 'when their health or human rights are in danger'. Amnesty said the rape of women in war zones such as Darfur caused them to change their policy.

a publication vilified Christianity and might lead to a breach of the peace, which could well apply to some media comments on Catholic attitudes to abortion and euthanasia.

▶ Some religious believers might feel that because their attitude to matters of life and death is based on what God says, it should not be criticised because God is beyond human criticism.

2. Arguments that the media should be free to criticise what religions say about matters of life and death

▶ All societies with democratic forms of government claim to believe in freedom of expression (it is Article 10 of the European Convention on Human Rights). In order for democracy to work, the electorate has to be able to make informed choices before they vote. For this they need a free media so that they can know what is going on in the world and in their own country, and they can then work out which political party will deal best with the problems of the country and the world. If the media have freedom of expression, then they must be free to criticise religious attitudes to matters of life and death.

▶ Many religious leaders use the media to criticise government policies on matters of life and death, for example, regulations on abortion. If religions wish to have the right to criticise the attitudes

When the Church's Pontifical Council for Justice and Peace urged Catholics to stop donating to Amnesty International because of its decision to promote women's right to abortion after they have been raped, there was much criticism of the Church's position in the press. Although Cardinal Renato Martino had defended the Church's position by saying, 'to justify it (abortion) selectively, in the event of rape, that is to define an innocent child in the belly of its mother as an enemy, as "something one can destroy"', some parts of the press criticised the Church not only for opposing the right to abortion for women made pregnant by soldiers raping them as an act of war, but also for putting the Church's teaching on abortion above the Church's teaching on human rights.

Should the media have the right to criticise official statements by the Church?

Nothing in this Part shall be read or given effect in a way which prohibits or restricts discussion, criticism or expressions of antipathy, dislike, ridicule, insult or abuse of particular religions or the beliefs or practices of their adherents, or of any other belief system or the beliefs or practices of its adherents, or proselytising or urging adherents of a different religion or belief system to cease practising their religion or belief system. The new offence therefore has an even higher threshold than the race hatred offence, recognising that religious beliefs are a legitimate subject of vigorous public debate.

Racial and Religious Hatred Act 2006

of other people on issues of life and death, they must be prepared to have their attitudes criticised.

▶ In a multi-faith society such as the United Kingdom, there must be freedom of religious belief and expression (as guaranteed by Article 9 of the European Convention on Human Rights). This means that the media must have the right to question and even criticise not only religious beliefs, but also what religions say about controversial issues such as abortion, euthanasia and aid to developing countries.

▶ Life and death issues are of such importance to everyone that people want to know what the right thing to do about them is. Society cannot find the truth by allowing religions to put forward opinions that no one can criticise. A free media gives religious people a chance to put forward their ideas whilst at the same time allowing non-religious people (or people from a different religion) the chance to put forward their ideas.

▶ Sir Karl Popper, one of the greatest twentieth-century philosophers, argued that freedom of expression is essential for human societies to make progress. He claimed that it is no accident that the most advanced societies also have the greatest freedoms for their citizens. According to Popper, progress is made by subjecting all ideas, policies and so on to scrutiny, discovering what is false in them and then putting forward a new form without the false elements. This can only happen if government policies and religious attitudes can be scrutinised by a free media.

Summary

Some people think that what religions say about matters of life and death should not be criticised by the media because they might:

- stir up religious hatred
- be offensive to religious believers.

Other people think the media should be free to criticise religious attitudes because:

- a free media is a key part of democracy
- if religions want to be free to say what they want, then the media must also be free to criticise religion.

Questions

b) Do you think the media should be free to criticise religion? Give two reasons for your point of view. **(4)**

c) Explain why people argue about the way the media treat religion. **(8)**

d) 'The media should not criticise religious attitudes to abortion.'

    (i) Do you agree? Give reasons for your opinion. **(3)**

    (ii) Give reasons why some people may disagree with you. **(3)**

Exam Tip

d) Use the answering evaluation questions advice from page 9. The arguments for could be three of the reasons from point 1 of this topic. Arguments against could be three of the reasons from point 2 of this topic.

Topic 3.2.9 How an issue from matters of life and death has been presented in one form of the media

You have to study how **one** issue from matters of life and death has been presented in one form of the media.

Your issue could be connected with:

▶ life after death
▶ abortion
▶ euthanasia
▶ world poverty.

You can choose the form but it should only be one of the following:

▶ a television programme
▶ a radio programme
▶ a film
▶ an article in the national press.

There are always life and death issues being presented in soap operas. The character Hayley Cropper from Coronation Street was diagnosed with terminal cancer and decided on euthanasia to allow her to die with dignity. In any issue you study you must concentrate on whether the way the issue was presented was fair to Christians and Christian beliefs.

You must choose both the issue and the type of media carefully to be able to answer questions on:

▶ why the issue is important
▶ how it was presented
▶ whether the presentation was fair to religious beliefs
▶ whether the presentation was fair to religious people.

He sees dead people...
and they annoy him.

RICKY   TÉA   GREG
GERVAIS   LEONI   KINNEAR

GHOST TOWN

September 19
GhostTownMovie.com

Is the presentation of life after death in *Ghost Town* fair to Christians and Christian beliefs?

To do this you must:

1. Select an issue and a form of media. It is very important that you select only one issue. Some films have several issues running through them. If you choose more than one issue, your answers are likely to be confused.
2. Decide why the issue is important (you may need to look at the views of different members of the particular religion and of the impact of the issue on society as a whole) and why you think the producers of the media decided to focus on this issue.
3. Write an outline of how the issue is presented, listing the main events and the way the events explore the issue.
4. Look closely at the way religious beliefs are treated in the presentation of the issue. Use this information to decide whether you think the presentation is fair to religious beliefs.
5. Look closely at the way religious people are treated in the presentation of the issue. Use this information to decide whether you think the presentation is fair to religious people.

Summary

When studying the presentation of an issue from matters of life and death in the media, you must be able to explain why the issue was chosen, how it is presented, whether the presentation treats religious people fairly and whether the presentation treats religious beliefs fairly.

Questions

b) Do you think the media presented an issue from matters of life and death fairly? Give two reasons for your point of view. **(4)**

c) Choose an issue from matters of life and death presented in one form of the media, and explain whether the presentation is fair to religious people. **(8)**

d) You are unlikely to be asked an evaluation question on this section as you only have to study one issue in one form of the media.

Exam Tip

c) One way to answer this question would be to state what the issue is and then briefly summarise the presentation. Decide whether you think the presentation of the issue is fair to religious people and give four reasons from the presentation to back up your opinion. Make sure you use specific details from the presentation (such as the names of characters) and specialist vocabulary from the issue.

Topic 3.2.10 The causes of world poverty

World poverty is a very complex issue. The countries of the West (such as the USA, United Kingdom, France and Australia) are regarded as rich. The countries of the East (such as Bangladesh and India) are regarded as poor. However, things are constantly changing as countries move from being poor to rich, for example, Dubai, Kuwait and Singapore; or from poor to less poor (not poverty stricken, but not rich), for example Mexico and Malaysia; or from less poor to poor, for example, Zimbabwe.

It is common for countries to be classified as:

▶ **MEDC** – more economically developed countries, for example, the USA
▶ **EDC** – economically developing countries, for example, Mexico
▶ **LEDC** – less economically developed countries, for example, Bangladesh.

There are many causes of world poverty and reasons for a country being less economically developed.

Natural disasters

Many LEDCs are situated in areas of the world where natural disasters (earthquakes, floods, droughts, etc.) are more frequent and more severe than anywhere else. An earthquake or a flood, for example, can destroy many thousands of homes and the farmland on which the inhabitants depend. If rain does not fall, crops will not grow unless people have the wealth to sink wells, install pumps and organise irrigation systems.

The Burj al Arab hotel in Dubai is the first seven-star hotel in the world, showing how Dubai has moved from LEDC to MEDC.

Debt

Most LEDCs have to borrow money from the banks of developed countries to survive and begin to develop. However, these banks charge interest, so a less developed country can find itself paying more in interest than it earns in foreign currency. The developing world now pays $1.3 in debt repayment for every $1 it receives in aid. According to World Bank data, between 1985 and 2010, developing countries paid $530 billion more in interest to banks and governments in rich countries than they received in aid and loans.

Because unpaid interest is added to the original debt, since 1990 the amount of money poor countries have had to pay in interest to rich countries has risen from £7.4 billion to £10.3 billion.

Wars

Many LEDCs have been badly affected by wars. In Africa, many civil wars (wars fought between people from the same country) have been caused by European empire-building in the nineteenth century. In the nineteenth

I am Tonganhe. I live in Mozambique. When the floods came, I got separated from my family. But Save the Children helped me find them again. I was so happy they were still alive. We had lost all our crops in the floods, but then Save the Children gave us food and seeds to grow new crops.

Letter from a boy in Mozambique in Africa, from Save the Children's publication Welcome to Our World

Refugees from the Syrian Civil War are causing major problems for neighbouring countries as well as for aid agencies.

century countries such as Ethiopia and Somalia were constructed, expanded or reduced by Europeans without any thought being given to ethnic links, language, or even traditional grazing rights. So different ethnic groups of people were sometimes artificially put together in one country. When these countries achieved independence, they were still artificial countries and civil war often ensued as various ethnic groups fought for control. Something similar happened in Europe in the 1990s when the various parts of Yugoslavia (artificially formed after the Second World War) fought bitter wars of independence.

LEDCs can also suffer from wars between countries, for example Ethiopia and Somalia, and from wars caused by corruption and political differences, for example Mozambique, Angola and Guatemala.

Wars destroy crops, homes, schools, hospitals, and so on, causing even more poverty. They also force many people to leave their homes and become refugees in other safer countries. These neighbouring countries may have been developing, but a sudden influx of refugees with no money or food can make the countries poor again.

Unfair trade

World trade is dominated by the rich countries of the world. It is often the rich countries that determine the prices paid for products from LEDCs.

Most people in poor countries work in agriculture and one way for them to become richer would be for them to grow surplus crops and export their surplus to earn money from MEDCs. However, the rich countries are using their wealth to protect their farmers. They pay subsidies to their farmers to grow crops, and put high tariffs (import taxes) on crops from poor countries so that their products are more expensive. Then, if the MEDC farmers produce more crops than are needed, they export them at lower prices than the LEDCs can produce them for.

Poor countries are also being kept poor by the trade policies of rich countries. The rich nations pay $350 billion in subsidies to their farmers and $57 billion in aid to poor countries. The World Bank estimates that if the subsidies and tariffs were halved, it would increase the economies of poor countries by $150 billion a year.

To overcome the problem, many LEDCs grow cash crops such as cotton, coffee, tea and tobacco, which they can sell to the developed world. Many people in LEDCs are starving because land is used to grow cash crops instead of food, and the prices for the cash crops go down because too many countries are growing them.

Goldman Sachs made more than a quarter of a billion pounds last year by speculating on food staples, reigniting the controversy over banks profiting from the global food crisis. Less than a week after the Bank of England Governor, Sir Mervyn King, slapped Goldman Sachs on the wrist for attempting to save its UK employees millions of pounds in tax by delaying bonus payments, the investment bank faces fresh accusations that it is contributing to rising food prices. Goldman made about $400m (£251m) in 2012 from investing its clients' money in a range of 'soft commodities', from wheat and maize to coffee and sugar, according to an analysis for *The Independent* by the World Development Movement (WDM). Christine Haigh of the WDM said: 'While nearly a billion people go hungry, Goldman Sachs bankers are feeding their own bonuses by betting on the price of food. Financial speculation is fuelling food price spikes and Goldman Sachs is the No 1 culprit.'

Tom Bawden, The Independent *20 January 2013*

Sugar costs £319 per tonne to grow in the EU. European farmers are guaranteed £415 per tonne and are protected against non-EU imports by a 140 per cent tariff. Farmers in LEDCs produce sugar cane rather than sugar beet and this only costs £183 per tonne to produce. EU farmers overproduce and the surplus of seven million tonnes is dumped onto the world market. This has depressed the world market price to £121 per tonne so that, although LEDC farmers produce sugar at roughly a third of the MEDC cost, they still cannot make a profit on it.

HIV/AIDS

This disease is sweeping LEDCs, especially in Southern Africa. The loss of so many earners and the presence of so many children who will not be able to have an education are causing many African countries to become poorer. This effect is going to get worse unless countries can stem the spread of the disease.

Other factors

There are other factors contributing to world poverty. Lack of education means that young people in LEDCs do not have the skills needed to work in industries that might improve the country. Lack of clean fresh water leads to disease and children dying at a young age; such low life expectancy leads families to have a large number of children so that a sufficient number will survive to look after their parents in their old age. Relying on one export (such as copper or oil) can lead to poverty because, if the value of the product goes down in the world market, the country will be making a loss instead of a profit. This can change a country from rich to poor almost overnight.

The price of coffee is now 30 per cent less in real terms than in 1960, leading to lower incomes and standard of living for 25 million households in coffee-producing areas.

Statistics

According to UN research, South Africa is the most Aids affected country in the world. 17.9 per cent of the adult population is infected and 45 per cent of all deaths in 2012 were HIV/AIDS related.

Questions

b) Do you think world poverty can be ended? Give two reasons for your point of view. **(4)**

c) Explain why some countries in the world are very poor. **(8)**

d) 'World poverty is caused by the greed of rich countries.'

    (i) Do you agree? Give reasons for your opinion. **(3)**

    (ii) Give reasons why some people may disagree with you. **(3)**

Exam Tip

d) Use the answering evaluation questions advice from page 9. The arguments for could come from such reasons as debt, unfair trade, war. The arguments against could be from natural disasters, HIV/AIDS, war.

Summary

The main causes of world poverty are:

- natural disasters
- wars
- debt
- unfair trade
- lack of education
- HIV/AIDS.

Topic 3.2.11 How and why CAFOD is trying to remove world poverty

Just as the commandment 'Thou shalt not kill' sets a clear limit in order to safeguard the value of human life, today we also have to say 'thou shalt not' to an economy of exclusion and inequality. Such an economy kills. How can it be that it is not a news item when an elderly homeless person dies of exposure, but it is news when the stock market loses two points? This is a case of exclusion. Can we continue to stand by when food is thrown away while people are starving? This is a case of inequality. Today everything comes under the laws of competition and the survival of the fittest, where the powerful feed upon the powerless. As a consequence, masses of people find themselves excluded and marginalised: without work, without possibilities, without any means of escape ... With this in mind, I encourage financial experts and political leaders to ponder the words of one of the sages of antiquity: 'Not to share one's wealth with the poor is to steal from them and to take away their livelihood. It is not our own goods which we hold, but theirs'.

'Evangelii Gaudium', Pope Francis, 24 November 2013

The major Catholic agency working for world development and supported by the Catholics of England and Wales is CAFOD (Catholic Fund for Overseas Development). It was established by the Catholic Bishops of England and Wales in 1962. It is the English and Welsh arm of Caritas International (a worldwide network of Catholic relief and development organisations) supporting 1000 development projects in over 60 countries.

How CAFOD is trying to end world poverty

1. Development programmes

CAFOD promotes long-term development so that LEDCs can become self-supporting and have the opportunities to become MEDCs. Some examples of CAFOD's development aid are:

▶ The area around Hola in south eastern Kenya is arid and poor. Its 12,000 people make a subsistence living as nomadic farmers moving around with their cattle. These people have no access to state health care. Since 1985 CAFOD has been helping the Hola Catholic Mission health programme. During this time three clinics have been opened and 40 health workers (chosen by the local community and working for no pay) have been trained to provide basic medical care and advice on hygiene, nutrition and child health.

▶ In Brazil, the richest 10 per cent of the 150 million population receive 53.2 per cent of the wealth whilst the poorest 10 per cent receive 0.6 per cent. This has led to about 6 million homeless children living on the streets. CAFOD is helping the parish of Piexnhos in Olinda (part of Helder Camara's old diocese) to run a scheme known as 'The Community Taking Responsibility for its Children'. Street educators give the children literacy classes and training in a number of key skills so that they can earn a living.

▶ In Bangladesh, floods in the district of Khulna often wipe out poor farmers' entire rice crops. CAFOD is helping the Organisation of Peasant Farmers which sets up savings schemes to help them when crops fail and which is starting up different farming projects such as duck-rearing units.

2. Disasters and emergencies

CAFOD has a disaster fund to deal with natural disasters and refugees, which often have to take priority over long-term aid. CAFOD has provided over £2 million to support Church partners in Syria provide food parcels, medical aid and relief supplies to refugees from the civil war. They have also helped people to find safe places to stay.

3. Raising awareness

About five per cent of CAFOD's budget is spent on educating the people and churches of England and Wales about the need for development and the ways in which Catholics can help less developed countries. It publishes a newspaper called *Friday* and many educational materials. These give information not only about what CAFOD is doing, but also about world development.

4. Speaking out on behalf of poor communities to bring social justice

CAFOD was heavily involved in the Make Poverty History campaign of 2005, the biggest ever global mobilisation to end poverty. It is now involved in the Trade Justice Campaign to change the rules and practices of international trade to help developing countries work themselves out of poverty. CAFOD is also campaigning to cancel the debt owed by some of the world's poorest countries. Many developing countries spend twice as much on debt repayments to rich creditors than they do on healthcare and education. CAFOD also promotes Fairtrade products to bring better prices, decent working conditions, local sustainability, and fair terms of trade for farmers and workers in the developing world.

Why CAFOD is trying to end world poverty

- According to the New Testament, riches must be used for the help of others, especially the poor.
- Jesus told the Parable of the Sheep and the Goats where he said, 'When I was hungry, you fed me. When I was thirsty, you gave me drink. When I was naked, you clothed me. When I was sick or in prison, you visited me.' The people wanted to know when they had ever done this and Jesus said, 'When you did it for the least of my brothers, you did it for me.' Catholics want to help Jesus and so they help the poor and suffering.
- The parable also teaches that the way to reach heaven is by helping those less fortunate than you, and Catholics want to get to heaven.
- In the **Sermon on the Mount** (Matthew 5–7), Jesus taught that Christians should share their time and possessions to help those in need. So Catholics should try to end world poverty.
- The Catholic Church teaches that Christians have a duty to help the poor and suffering. Pope Francis has made many statements reminding Catholics of their duty to try to end poverty.
- The Golden Rule for Christians is to treat other people in the way you would like to be treated. CAFOD believes that they would want rich Christians to try to end world poverty if they were suffering from it.

Questions

b) Do you think all Catholics should help CAFOD? Give two reasons for your point of view. **(4)**

c) Explain how CAFOD is trying to end world poverty. **(8)**

d) 'If everyone was Catholic, there would be no world poverty.'

    (i) Do you agree? Give reasons for your opinion. **(3)**

    (ii) Give reasons why some people may disagree with you. **(3)**

Exam Tip

c) One way to answer this question would be to give a brief outline of four CAFOD activities explaining how each activity is trying to end world poverty. Make sure you use some specialist vocabulary such as LEDC, MEDC, long-term development, emergency aid.

Summary

CAFOD works for world development by:

- promoting long-term development schemes
- responding to emergencies
- raising public awareness of the causes of poverty
- speaking out on behalf of poor communities.

It works to end world poverty because:

- Jesus taught that Christians should help the poor.
- The Catholic Church teaches that Catholics should help the poor.
- It believes it is the way to follow the Golden Rule.

How to answer exam questions

a) What is meant by 'paranormal'? (2)

Paranormal means unexplained things which are thought to have spiritual causes, for example, ghosts and mediums.

b) Do you think belief in life after death should affect the way Catholics live their lives? (4)

Yes I do because Catholics believe that only if they have lived a good Catholic life will they be allowed into heaven. This is bound to affect their lives because to live a good Catholic life they have to love God by praying and by attending Mass. Living a good Catholic life also means trying to love your neighbour as yourself which is bound to affect a Catholic's life, as they have to help the suffering and those in need.

c) Explain why euthanasia is a controversial issue. (8)

Euthanasia is a controversial issue because people have such conflicting views about it. Many people think euthanasia should be illegal because doctors would face a big problem if they started to kill patients, even though the patient requested it. However, other people want euthanasia to be made legal because advances in medicine have led to people being kept alive who would previously have died, but they have little quality of life.

Then there are arguments about who would decide to allow the euthanasia to take place, and what safeguards there could be to ensure that only people who need euthanasia were allowed to die.

However, there is another argument that it is a basic human right to have control about ending your life. If people have the right to commit suicide, then they have the right to assisted suicide.

d) 'The media should not be allowed to criticise what religions say about matters of life and death.'
   In your answer you should refer to Roman Catholic Christianity.
   (i)   Do you agree? Give reasons for your opinion. (3)
   (ii) Give reasons why some people may disagree with you. (3)

i) As a Catholic, I disagree with this statement because criticising what religions say about issues like abortion and euthanasia is a way of stirring up religious hatred, which is banned by the Racial and Religious Hatred Act of 2007. Also I think that there should be some restrictions on the freedom of the media because criticism of the teachings of the Church can cause serious offence to Catholics. The teachings of the Church are based on what God says, and the media has no right to criticise because God is beyond human criticism.

ii) Some people might disagree with me because freedom of expression is guaranteed in Article 10 of the European Convention on Human Rights. They might also believe that in order for democracy to work, the electorate has to be able to make informed choices which needs the media to be free to criticise religious attitudes to matters of life and death. Finally, they might think that life and death issues are of such importance that we cannot allow religions to put forward opinions no one can criticise.

Question a
A high mark answer because it is a correct definition of the key word.

Question b
A high mark answer because an opinion is backed up by two developed reasons.

Question c
A high mark answer because it explains why euthanasia is a controversial issue with four reasons. There is good use of specialist vocabulary such as role of doctors, dedication, advances in medicine, quality of life, painless death, safeguards, suicide, assist their≈suicide.

Question d
A high mark answer because it states the candidate's own opinion and backs it up with three clear Catholic reasons for thinking that the media should not be free to criticise what religions say about matters of life and death. It then gives three reasons for people disagreeing and believing that the media should be free to criticise what religion says.

Section

3.3

Marriage and the family

Introduction

This section of the examination specification requires you to look at issues surrounding sex and marriage, divorce, family life, homosexuality and contraception.

Sex and marriage

You will need to understand the effects of, and give reasons for your own opinion about:

▶ changing attitudes to marriage, divorce, family life and homosexuality in the UK
▶ Christian attitudes to sex outside marriage
▶ the purposes of marriage in Catholic Christianity and how this is shown in the wedding ceremony.

Divorce

You will need to understand the effects of, and give reasons for your own opinion about different Christian attitudes to divorce and the reasons for them.

Homosexuality

You will need to understand the effects of, and give reasons for your own opinion about Christian attitudes to homosexuality and the reasons for them.

Family life

You will need to understand the effects of, and give reasons for your own opinion about:

▶ Catholic teachings on family life and its importance
▶ how Catholic parishes help with the upbringing of children
▶ how Catholic parishes help to keep the family together.

Contraception

You will need to understand the effects of, and give reasons for your own opinion about:

▶ different methods of contraception and the reasons for them
▶ different Christian attitudes to contraception and the reasons for them.

The media and marriage and family life

You will need to understand the effects of, and give reasons for your own opinion about:

▶ how an issue from marriage and the family has been presented in one form of the media
▶ whether the treatment of the issue in the media is fair to religious beliefs and religious people.

Topic 3.3.1 Changing attitudes to marriage, divorce, family life and homosexuality in the UK

KEY WORDS

Civil partnership – a legal ceremony giving a homosexual couple the same legal rights as a husband and wife

Cohabitation – living together without being married

Contraception – intentionally preventing pregnancy from occurring

Homosexuality – sexual attraction to a same sex partner

Nuclear family – mother, father and children living as a unit

Re-constituted family – where two sets of children (stepbrothers and stepsisters) become one family when their divorced parents marry each other

Re-marriage – marrying again after being divorced from a previous marriage

In the United Kingdom in the 1960s, it was expected that: young people would not have sex until they were married; most people would be married in church by the age of 25; most marriages would last for life; most families would consist of husband, wife and their children (nuclear family); homosexual behaviour would not be seen in public because homosexual sex between adult males was a criminal offence.

How attitudes have changed

- Most people now have sex before they get married.
- It is now socially quite acceptable for couples to live together (cohabit) rather than marry and a greater percentage are doing so (5.9 million people were cohabiting in 2012, twice as many as in 1996).
- The average age for marrying has increased enormously (32.2 for men and 30.2 for women in 2011).
- Only a minority of marriages now take place in church (60 per cent in 1970, 30 per cent in 2011).
- Divorce is accepted as a normal part of life, and no one is looked down on for being divorced. There has been a great increase in the number of divorces.
- Single-parent families have increased considerably as more couples divorce.
- There are far more families where the children are being brought up by cohabiting parents (25.5 per cent of all families in 2013).
- Re-constituted families are increasing rapidly as more people divorce and re-marry.
- Homosexual sex in private between two consenting adults (over 21) was made legal in 1967 and subsequent reforms have led to society treating homosexual sex in the same way as heterosexual sex.
- The Civil Partnerships Act 2004 provided same sex couples who entered into a civil partnership with the same rights and treatment as opposite sex couples who married. The Marriage (same sex couples) Act 2013 allowed same sex couples to marry in just the same way as heterosexual couples, but did not require religions to provide same sex marriage ceremonies.

Reasons for the changes

Cohabitation and marriage

▶ The increased availability of effective contraception (especially the contraceptive pill) has made it safer to have sex without becoming pregnant.

▶ Christianity has lost its influence as fewer people go to church and so are not encouraged to refrain from sex until they marry.

▶ There is increased media publicity of celebrities, which has made cohabitation appear respectable and led to it becoming more popular.

▶ The presentation on television and in films of sexual relationships outside marriage as the norm has led to more people regarding sex outside marriage as acceptable.

Divorce

▶ In 1969, new laws made divorce much cheaper and easier to obtain for ordinary people. This has led to a huge increase in the number of divorces.

▶ Expectations of what marriage should be like have changed greatly. Increased **equality** for women means that women are no longer prepared to accept unequal treatment from men. Women expect to have as good a life as their husbands and if their husbands treat them badly, they will divorce them.

▶ Before the equal rights legislation (see Topic 3.4.1), married women were often dependent on their husbands for financial support. Nowadays, many women are financially independent and can afford to support themselves after a divorce.

▶ Demographic changes – there has also been a great change in how long people are likely to be married. A hundred years ago, many men could expect to have more than one wife because so many women died in childbirth. Most divorces occur after ten years of marriage, which was the average length of a marriage 100 years ago.

Family life

▶ The increase in the number of cohabiting couples means that there are now many more families where the parents are not married.

▶ The increase in divorce has led to an increase in re-marriage (most people who divorce before the age of 50 re-marry). This means that there are now many more re-constituted families.

▶ The extended family is becoming more popular as more mothers are in paid employment and use retired grandparents or non-working close relatives to look after their children.

▶ The increase in the number of divorces plus the acceptance by society of unmarried mothers has led to an increase in the number of single-parent families.

Lots of cohabiting couples believe that they have the same legal rights as a married couple if they separate, because they are 'common law' partners. However, this is not the case in British law. Even if an unmarried couple have been living together in a family home or running a family business, each party would only retain the assets that are in their name if they were to split up. If one partner wants to challenge this, they have to find documentation to prove that there was a joint intention for them to have an interest in the asset.

Adapted from news reports in February 2013 when a woman cohabiting with a man for 30 years lost a court case for part of the property when they separated

Do you think this nuclear family would be any different if the parents were cohabiting rather than married?

Homosexuality

▶ The various changes in the law on homosexuality have made it easier to be openly homosexual and made society more aware and accepting of homosexuality.

▶ Medical research has shown that homosexuality is most probably genetic. As society begins to realise that at least five per cent of the population is homosexual, so people are accepting equal status and rights for homosexual couples.

▶ The increased openness of gay celebrities has led to a greater acceptance of all gay people.

▶ The work of such organisations as Stonewall has changed many people's attitudes and led to a greater acceptance of equal rights for homosexuals.

The first gay marriages in Britain took place on 29 March 2014.

Summary

Fifty years ago, most people only had sex in marriage, and they married in church. Now, people have sex before they marry, cohabiting is socially acceptable and most marriages do not take place in church. This could be caused by safer contraception and fewer people being influenced by religion.

Divorce and re-marriage used to be rare but are accepted today, and two in five marriages end in divorce. The changes may have been caused by cheaper divorce and women having more equality.

Family life has changed so that, although most children are still brought up by a mother and a father, the parents may not be married or they may have been married more than once. These changes are probably caused by the changing attitudes to sex, marriage and divorce.

Homosexuality used to be illegal, but now homosexuals have the same rights as heterosexuals including same sex marriage. These changes are probably due to discoveries showing homosexuality is natural and changes to the law.

Questions

b) Do you think homosexuals should be allowed to marry? Give two reasons for your point of view. **(4)**

c) Explain why attitudes to marriage and divorce have changed. **(8)**

d) 'There's no difference between living with a partner and being married to them.'

    (i) Do you agree? Give reasons for your opinion. **(3)**

    (ii) Give reasons why some people may disagree with you. **(3)**

Exam Tip

c) One way to answer this question would be to give two reasons why attitudes to marriage have changed (any two of the reasons under cohabitation and marriage) and two reasons why attitudes to divorce have changed. Make sure to use some specialist vocabulary such as: effective contraception, refrain from sex, cohabitation, media publicity, new laws, equal rights legislation, demographic changes.

Topic 3.3.2 Christian attitudes to sex outside marriage

Christianity teaches that sex should only take place between a man and woman married to each other. Therefore most Christians believe that sex outside marriage is wrong because:

▶ Christianity teaches that sex was given to humans by God for the joy, pleasure and bond of a married couple and for the procreation of children, and children should be brought up in a Christian family so sex should only take place within marriage.

▶ The Bible says that fornication (a word used in religion for both pre-marital sex and promiscuity) is sinful and Christians should follow the teachings of the Bible.

▶ The Catechism of the Catholic Church teaches that pre-marital sex is wrong and Catholics are encouraged to follow the teachings of the Church.

▶ All Christians are against adultery because it breaks the wedding vows to be faithful to each other.

▶ Christians are also against adultery because it is condemned in the Ten Commandments, which all Christians should follow.

▶ Adultery is condemned by Jesus in the Gospels and all Christians should follow the teachings of Jesus.

Some Christians accept that couples may live together before marriage, but they would expect them to marry when starting a family and would only accept a sexual relationship between two people committed to a long-term relationship.

KEY WORDS

Adultery – a sexual act between a married person and someone other than their marriage partner

Pre-marital sex – sex before marriage

Procreation – making a new life

Promiscuity – having sex with a number of partners without commitment

In an extensive interview in the current issue of the Dublin-based magazine, *Hot Press*, the Archbishop of Dublin, Dr John Neill, has said that 'the ideal – and right place – is for sex within marriage', but added that he 'certainly would not condemn anybody in a loving relationship'. Asked if the Anglican Church considered pre-marital sex as a sin, Dr Neill said: 'I think that making hard and fast statements about listing things as sins would be less common nowadays'.

Hot Press, *16 August 2007*

Questions

b) Do you think Christians should be allowed to have sex before marriage? Give two reasons for your point of view. **(4)**

c) Explain why most Christians are against sex outside marriage. **(8)**

d) 'Christians should never have sex outside marriage.'

    (i) Do you agree? Give reasons for your opinion. **(3)**

    (ii) Give reasons why some people may disagree with you. **(3)**

Exam Tip

c) One way to answer this question would be to give two reasons why Christians are against sex before marriage and two reasons why Christians are against adultery. Make sure to use some specialist vocabulary such as: pre-marital sex, adultery, procreation, bond of marriage, promiscuity, Bible, Catechism, wedding vows, Ten Commandments.

Summary

● All Christians believe adultery is wrong as it breaks one of the Ten Commandments.

● Most Christians believe that sex before marriage is wrong because the Church and the Bible teach this.

Topic 3.3.3 The purposes of marriage in Catholic Christianity

KEY WORD

Faithfulness – staying with your marriage partner and having sex only with them

> The matrimonial covenant, by which a man and a woman establish between themselves a partnership of the whole of life, is by its nature ordered toward the good of the spouses and the procreation and education of offspring; this covenant between baptised persons has been raised by Christ the Lord to the dignity of a sacrament.
>
> *Catechism of the Catholic Church 1601*

The Catholic Church teaches that God created man and woman for each other in the sacrament of marriage. The purposes of Catholic marriage are:

▶ so that a couple can have a life-long relationship of love and faithfulness
▶ so that a couple can have the support and comfort of each other
▶ for the procreation of children
▶ for the bringing up of a Christian family.

Marriage is one of the seven sacraments of the Church and as such it is a sign of grace, instituted by Christ himself and, through the Church, imparting God's grace and strength. As a sacrament, Catholic marriage involves not only the bride and groom, but also God himself. It can be argued its sacramental nature is a further purpose of marriage in Catholic Christianity.

How the purposes of marriage are shown in the wedding ceremony

The life-long relationship of love and faithfulness is shown in:

▶ the exchange of vows committing the partners to lifetime marriage and restricting sex to each other
▶ the exchange of rings symbolising the unending nature of marriage
▶ the priest's introduction to the service which emphasises the fact that marriage is a special sacrament which cannot be broken by the husband or wife
▶ readings from the Bible and a sermon or homily given by the priest or deacon on the nature of Christian marriage as a life-long relationship of love and faithfulness.

The couple having the support and comfort of each other is shown in:

▶ a preparation course which the couple must take before the wedding ceremony. This is religious counselling between the bride, the groom and a priest or deacon (sometimes assisted by a relationship counsellor) before the wedding ceremony takes place. This helps the couple to understand the nature of Catholic marriage and how to provide support and comfort for each other
▶ the priest asking the couple if they will honour and love one another as husband and wife for the rest of their lives. He asks this before the marriage vows, and they must agree to this promise of love and support for the ceremony to continue

The exchange of vows and the signing of the register make a Catholic wedding legal according to UK law.

- the marriage vows and exchange of rings (see margin)
- the readings and homily are also likely to refer to the need for support and comfort
- the prayers and Nuptial Mass give the couple God's grace and strength to support and comfort each other.

The procreation of children is shown in:

- the priest asking the couple if they will accept children from God lovingly and bring them up according to the law of Christ and his Church. He asks this before the marriage vows and the couple must agree to this for the wedding ceremony to continue
- the readings, homily and prayers all refer to the acceptance of children as an essential feature of Catholic marriage.

The bringing up of a Christian family is shown in:

- the preparation course, which will involve discussion about how the couple should bring up their children, with reference to baptism, first confession, communion and confirmation, and the Catholic schools connected with the parish
- the priest asking the couple if they will accept children from God lovingly and bring them up according to the law of Christ and his Church. He does this before the marriage vows.

Bringing children up in this way (and the couple living in a marriage of love and faithfulness) is what makes a Christian family.

The vows

Priest: Do you take ___ as your lawful wife/husband, to have and to hold, from this day forward, for better or for worse, for richer or for poorer, in sickness and in health, to love and cherish until death do you part?

Bride/Groom: I do.

The exchange of rings

Bride/Groom: I take this ring as a sign of my love and faithfulness in the name of the Father, the Son and the Holy Spirit.

Priest: Are you ready; freely and without reservation to give yourselves to each other in marriage? Are you ready to love and honour each other as man and wife for the rest of your lives? Are you ready to accept children lovingly from God, and bring them up according to the law of Christ and his Church?

Source: Catholic Rite of Marriage During Mass

Questions

b) Do you think the Catholic wedding ceremony helps a Catholic marriage to work? Give two reasons for your point of view. **(4)**

c) Explain the purposes of Christian marriage that are shown in a Catholic wedding ceremony. **(8)**

d) 'The main purpose of a Catholic marriage is to have children.'

    (i) Do you agree? Give reasons for your opinion. **(3)**

    (ii) Give reasons why some people may disagree with you. **(3)**

Exam Tip

b) You should already have thought about this, and you just have to give two reasons for your opinion. For example, if you agree you could explain how the exchange of vows and exchange of rings might help.

Summary

Catholic marriage is for a life-long relationship of love and faithfulness and bringing up a Catholic family. These purposes can be seen in the marriage ceremony where the exchange of vows and rings, Bible readings, homily and prayers all emphasise them.

Topic 3.3.4 Christian attitudes to divorce

During a morning Mass on Friday, Pope Francis said those divorced should be 'accompanied', not 'condemned'. The pontiff went on to say that those around a divorcing couple should not give in to the temptation of casuistry, a specific-instance based reasoning often used in debating ethical questions. 'It is always the small case. And this is the trap, behind casuistry, behind casuistical thought, there is always a trap,' the Pope said. 'Against people, against us, and against God, always.' He recalled the story of Adam and Eve, how they joined together to become one, and encouraged the faithful to 'see how beautiful love is, how beautiful marriage is, how beautiful the family is, how beautiful this journey is, and how much love we too (must have), how close we must be to our brothers and sisters who in life have had the misfortune of a failure in love'.

Vatican news network

There are different attitudes to divorce in Christianity.

1. The Catholic attitude

The Catholic Church does not allow religious divorce or re-marriage. Catholic marriage is a sacrament and the exchange of vows means that the only way a marriage between baptised Catholics can be dissolved (religiously) is by the death of one of the partners or if the marriage is annulled.

However, the Catholic Church does allow for the legal separation of spouses if they find it impossible to live together, and even civil divorce (an ending of the marriage according to the laws of the country but not the Church) if that will ensure the proper care of the children and the safety and security of the married partner. Neither of these routes, however, has ended the marriage: the couple are still married in the eyes of God and the Church, and so cannot re-marry. Catholics have this attitude because:

▶ Jesus taught that divorce is wrong in Mark's Gospel and Christians should follow the teachings of Jesus.
▶ The couple have made a covenant with God in the sacrament of marriage and that covenant cannot be broken by any earthly power.
▶ The Church teaches very clearly in the Catechism that a marriage cannot be dissolved and so religious divorce is impossible. Catholics should follow the teachings of the Church and so should not divorce.
▶ As there can be no religious divorce, there can be no re-marriage because that would be the same as **bigamy** and adultery, both of which are very serious sins. Catholics who re-marry may be refused communion.

However, the Catholic Church does allow **annulment** if it can be proved that the marriage was never consummated or that it was not a true Christian marriage.

What type of Christian do you think might have drawn this cartoon?

2. The attitude of non-Catholic Christians

Most non-Catholic Churches think that divorce is wrong, but allow it if the marriage has broken down. Most of these Churches allow divorced people to re-marry, but they usually require them to talk to the priest/minister about why their first marriages failed. They are sometimes asked to show repentance for the failure and required to promise that this time their marriage will be for life.

Non-Catholic Churches allow divorce because:

▶ Jesus allowed divorce in Matthew 19:9 for a partner's adultery, therefore Jesus showed that divorce can happen if the reasons for it are sufficiently severe.

▶ They believe that there are certain situations where Christians must choose 'the lesser of two evils'. If a marriage has really broken down then the effects of the couple not divorcing would be a greater evil than the evil of divorce itself.

▶ Christians are allowed forgiveness and a new chance if they confess their sins and are truly repentant. This belief in forgiveness should apply to divorce and re-marriage as much as anything else. So a couple should have another chance at marriage as long as they are determined to make it work the second time.

▶ It is the teaching of these Churches that it is better to divorce than live in hatred and quarrel all the time.

Questions

b) Do you think divorce is better than an unhappy marriage? Give two reasons for your point of view. **(4)**

c) Explain why some Christians allow divorce and some do not. **(8)**

d) 'No Christian should ever get divorced.'

    (i) Do you agree? Give reasons for your opinion. **(3)**

    (ii) Give reasons why some people may disagree with you. **(3)**

Exam Tip

b) You should already have thought about this, and you just have to give two reasons for your opinion. For example, if you agree with divorce you could use two reasons for non-Catholic Churches agreeing with divorce.

Summary

● Catholics do not allow religious divorce and re-marriage because they believe the marriage vows cannot be broken.

● Other Christians disapprove of divorce, but allow religious divorce and re-marriage if the marriage has broken down, because Christianity teaches forgiveness.

For those who have taken their vows before God as Christians, there is no divorce. But most Baptists would acknowledge that human beings can make mistakes, and what appeared as a life-long relationship may eventually break down.

Statement by the Baptist Church in What the Churches Say on Moral Issues

---

I tell you that anyone who divorces his wife, except for marital unfaithfulness, and marries another woman commits adultery.

Matthew 19:9

When they were in the house again, the disciples asked Jesus about this. He answered 'Anyone who divorces his wife and marries another woman commits adultery against her. And if she divorces her husband and marries another man, she commits adultery.'

Mark 10:10–12

Why do you think divorce is sometimes considered the lesser of two evils?

Topic 3.3.5 Why family life is important for Catholics

> The family is the original cell of social life ... The family is the community in which, from childhood, one can learn moral values, begin to honour God and make good use of freedom. Family life is an initiation into life in society.
>
> *Catechism of the Catholic Church 2207*

> Children, obey your parents in the Lord, for this is right. 'Honour your father and mother' – which is the first commandment with a promise – 'that it may go well with you and that you may enjoy long life on the earth.'
>
> Fathers, do not exasperate your children; instead, bring them up in the training and instruction of the Lord.
>
> *Ephesians 6:1–4*

Family life is important for Catholics because:

- One of the main purposes of Catholic marriage is to have children and bring them up in a secure and loving Catholic environment so that they will love God and follow Jesus.
- Catholicism teaches that the family was created by God as the basic unit of society and as the only place in which children should be brought up. Therefore it is the most important part of society and without the family society would collapse.
- Catholic teaching on divorce makes it clear that Catholic parents should stay together wherever possible and bring up their children together because the family is so important.
- The family is the place where children learn the difference between right and wrong, so without the family there would be much more evil in the world.
- The family is the place where children are introduced to the faith through baptism and then through being taken to church for Mass, **first communion** and so on. This means that the family is very important for Christianity to continue and grow.
- Having a family is an expected outcome of Catholic marriage.
- Christian children are expected to care for their parents when they are no longer capable of caring for themselves. This is based on the fourth commandment and the teachings of Jesus.

However, there is a strong Catholic tradition dating back to Jesus, which says that the Christian family is more important than the human family. Priests, nuns and monks leave their families to serve God. Jesus himself never married.

Exam Tip

d) Use the answering evaluation questions advice from page 9. Arguments for the statement would be the reasons why family life is important for Catholics. Arguments against would have to come from your class discussion or your own ideas. For example, if your own family is not religious, you could give examples of how important your family is to you and your parents.

Questions

b) Do you think families need a mother and father who are married? Give two reasons for your point of view. **(4)**

c) Explain why family life is important for Catholics. **(8)**

d) 'Family life is more important for Catholics than for non-religious people.'

    (i) Do you agree? Give reasons for your opinion. **(3)**

    (ii) Give reasons why some people may disagree with you. **(3)**

Summary

Catholics believe that the family is important because: it is taught in the Bible; Catholic marriage services refer to bringing up a family as the main purpose of marriage; they believe that the family was created by God.

Topic 3.3.6 How Catholic parishes help with the upbringing of children

▶ Most **parishes** have a local Catholic primary and secondary school connected to them. These provide Catholic education and worship in addition to the standard education. (The school buildings are provided and maintained by the Church. The teachers and equipment are paid for by the state.) This education helps parents because it teaches children right from wrong and helps parents to fulfil their marriage and baptism promises to bring their children up as Catholics.

▶ Parishes run classes to prepare children for first confession, communion and confirmation. These help parents with the Catholic upbringing of their children as they bring children into full membership of the Church.

The Church has an important role to play in the upbringing of Catholic children. This photo shows a children's liturgy.

▶ Some parishes run children's liturgies to help young children understand the Church and the Mass, and to allow parents to be at Sunday worship. This helps parents to bring their children up as good Catholics and gives parents and their children the spiritual strength of the Mass.

▶ Some parishes also run youth clubs and youth activities so that children are kept off the streets and away from bad influences. Again this helps parents to bring up their children as good Catholics.

> Education in the faith by the parents should begin in the child's earliest years ... The parish is the Eucharistic heart of the liturgical life of Christian families; it is a privileged place for the catechesis of children and parents.
>
> *Catechism of the Catholic Church 2226*

Questions

b) Do you think Catholic children should go to a Catholic school? Give two reasons for your point of view. **(4)**

c) Explain how parishes support parents in the Catholic upbringing of their children. **(8)**

d) 'You can't be a good Catholic if you don't go to a Catholic school.'

    (i) Do you agree? Give reasons for your opinion. **(3)**

    (ii) Give reasons why some people may disagree with you. **(3)**

Exam Tip

c) One way to answer this question would be to give four examples of parish activities and how they help Catholic parents to bring up their children. Make sure to use some specialist vocabulary such as: marriage promises, baptism promises, first confession, first communion, confirmation, children's liturgy, Mass, spiritual strength.

Summary

Catholic parishes help parents with the upbringing of their children by:

● supporting the local Catholic schools
● running classes for first communion and confirmation
● running children's liturgies
● running youth clubs and youth activities.

Topic 3.3.7 How Catholic parishes help to keep families together

> Lord, by this sacrament you make us one family in Christ your Son, one in the sharing of his body and blood, one in the communion of his Spirit. Help us to grow in love for one another and come to the full maturity of the Body of Christ.
>
> *Prayer from the Baptismal Mass*

Because family life is so important, Catholic parishes offer lots of help to keep families together:

- During Mass the priest may remind parents of the vows they made in their marriage ceremony and also of other reasons not to divorce.
- The parish priest is always available to give help and advice to couples having family problems.
- Celebrating Family: Blessed, Broken, Living Love is the national programme of support for marriage and family life within the Catholic community in England and Wales. The Marriage and Family Life Project Office provides support, resources and advice to parishes as they respond to families' expressed needs.
- The Church has provided a package titled 'Everybody's Welcome? Helping Your Parish to Become More Friendly for Families of All Kinds' to help parishes explore new ways to be more family friendly. Parishes try to be family friendly so that family life can be strengthened by families celebrating Mass together.
- The Church has produced a series of leaflets – 'What is Life Like?' – to help parishes understand and meet the needs of families facing specific challenges: divorce and re-marriage, bereavement, disability, mental ill-health, living without a shared faith in God, belonging to two Christian communities, and dealing with gay or lesbian family members.
- Many parishes also provide financial support if, for example, the family wage-earner is ill or made redundant, and have links to national Catholic charities to help family life, for example: Catholic Marriage Care, the National Catholic Child Welfare Council.

A Catholic family celebrating Mass together.

Summary

Catholic parishes help to keep families together by:

- welcoming families to worship together
- the priest offering help and advice for family problems
- homilies at Mass encouraging and strengthening family values
- providing leaflets on how to deal with family problems
- providing financial support and links to Catholic family charities.

Questions

b) Do you think parishes provide enough support for family life? Give two reasons for your point of view. **(4)**

c) Explain how parishes support Catholic family life. **(8)**

d) 'Catholic parishes spend too much time helping families.'

    (i) Do you agree? Give reasons for your opinion. **(3)**

    (ii) Give reasons why some people may disagree with you. **(3)**

Exam Tip

d) Use the answering evaluation questions advice from page 9. Arguments for the statement could be the things parishes are doing to help families. Arguments against could be from the importance of family life in Topic 3.3.5, showing that family life is so important that it needs a lot of time spending on it.

Topic 3.3.8 Christian attitudes to homosexuality

There are several attitudes to homosexuality in Christianity. The main ones are:

1. The Catholic attitude

The Catholic attitude towards homosexuality is that being a homosexual is not a sin but that homosexual sexual relationships are a sin. The Catholic Church asks homosexuals to live without any sexual activity (i.e. be celibate). They believe that the sacraments of the Church will help them do this. The Church does not accept same sex marriage, but is less opposed to civil partnerships. However, the Church teaches that it is sinful to harass homosexuals or attack their behaviour. Catholics have this attitude because:

▶ The Bible condemns homosexual sexual activity.
▶ It is the tradition of the Church that sexual activity should be creative as well as unitive (see page 72), and it is not possible for homosexuals to have procreative sex.
▶ The Catechism of the Catholic Church, which all Catholics should believe, teaches that marriage is for a man and a woman to join as one and to raise a family.
▶ The Church teaches that people cannot help their sexual orientation (but they can control their sexual activity). Therefore discriminating against people because of their sexual orientation is wrong.
▶ The Bible teaches that everyone has human dignity because they are made in the image of God.
▶ The Church does not refer to 'heterosexual' or 'homosexual' alone, but speaks about homosexual persons whose identity is as a child of God.

In receiving Royal Assent, the Marriage (Same Sex Couples) Act marks a watershed in English law and heralds a profound social change. This fact is acknowledged by both advocates and opponents of the Act. Marriage has, over the centuries, been publicly recognised as a stable institution which establishes a legal framework for the committed relationship between a man and a woman and for the upbringing and care of their children. It has, for this reason, rightly been recognised as unique and worthy of legal protection. The new Act breaks the existing legal links between the institution of marriage and sexual complementarity. With this new legislation, marriage has now become an institution in which openness to children, and with it the responsibility on fathers and mothers to remain together to care for children born into their family unit, are no longer central. That is why we were opposed to this legislation on principle.

Statement by the President and Vice-President of the Catholic Bishops Conference of England and Wales 17 July 2013

The Church utterly condemns all forms of unjust discrimination, violence, harassment or abuse directed against people who are homosexual. Consequently, the Church teaches that homosexual people 'must be accepted with respect, compassion, and sensitivity'.

Cherishing Life, Catholic Bishops' Conference of England and Wales 2004

2. The Evangelical Protestant attitude

Many Evangelical Protestants believe that homosexuality is a sin. They believe that there should be no homosexual Christians and hold special prayer meetings to give homosexuals the power of the Spirit to change their sexual preference (orientation). The reasons for this attitude are:

▶ They believe that the Bible is the direct word of God and as the Bible condemns homosexuality in some passages of both the Old and New Testaments, it must be wrong.
▶ They believe that the salvation of Christ can remove all sins, including homosexuality.
▶ They believe it because all the Churches have taught it, even though some now say homosexuality is acceptable.

However, the Evangelical Alliance has recently made this statement: 'At the same time we utterly repudiate **homophobia** and call upon Churches to welcome those of a homosexual orientation as they would welcome any other person.'

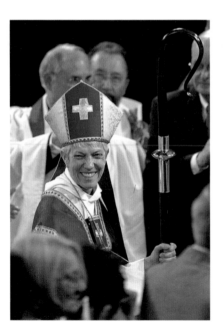

Mary Glasspool, Bishop of Los Angeles, was the first openly lesbian woman to be elected an Anglican bishop.

> We recognise the many reasons why couples wish their relationships to have a formal status. These include the joys of exclusive commitment and also extend to the importance of legal recognition of the relationship. To that end, civil partnership continues to be available for same sex couples. Those same sex couples who choose to marry should be welcomed into the life of the worshipping community and not be subjected to questioning about their lifestyle. Neither they nor any children they care for should be denied access to the sacraments ... same sex weddings in church will not be possible. As with civil partnership, some same sex couples are, however, likely to seek some recognition of their new situation in the context of an act of worship. The 2005 pastoral statement said that it would not be right to produce an authorised public liturgy in connection with the registering of civil partnerships and that clergy should not provide services of blessing for those who registered civil partnerships. The House did not wish, however, to interfere with the clergy's pastoral discretion about when more informal kind of prayer, at the request of the couple, might be appropriate in the light of the circumstances ... Services of blessing should not be provided. Clergy should respond pastorally and sensitively in other ways.
>
> *Church of England House of Bishops Pastoral Guidance on Same Sex Marriage, 15 February 2014*

3. The Liberal Protestant attitude

Many Liberal Protestants have the attitude that lifelong homosexual relationships are acceptable and homosexuals are welcomed into the Church. They are happy to provide blessings for civil partnerships but not same sex marriages which they believe cannot be equated to Christian marriage. However, some, such as the Quakers, are happy to celebrate same sex weddings in church. They are happy for homosexuals to be ministers and priests. The reasons for this attitude are:

▶ They believe that the teachings of the Bible need re-interpreting in the light of modern knowledge and that the anti-homosexual texts in the Bible are a reflection of the Jewish culture at the time rather than the word of God.

▶ They feel that the major Christian belief in love and acceptance means that homosexuals must be accepted.

▶ Recent scientific research shows that homosexuality may well be genetic and so is part of people's nature.

▶ They believe that Christians should be open and honest and refusing rights to gay Christians encourages them to be dishonest and hypocritical about their nature and life.

Quakers in Britain welcome the Marriage (Same Sex Couples) Act. The legislation received Royal Assent on 17 July 2013. The Act is being implemented in a phased way and the first marriages in England and Wales under the new law may be from 29 March 2014.

Quakers see God in everyone and that leads us to say that all committed loving relationships are of equal worth and so Quakers in Britain wish to celebrate them in the same way.

Quakers in Britain, December 2013

Questions

b) Do you think homosexuals should have equal rights? Give two reasons for your point of view. **(4)**

c) Explain why some Christians accept homosexuality and some do not. **(8)**

d) 'No Christian should be homosexual.'

  (i) Do you agree? Give reasons for your opinion. **(3)**

  (ii) Give reasons why some people may disagree with you. **(3)**

Exam Tip

d) Use the answering evaluation questions advice from page 9. Arguments for the statement would be the reasons for the Evangelical Protestant view. Arguments against would be the reasons for the Liberal Protestant view.

Summary

● Catholics are opposed to any bias against homosexuals, but are opposed to same sex marriage and believe homosexuals should refrain from sexual activity because this is the teaching of the Church.

● Evangelical Protestants believe that homosexuality is sinful and are opposed to same sex marriage because homosexuality is condemned in the Bible.

● Liberal Protestants believe that homosexuality is acceptable because it is natural and Christians should love and accept everyone.

Christian ministers who gave church blessings to civil partnerships are likely to offer Christian same sex marriage ceremonies.

Topic 3.3.9 Different methods of contraception

Throughout history people have tried to control the number of children they have for a number of reasons:

▶ for the health of the mother
▶ to ensure there is enough food for the family unit
▶ to provide a better standard of living for the family unit.

Contraception is something that allows sex to happen without conception occurring, so allowing a couple to control the number of children they have. The use of contraception in the West has become very popular (it is now estimated that 90 per cent of the sexually active population of childbearing age in the UK use some form of contraception).

There are two fundamentally different types of contraception:

1. Natural methods of contraception

The most common form of natural contraception is known as natural family planning (NFP), or fertility awareness. It involves reducing the chance of becoming pregnant by planning sex around the most infertile times during the woman's monthly cycle. To be as effective as possible, it should be taught by an experienced NFP teacher.

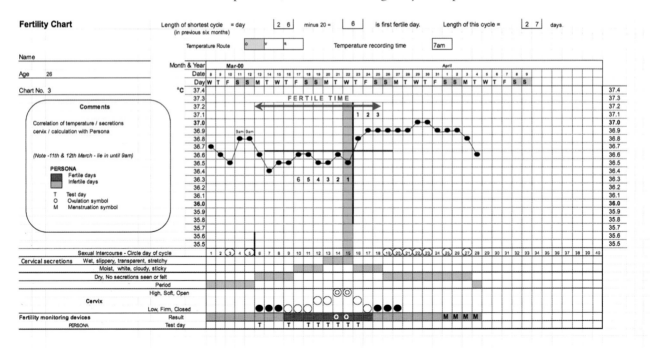

A completed fertility chart combining several indicators or signs of fertility.

Another method uses a device to measure hormone levels in the urine. If used according to the instructions, these methods can be 94 per cent effective.

Natural methods require a couple to be in a loving, stable relationship as they require planning and sufficient love and concern for the partner to give up sex at certain times of the month. As they are natural they do not involve any drugs or any risk of promoting an early abortion. Natural methods do not prevent sexually transmitted diseases, but these will not affect a couple who only have sex with each other as required in Catholic marriage.

2. Artificial methods of contraception

There are several types of artificial contraception. Barrier methods such as condoms prevent the sperm from reaching the egg. Hormonal drugs (the pill) stop a woman from producing eggs. There are also methods such as the coil (IUD/IUS) and the morning-after pill, which prevent a fertilised egg from attaching itself to the womb wall (these methods are sometimes called abortifacients).

Artificial methods can be used without any planning, and in any form of sexual relationship, however casual. They involve either changes to a woman's body or interfering with the normal sexual process. Condoms are also effective in preventing the transmission of sexually transmitted diseases (especially AIDS).

Questions

b) Do you think contraception should be used? Give two reasons for your point of view. **(4)**

c) Explain the main differences between natural and artificial methods of contraception. **(8)**

d) 'It doesn't matter what type of contraceptive you use.'

    (i) Do you agree? Give reasons for your opinion. **(3)**

    (ii) Give reasons why some people may disagree with you. **(3)**

Exam Tip

c) One way to answer this question would be to use information from the last paragraph of natural methods then use the last paragraph of artificial methods to show the differences, for example, natural methods require a couple to be in a loving stable relationship, artificial methods do not. Try to use some specialist vocabulary such as: NFP, fertility awareness, abortifacient, condoms, sexually transmitted diseases, AIDS.

Summary

Natural methods of contraception require planning, love and commitment by avoiding having sex during a woman's fertile period.

Artificial methods of contraception either prevent the sperm from meeting the egg, stop a woman producing eggs, or stop the fertilised egg from implanting in the womb. They can be used in any type of sexual relationship.

Topic 3.3.10 Different Christian attitudes to contraception

The methods of birth regulation based on self-observation and the use of infertile periods ... respect the bodies of the spouses, encourage tenderness between them ... In contrast, 'every action which, whether in anticipation of the conjugal act, or in its accomplishment, or in the development of its natural consequences, proposes, whether as an end or as a means, to render procreation impossible' is intrinsically evil.

Catechism of the Catholic Church 2370

Statistics

In 2014, 45 years after Pope Paul VI's encyclical *Humanae Vitae* forbade all forms of artificial contraception, Univision conducted a survey of 12,000 Catholics from five continents. The survey discovered that in Latin America, overall support for artificial contraceptives was 91 percent, in Europe it was 89 percent, and in the United States 79 percent.

Do you find this surprising?

There are two main attitudes to contraception among Christians.

1. The Catholic attitude

The Catholic Church has always taught responsible parenthood. The Church teaches that sexual intercourse is a gift from God as a source of joy and pleasure to married couples (the unitive purpose) as well as a means of creating a family (the creative purpose). Responsible parenthood involves deciding on the number of children to have and when to have them. However, the Catholic way to achieve this is through using natural family planning (see page 70). The Church in its documents always refers to natural and artificial methods of birth 'regulation', but the examination specification uses the word 'contraception'. The Church teaches that using artificial methods of contraception is going against God's intentions. Catholics believe this because:

▶ In *Casti Connubii*, published in 1930, Pope Pius XI condemned all forms of artificial contraception.
▶ In 1951, Pope Pius XII declared that Catholics could use natural methods of contraception as these are natural and so part of God's creation.
▶ In 1968, Pope Paul VI's encyclical *Humanae Vitae* affirmed the teaching of previous Popes that the only allowable forms of contraception are natural methods. This teaching has been confirmed in the Catechism of the Catholic Church.
▶ Artificial methods of birth control separate the unitive and creative aspects of sex, which is not what God intended.
▶ Some contraceptives have abortifacient effects (they bring about a very early abortion) and so are against the teaching of the Church.
▶ The Catholic Church regards contraception as a major cause of sexual promiscuity, broken families, the rise in the divorce rate and sexually transmitted diseases.

2. The attitude of non-Catholic Christians

Almost all non-Catholic Christians believe that all forms of contraception are permissible as long as they are used to restrict the size of the family and not simply to stop having children altogether. They have this attitude because:

▶ Christianity is about love and justice, and contraception improves women's health and raises the standard of living of children as families are smaller.

- God created sex for enjoyment and to cement the bonds of marriage. Within marriage, contraception allows the role of sex to be separated from making children and this is not against God's will.
- There is nothing in the Bible that forbids the use of contraception.
- In 1930, the Lambeth Conference of the worldwide Anglican Communion (Church of England) declared it was legitimate for Christians to use contraception to limit family size. This has been followed by the major Protestant Churches and the Orthodox Churches.
- They believe that it is better to combat HIV/AIDS by using condoms than by expecting everyone to follow Christian rules about sex and marriage.

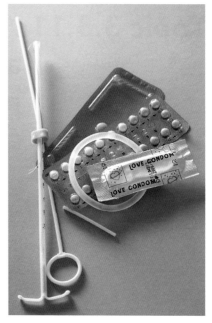

There are many types of artificial contraceptives.

Contraception is seen as a gift from medical science under God's sovereignty. Choosing not to have or space families is morally defensible, considering the needs of the world, population size and family responsibility. However, those contraceptives that have an abortifacient function (for example, IUD and various pills) are considered to take human life and should be avoided.

Statement by the Baptist Church in What the Churches Say

Questions

b) Do you think it is wrong for Christians to use artificial methods of contraception? Give two reasons for your point of view. **(4)**

c) Explain why some Christians allow artificial methods of contraception and some do not. **(8)**

d) 'Christians should never use contraceptives.'

    (i) Do you agree? Give reasons for your opinion. **(3)**

    (ii) Give reasons why some people may disagree with you. **(3)**

Exam Tip

b) You should already have thought about this, and you just have to give two reasons for your opinion. For example, if you think it is wrong you could use two reasons for the Catholic Church disagreeing with artificial methods of contraception.

Summary

The Catholic Church teaches that using artificial methods of contraception to stop a baby being conceived is wrong. God gave sex in order to create children as well as strengthening the marriage. Natural methods of contraception are acceptable.

Other Christians allow the use of contraception because they believe God gave sex to strengthen a married relationship.

Topic 3.3.11 How an issue from marriage and the family has been presented in one form of the media

You have to study how one issue from marriage and the family has been presented in one form of the media.

Your issue could be connected with:

▶ sex outside marriage
▶ adultery
▶ divorce
▶ re-marriage
▶ family life
▶ homosexuality
▶ contraception.

You can choose the media but it should only be one of the following:

▶ a television programme
▶ a radio programme
▶ a film
▶ an article in the national press.

If you study a film such as *Keeping Mum*, where Rowan Atkinson stars as a Church of England vicar whose preoccupation with the Church leads his wife to adultery and his daughter to promiscuity, you need to investigate whether the way the film presents the issue is fair to religious people and religious beliefs.

You must choose both the issue and the type of media carefully to be able to answer questions on:

◗ why the issue is important
◗ how it is presented
◗ whether the presentation is fair to religious beliefs
◗ whether the presentation is fair to religious people.

To do this you must:

1. Select an issue and a form of media. It is very important that you select only one issue. Some films have several issues running through them. If you choose more than one issue, your answers are likely to be confused.
2. Decide why the issue is important (you may need to look at the views of different members of the particular religion and of the impact of the issue on society as a whole) and why you think the producers of the media decided to focus on this issue.
3. Write an outline of how the issue is presented, listing the main events and the way the events explore the issue.
4. Look closely at the way religious beliefs are treated in the presentation of the issue. Use this information to decide whether you think the presentation is fair to religious beliefs.
5. Look closely at the way religious people are treated in the presentation of the issue. Use this information to decide whether you think the presentation is fair to religious people.

Hollyoaks features many storylines on Catholics and marriage and family issues. In 2008 a young Catholic priest, Kieron Hobbs, had a homosexual affair with John Paul McQueen, a Catholic student teacher. If you study one of these issues, you must investigate whether the presentation of the issue is fair to Catholic beliefs and Catholic people.

Questions

b) Do you think the media presented an issue from marriage and the family fairly? Give two reasons for your point of view. **(4)**

c) Choose an issue from marriage and the family presented in one form of the media and explain whether the presentation is fair to religious people. **(8)**

d) You are unlikely to be asked an evaluation question on this section as you only have to study one issue in one form of the media.

Exam Tip

c) One way to answer this question would be to state what the issue is and then briefly summarise the presentation. Decide whether you think the presentation of the issue is fair to religious people and give four reasons from the presentation to back up your opinion. Make sure you use specific details from the presentation (such as the names of characters) and specialist vocabulary from the issue.

Summary

When studying the presentation of an issue from marriage and the family in the media, you must be able to explain why the issue was chosen, how it is presented, whether the presentation treats religious people fairly and whether the presentation treats religious beliefs fairly.

How to answer exam questions

a) What is meant by a nuclear family? (2)

A nuclear family is a family with a mother, father and children living together as a unit.

b) Do you think all Christians should accept homosexuality? (4)

Yes I do because the Catholic Church teaches that it is not wrong to be homosexual and that it is very wrong to discriminate against homosexuals and so Catholics should accept homosexuality. Also there is scientific evidence that homosexuality comes from a person's genetic make-up which means that homosexuality is natural and so should be accepted.

c) Explain how Roman Catholic parishes help to keep families together. (8)

One way parishes help keep families together is when during Mass the priest may remind parents of the vows they made in their marriage ceremony and also of other reasons not to divorce.

Another way is by implementing the Church package 'Everybody's Welcome? Helping Your Parish to Become More Friendly for Families of All Kinds' which helps strengthen family life by families celebrating Mass together so keeping them together.

The Church has also produced a series of leaflets – 'What is Life Like?' – for parishes to use to meet the needs of families facing specific challenges, such as divorce and re-marriage, bereavement and living without a shared faith in God.

Finally, many parishes also provide financial support for families in financial difficulties and have links to national Catholic charities to help family life, for example: Catholic Marriage Care.

d) 'Sex before marriage is always wrong.'

In your answer you should refer to Roman Catholic Christianity.

    i)   Do you agree? Give reasons for your opinion. (3)

    ii)   Give reasons why some people may disagree with you. (3)

i) As a Catholic, I agree with this statement because the Church teaches that sex was given to humans by God for the joy, pleasure and bond of a married couple and for the procreation of children, and children should be brought up in a Christian family so sex should only take place within marriage. Also the Bible says that fornication (a word used in religion for both pre-marital sex and promiscuity) is sinful and Christians should follow the teachings of the Bible. Finally, the Catechism of the Catholic Church teaches that pre-marital sex is wrong and as a Catholic, I believe I should follow the teachings of the Church.

ii) Some people might disagree with me because they think that sex is a natural result of two people being in love, and there is no reason for them waiting until they are married. They might also believe that modern contraception methods are so effective that a couple can have sex without the risk of pregnancy, so unwanted children are not likely to result from sex before marriage. Finally, they might point to the fact that sex before marriage is now accepted by society and very few people think it is wrong.

Question a

A high mark answer because it gives a correct definition.

Question b

A high mark answer because an opinion is backed up by two developed reasons.

Question c

A high mark answer because it explains four ways in which Catholic parishes help to keep families together. There is good use of specialist vocabulary such as: Mass, vows, marriage ceremony, celebrating Mass, divorce and re-marriage, bereavement, disability, mental ill-health, shared faith, Christian communities, national Catholic charities, Catholic Marriage Care, the National Catholic Child Welfare Council.

Question d

A high mark answer because it states the candidate's own opinion and backs it up with three clear Catholic reasons for believing sex before marriage is always wrong. It then gives three reasons for people disagreeing and believing that sex before marriage should be allowed.

Section 3.4

Religion and community cohesion

Introduction

This section of the examination specification requires you to look at issues surrounding the roles of men and women, racial harmony, religious harmony and the media and community cohesion.

Roles of men and women

You will need to understand the effects of, and give reasons for your own opinion about:

▶ how and why attitudes to the roles of men and women have changed in the United Kingdom
▶ different Christian attitudes to equal rights for women in religion and the reasons for them.

Racial harmony

You will need to understand the effects of, and give reasons for your own opinion about:

▶ the nature of the United Kingdom as a multi-ethnic society including problems of discrimination and racism
▶ government action to promote community cohesion in the United Kingdom, including legislation on equal rights for ethnic minorities and religions
▶ why Catholics should help to promote racial harmony
▶ the work of the Catholic Church to help asylum seekers and/or immigrant workers in the United Kingdom.

Religious harmony

You will need to understand the effects of, and give reasons for your own opinion about:

▶ the United Kingdom as a multi-faith society, including the benefits of living in a multi-faith society
▶ differences among Christians in their attitudes to other religions
▶ issues raised for religion by a multi-faith society – conversion, bringing up children, mixed-faith marriages
▶ ways in which religions work to promote community cohesion in the United Kingdom.

The media and community cohesion

You will need to understand the effects of, and give reasons for your own opinion about:

▶ how an issue from religion and community cohesion has been presented in one form of the media
▶ whether the treatment is fair to religious beliefs and religious people.

Topic 3.4.1 How and why attitudes to the roles of men and women have changed in the United Kingdom

KEY WORDS

Discrimination – treating people less favourably because of their ethnicity/gender/colour/sexuality/age/class

Sexism – discriminating against people because of their gender (being male or female)

Women make up 84 per cent of employees in personal services (care assistants, child minders, hairdressers, etc).

Men make up 66 per cent of managers, senior officials, professionals.

Source: Census 2001

Statistics

The gender pay gap (the difference between men's and women's median hourly pay) was narrowing but widened again during the recession

1986	26%
2002	19%
2007	12.6%
2013	15.7%

Average minutes spent per day

Activity	Men	Women
Cooking	27	54
Cleaning	13	47
Laundry	4	18
Caring for children	22	42

Source: Office of National Statistics

How attitudes have changed

Women in the UK have always had the right to own property and earn their own living, but in the past they did not have the same rights as men and, when women married, their husbands had the right to use their property. During the second half of the nineteenth century, it became the accepted view that married women should stay at home and look after the children (in 1850 about 50 per cent of married women had been in employment, but by 1900 this was down to about 15 per cent).

During the late nineteenth and early twentieth centuries, women began to campaign against sexism and to be treated as the equals of men. The growth of equal rights for women began with the Married Women's Property Act 1882, which allowed married women to keep their property separate from their husband's. In 1892, the Local Government Act gave women the right to stand as councillors. In 1918, the Representation of the People Act allowed women over 30 to vote in parliamentary elections (men could vote at 21). However, it was not until 1928 that the Electoral Reform Act gave equal voting rights to women.

Equal rights in employment did not arrive until the Equal Pay Act 1970, which required employers to give women the same pay as men – equal pay for like work, regardless of the employee's sex. Then, in 1975, the Sex Discrimination Act made discrimination on the grounds of gender or whether someone is married (though religion was given an opt-out) in employment illegal. These Acts gave women the right to take employers to court if they treated them differently from their male colleagues.

Although women achieved equal rights in law, attitudes to the roles of men and women have been even slower to change.

Men's attitudes to the roles of men and women have changed considerably – in 1989, 32 per cent of men agreed that, 'a man's job is to earn money, a woman's job is to look after the home and family'

Firms like Land Rover now employ more women engineers, but most are still men. Why do you think this is?

whereas in 2008 only 17 per cent of men agreed with the statement. However, there has been less progress in who actually does the work around the home. The Public Policy Research Think Tank showed that in 2012 80 per cent of married women did more housework than their husbands.

Why attitudes have changed

▶ During the First and Second World Wars, women had to take on many of the jobs previously done by men and proved they could do them just as well.

▶ The development of equal rights for women in other countries (New Zealand was the first country to give women equal political rights) made it difficult to claim it was not needed in Britain.

▶ The success of women as councillors and the important contribution of women to developments in health and social care showed that women were the equals of men in these areas.

▶ The work of the suffragette movement to gain equal voting and political rights for women showed the men in authority that women were no longer prepared to be treated as second class citizens.

▶ Social and industrial developments in the 1950s and 1960s led to the need for more women workers and for married women to provide a second income.

▶ The UN Declaration of Human Rights and the development of the Feminist Movement put forward a case for equal rights that could not be contradicted.

▶ The Labour Governments of 1964–70 and 1974–79 were dedicated to the equal rights campaign and passed the Equal Pay Act and the Sex Discrimination Act.

Why might this Second World War poster have helped women gain equal rights?

Everyone is entitled to all the rights and freedoms set forth in this Declaration, without distinction of any kind, such as race, colour, sex, language, religion, political or other opinion, national or social origin, property, birth or other status. Furthermore, no distinction shall be made on the basis of the political, jurisdictional or international status of the country or territory to which a person belongs, whether it be independent, trust, non-self-governing or under any other limitation of sovereignty.

Article 2 of the UN Declaration of Human Rights

Questions

b) Do you think men should share housework with women? Give two reasons for your point of view. **(4)**

c) Explain how attitudes to the roles of men and women have changed. **(8)**

d) 'Men and women should have equal roles in life.'

    (i) Do you agree? Give reasons for your opinion. **(3)**

    (ii) Give reasons why some people may disagree with you. **(3)**

Exam Tip

c) One way to answer this question would be to use four changes from page 78, beginning with what the attitude used to be and explaining how it has changed. Your answer should be four short paragraphs. Make sure you use some specialist vocabulary such as: Married Women's Property Act, electoral reform, Equal Pay Act, Sex Discrimination Act, gender pay gap, domestic work.

Summary

Attitudes to the roles of men and women have changed greatly. Women now have equal rights, and men and women are expected to share roles in the home. Attitudes have changed because of the Feminist Movement, social and industrial changes and the effects of the World Wars.

Topic 3.4.2 Different Christian attitudes to equal rights for women in religion

> A wife is to submit graciously to the servant leadership of her husband even as the Church willingly submits to the leadership of Christ … she, being in the image of God, as is her husband and thus equal to him, has the God-given responsibility to respect her husband and to serve as his helper.
>
> *Statement by the Southern Baptist Convention of the USA, June 1998*

> The Lord Jesus chose men to form the college of the twelve **apostles**, and the apostles did the same when they chose collaborators to succeed them in their ministry … for this reason, the ordination of women is impossible.
>
> *Catechism of the Catholic Church 1577*

1. Catholic attitudes

The Catholic Church teaches that men and women should have equal roles in life and equal rights in society. As far as ministry is concerned, women are able to study and teach in theological colleges. Women can also be extraordinary ministers of Holy Communion (people who give out the bread and wine which has been consecrated by a priest), visit the sick, take funerals in certain circumstances, and so on. Indeed it is estimated that over 80 per cent of religious teachers and pastoral visitors in the USA Catholic Church are women. Over half of the lectors and extraordinary ministers in the British Catholic Church are women.

However, the Catholic Church teaches that only men can be ordained priests. It teaches that this does not affect the equal status of women. It is because of the special function of the priest representing Jesus at the Mass. This teaching is based on:

▶ Genesis 1:27 which teaches that God created men and women at the same time and both in the image of God. So the Church teaches that men and women have equal status in the sight of God
▶ the teaching of the Catholic Catechism that men and women are equal, and should have equal rights in life and society, and Catholics should follow the teachings of the Catechism
▶ the 1971 report, 'Justice in the World', in which the Third World Synod of Bishops called for women to 'participate in, and share responsibility for, the life of society and of the Church'
▶ the teaching of the Catechism that only men can be priests because the apostles were all men, and priests and bishops are successors of the apostles
▶ the teaching of the Catechism that only men can be priests because Jesus was a man and the priest represents Jesus in the Mass.

2. The traditional attitude of Protestant Christianity

Many Evangelical Protestants teach that men and women have separate and different roles and so cannot have equal rights in religion. It is the role of women to bring up children and run a Christian home. Women should not speak in church and must submit to their husbands. It is the role of men to provide for the family and to lead the family in religion. Men must love their wives as themselves, but only men can be Church leaders and teachers.

They have this attitude because:

▶ It is the teaching of the New Testament, which they believe is the final word of God. St Paul teaches that women should not teach or speak in church.

- St Paul also uses the story of Adam and Eve in Genesis to show that men have been given more rights by God because Adam was created first and it was the woman who was led astray by Satan and then led man astray.
- Although Jesus had women followers, he chose only men as his twelve apostles.
- It has been the tradition of the Church from the beginning that only men should have leadership rights in the Church.

3. The modern attitude of Protestant Christianity

Many Protestant Churches now accept that men and women should have equal rights, and they have women ministers and priests (for example, Church of England, Methodist, United Reformed Church and Baptist). This teaching is based on:

- the creation story in Genesis 1, which says that God created male and female at the same time and of equal status because both were created in the image of God
- some letters of Paul where he teaches that in Christ there is neither male nor female, therefore men and women should have equal rights
- the evidence from the Gospels that Jesus treated women as his equals. He preached in the Court of Women in the Jerusalem Temple (Matthew 21:23–22:14). He treated a Samaritan woman as his equal (John 4). He had women disciples who stayed with him at the cross (Matthew 27:55, Mark 15:40–41, Luke 23:27, John 19:25–27) unlike the male disciples who ran away. It was to women that Jesus first appeared after the resurrection
- some evidence that there were women priests in the early Church. The Council of Laodicea banned women priests in the fourth century and it would not have banned something that did not exist.

Pat Storey became the UK and Ireland's first female bishop when she was consecrated at a ceremony in Dublin in November 2013.

Questions

b) Do you think women should have equal rights in religion? Give two reasons for your point of view. **(4)**

c) Explain why some Christians give equal roles to women in religion and some do not. **(8)**

d) 'Women should have equal roles in Christianity.'

    (i) Do you agree? Give reasons for your opinion. **(3)**

    (ii) Give reasons why some people may disagree with you. **(3)**

Exam Tip

b) You should already have thought about this, and you just have to give two reasons for your opinion. For example, if you agree with equal rights for women in religion except for the priesthood, you could use two reasons for the Catholic attitude.

Summary

- Catholics believe men and women should have equal rights, but only men can become priests because Jesus was a man and the priest is representing him at Mass.
- Traditional Protestants believe only men should be religious leaders because this is what the Bible teaches.
- Liberal Protestants believe men and women have equal rights in religion because Jesus had women disciples.

Topic 3.4.3 The nature of the UK as a multi-ethnic society

KEY WORDS

Ethnic minority – a member of an ethnic group (race) which is much smaller than the majority group

Multi-ethnic society – many different races and cultures living together in one society

Prejudice – believing some people are inferior or superior without even knowing them

Racism – the belief that some races are superior to others

The United Kingdom has always been a mixed society – Celts, Romans, Angles, Saxons, Jutes, Danes, Vikings and Normans are all ancestors of the British.

The United Kingdom has always believed in human freedom and offered asylum to those suffering persecution; for example, to French Protestants (Huguenots) in the seventeenth century, to Russian Jews in the nineteenth century, to European Jews escaping Hitler in the twentieth century.

In the nineteenth century the United Kingdom built up an empire around the world. In exchange for being ruled by Britain, citizens of the Empire were allowed to settle in the United Kingdom. Slaves who set foot on British soil immediately became free. As a result, small black communities grew up in Bristol, Liverpool and Cardiff.

The Empire became known as the 'Commonwealth' as nations gained their independence from the United Kingdom. In the 1950s there was substantial immigration from the Commonwealth. People came from India, Pakistan, Bangladesh, West Africa and the Caribbean to lessen a labour shortage in the United Kingdom. Many of these workers had fought for the United Kingdom in the Second World War (there were more people in the British armed forces from the Commonwealth than from the United Kingdom itself).

Immigration from the Commonwealth has continued on a smaller scale, but the extension of the European Union at the beginning of this century led to a large influx of East Europeans, and wars and racial/religious persecutions have led to an increase of asylum seekers (people wanting to live in the United Kingdom because their lives are at risk in their own countries).

Although only 13 per cent of the total United Kingdom population is classed as being from an ethnic minority, there are big differences in different areas. For example, over 50 per cent of London's population is an ethnic minority, as opposed to less than 2 per cent of the population of South West England. There are also more than a million people who class themselves as mixed race.

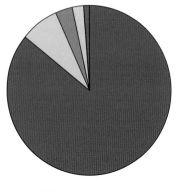

- ■ 86% White British
- □ 7.5% Asian British
- ■ 3.3% Black British
- □ 2.2% Mixed British
- ■ 1% Other Ethnic Groups

The different ethnicities in the UK, according to the 2011 census.

Discrimination and racism

Racism is a type of prejudice that can cause major problems in a multi-ethnic society because of the discrimination it leads to. Racist people believe the ethnic group to which they belong to be superior to all other ethnic groups. Therefore they believe that all other races are inferior. Religiously prejudiced people believe that everyone who does not believe in their religion is wrong.

Notting Hill Carnival celebrates the benefits of Britain's multi-ethnic society.

Statistics

A report by the University of Manchester's Centre on Dynamics of Ethnicity published in 2014 showed that most immigrants are better qualified than the existing population:

Number with no qualifications

Bangladeshi	28%
Pakistani	26%
White British	24%
Black Caribbean	19%
Chinese	16%
Indian	15%
Black African	11%

Numbers of graduates

Bangladeshi	20%
Pakistani	24%
White British	26%
Black Caribbean	26%
Black African	40%
Indian	42%
Chinese	43%

The problems of discrimination and racism:

▶ Racially prejudiced employers will not give jobs to certain ethnic groups, religiously prejudiced employers will not give jobs to certain religious groups (it is easy, for example, for employers to discriminate against Muslims, Sikhs and **Orthodox Jews**).

▶ Prejudiced landlords are likely to refuse accommodation to certain ethnic groups or religions.

▶ If teachers are prejudiced against certain ethnic minorities or religious groups, they will discriminate against them in their teaching, so that those pupils do not achieve the results (and so gain the jobs) of which they are capable. Teachers could try to get pupils excluded from school, put them into lower ability groups than their actual ability, and so on.

▶ Prejudiced police officers could potentially discriminate against certain ethnic or religious groups, for example, by: stopping and searching them if they have no real reason for doing so; not treating evidence from people against whom they are prejudiced in the same way that they treat evidence from people against whom they are not prejudiced.

Research in 2013 showed that: EU migrants to the UK contribute three times more to the UK economy than they take out in benefits; the number of EU migrants living in the UK is roughly the same as the number of Britons living elsewhere in the EU; 40 per cent of UK nurses come from abroad, meaning the NHS would collapse without migrants.

The effects of discrimination and racism

The effects of discrimination and racism can be quite devastating for a multi-ethnic society:

▶ If certain groups feel that they are being treated unfairly by society, then they will begin to feel alienated and so work against that society.

▶ Some politicians believe that young black people turn to crime because they feel they will not be able to get good well-paid jobs because of racism and discrimination and so they might as well earn good money from crime. If true, this might lead to an increase in crime.

▶ Some politicians believe that some young people have been turning to extremist Islamic groups because they feel they have no chance of success in a prejudiced British society that discriminates against their religion. This can then lead them to commit terrorist acts.

▶ Racism and discrimination can lead to the rise of groups like the English Defence League (EDL), which stir up hatred of different ethnic groups, leading to violence and communal warfare.

If a multi-ethnic society is to function well, it must treat all its members fairly, and give equal opportunities to all its members to achieve their best.

Most people in the UK do not want racist groups like the EDL stirring up hatred.

The benefits of living in a multi-ethnic society

Multi-ethnic societies bring far more benefits than problems:

▶ There is likely to be less chance of war because people of different ethnic groups and nationalities will get to know and like each other, and probably intermarry.

▶ More progress will be made in a multi-ethnic society because new people will bring in new ideas and new ways of doing things.

Societies that are cut off and do not mix with other cultures tend to be less progressive, for example, the Amazonian Indians.

) Life is more interesting with a much greater variety of food, music, fashion and entertainment.

) A multi-ethnic society helps people to see that different ethnic groups are all part of the human race and we have more in common than we have differences. This is vital in a world of multi-national companies and economic interdependence between all nations.

Barack Hussein Obama was elected the 44th president of the United States on Tuesday, sweeping away the last racial barrier in American politics with ease as the country chose him as its first black chief executive ...

Tens of thousands of people turned out to hear Mr. Obama's victory speech in Grant Park Chicago.

'If there is anyone out there who still doubts that America is a place where all things are possible, who still wonders if the dream of our founders is alive in our time, who still questions the power of our democracy, tonight is your answer.

It's been a long time coming, but tonight, because of what we did on this date in this election at this defining moment, change has come to America.'

Adapted from The New York Times *November 4th 2008*

Why do you think the Obama family being the USA's first family helps community cohesion?

Questions

b) Do you think we need laws against racism? Give two reasons for your point of view. **(4)**

c) Explain why discrimination and racism cause problems in a multi-ethnic society. **(8)**

d) 'Prejudice and discrimination should be banned.'

    (i) Do you agree? Give reasons for your opinion. **(3)**

    (ii) Give reasons why some people may disagree with you. **(3)**

Exam Tip

c) 'Explain why' means give reasons. One way to answer this question would be to use four effects of discrimination and racism from page 84. Make sure you use some specialist vocabulary such as: alienated, extremist, Islamic, terrorist acts, ethnic groups, communal warfare, English Defence League.

Summary

● Britain has many ethnic minorities and so is a multi-ethnic society.
● Multi-ethnic societies have many benefits, such as advancing more quickly because they have a greater variety of ideas.
● A multi-ethnic society needs equal opportunities and treatment to work, and prejudice and discrimination cause major problems in such a society because they do not treat everyone equally.

Topic 3.4.4 Government action to promote community cohesion in the United Kingdom

KEY WORDS

Community cohesion – a common vision and shared sense of belonging for all groups in society

Multi-faith society – many different religions living together in one society

'The Cantle Report' into the race riots in Bradford, Oldham and Burnley in 2001 noted how riots had not arisen in diverse areas, such as Southall and Leicester, where pupils learnt about different religions and cultures in local schools. As a result, the 2006 Education and Inspections Act introduced a duty upon all maintained schools in England to promote community cohesion, and on Ofsted to report on the contributions made in this area when undertaking school inspections. The Coalition Education Act 2011 confirmed that schools have a duty to promote community cohesion, but removed the need for Ofsted to report on school's community cohesion policies.

What does your school do to promote community cohesion?

The United Kingdom believes that a multi-ethnic society needs to promote community cohesion in order to overcome the problems of prejudice, discrimination and racism. The British Government promotes community cohesion by:

◗ financially supporting groups that are working for community cohesion
◗ making community cohesion part of the national education curriculum. The Education and Inspections Act 2006 introduced a duty on all maintained schools in England to promote community cohesion and on Ofsted to report on the contributions made in this area
◗ funding research into the best ways of achieving community cohesion
◗ appointing cabinet ministers, judges, etc., from ethnic minorities
◗ passing the Race Relations Act, which makes it unlawful to discriminate against anyone because of race, colour, nationality, ethnic or national origin, use threatening or abusive or insulting words in public that could stir up racial hatred; publish anything likely to cause racial hatred
◗ passing the Crime and Disorder Act, which allows higher maximum penalties where there is evidence of racial or religious motivation or hostility
◗ passing the Racial and Religious Hatred Act, which makes it an offence to use threatening words or behaviour intended to incite groups of people defined by their religious beliefs or lack of belief
◗ establishing the Equality and Human Rights Commission, which champions equality and human rights for all
◗ ensuring that the Labour Party, the Conservative Party and the Liberal Democrat Party oppose racism in any form, particularly by encouraging members of ethnic minorities to become MPs.

Why community cohesion is important

Community cohesion is important for all multi-ethnic and multi-faith societies because:

◗ Without community cohesion, different groups in society have different visions of what society should be like and this can lead to violence and civil unrest.
◗ A lack of community cohesion in Oldham, Burnley and Bradford led to racially/religiously motivated street rioting in 2001. According to the Government Cantle report, the rioting was caused

by: different communities living 'parallel lives', ignorance about other communities being exploited by extremists and weak local leadership and policing. Single-faith schools were also criticised for raising the possibility of deeper divisions.

◗ The 7 July 2007 bombers on the London Underground were British citizens who had lost their sense of allegiance to Britain and, indeed, were prepared to kill, maim and injure their fellow citizens.

◗ In places without community cohesion (such as Iraq and Kashmir) violence becomes a way of life.

◗ Lack of community cohesion leads to different communities leading separate lives, making civilised living impossible.

Community cohesion may have prevented atrocities like the 7 July 2007 London bombings.

Community cohesion is therefore about: how to avoid the bad effects of intolerance and harassment that can break down society; how to encourage different groups to work together and treat each other as fellow citizens; how to ensure respect for diversity whilst building up a commitment to common and shared bonds as citizens of the same society.

Questions

b) Do you think the government should spend money promoting community cohesion? Give two reasons for your point of view. **(4)**

c) Explain how the government is trying to promote community cohesion. **(8)**

d) 'Promoting community cohesion is the most important thing a government can do in a multi-ethnic society.'

    (i) Do you agree? Give reasons for your opinion. **(3)**

    (ii) Give reasons why some people may disagree with you. **(3)**

Exam Tip

c) One way to answer this question would be to use four government actions from this topic, and for each action explain how it should improve community cohesion. Make sure you use some specialist vocabulary such as: Education and Inspections Act, Ofsted, maintained schools, ethnic minority, Race Relations Act, racial motivation, religious motivation, Equality and Human Rights Commission.

Summary

The government is promoting community cohesion in the UK by passing laws against racism and discrimination, and by making community cohesion part of the national curriculum. Community cohesion is important because without it a multi-ethnic society could become violent and divided.

Topic 3.4.5 Why Catholics should help to promote racial harmony

KEY WORD

Racial harmony – different races/colours living together happily

The Catholic Church has members from every country in the world. Almost 30 per cent of the world's population is Catholic and over 70 per cent of Catholics are non-white, non-European.

Catholics should try to promote **racial harmony** because:

▶ In the Parable of the Good Samaritan (Luke 10:25–37), Jesus taught that Christians should love their neighbours and that 'neighbour' means people of all races. Jews and Samaritans were different races who, according to the Gospels, hated each other. In the parable, Jesus taught that the Good Samaritan treated the Jew who was attacked as his neighbour, so showing that Christians have to treat people of every race as their neighbour who they have to love.

▶ Scholars point out that Simon of Cyrene, who helped Jesus carry his cross, was a black African.

▶ Jesus treated a Samaritan woman as his equal (John 4) and healed a Roman centurion's servant (Luke 7).

▶ St Peter was given a vision by God (Acts 10) in which God sent down a sheet filled with all sorts of animals and told Peter to eat from them, but Peter refused because, according to Jewish law, they were unclean. A voice from heaven told him, 'What God has made clean, you have no right to call profane.' Peter believed that God was showing him that God treats all races the same and accepts the worship of anyone who does right, whatever their race.

> 'Which of these three do you think, was a neighbour to the man who fell into the hands of robbers?' The expert in the law replied, 'The one who had mercy on him'. Jesus told him, 'Go and do likewise'.
>
> *Luke 10:36–37*

> Then Peter began to speak: 'I now realise how true it is that God does not show favouritism but accepts men from every nation who fear him and do what is right.'
>
> *Acts 10:34–35*

> The Church rejects as foreign to the mind of Christ, any discrimination against men or harassment of them because of their race, colour, condition of life, or religion.
>
> *Declaration on the Relationship of the Church to non-Christians by Pope Paul VI*

The Good Samaritan by Vincent van Gogh. How does the Parable of the Good Samaritan encourage Christians to promote racial harmony?

- St Paul taught in Galatians 3:26–29 that everyone is equal in Christ and so there can be no divisions of race among Christians.
- St Paul also taught that as God created all nations from one man, Adam, all nations are therefore equal to each other.
- There are Catholic **cardinals** and bishops of every race and colour of skin, and the Church is dedicated to fighting racism in all its forms.
- Many Christians and Christian groups have worked for racial harmony. A major Catholic organisation working to promote racial harmony in the UK and in the Church is the Catholic Association for Racial Justice (CARJ). You can find details of their work on www.carj.org.uk. St Martin de Porres (1579–1639) was born of mixed race parents and is the patron saint of inter-racial justice. Blessed Katharine Drexel (1858–1955) founded the Sisters of the Blessed Sacrament to work for racial harmony in the USA. You may have studied the work of Mary Seacole (who was voted the greatest black Briton in history) during Key Stage 3.

Non-white cardinals at the Congregation of Cardinals, helping the Catholic Church promote racial harmony.

> Respect for the humanity we share with each and every neighbour is the only basis for a peaceful and good society. Any attack on the dignity and human rights of any racial or religious group damages all of us.
>
> *From the Churches Together letter to the press, May 1998*

Questions

b) Do you think Catholics should help to promote racial harmony? Give two reasons for your point of view. **(4)**

c) Explain why Catholics should help to promote racial harmony. **(8)**

d) 'If everyone were religious, there would be no racism.'

    (i) Do you agree? Give reasons for your opinion. **(3)**

    (ii) Give reasons why some people may disagree with you. **(3)**

Exam Tip

b) You should already have thought about this, and you just have to give two reasons for your opinion. For example, if you agree with Catholics promoting racial harmony, you could use two reasons from this topic.

Summary

Catholics should promote racial harmony because of the teachings of the Bible and Church against racism and because they should follow the example of Jesus.

Pope Francis has strongly condemned anti-Semitism while addressing a delegation of the Jewish Simon Wiesenthal Centre, yesterday in Rome.

Pope Francis stressed the need to 'fight all forms of racism, intolerance and anti-Semitism, while preserving the memory of the Holocaust and promoting mutual understanding through training and social commitment'.

In particular, the Pope said, 'the problem of intolerance should be dealt with as a whole: every time a minority is persecuted and marginalised because of his religious beliefs or ethnicity, the good of the whole society is in danger'.

Catholic Herald 23 October 2013

Topic 3.4.6 The work of the Catholic Church to help asylum seekers and immigrant workers

Globalisation and a more mobile labour market is bringing numbers of people to our parishes. They come with many spiritual and pastoral needs ... The Church has a responsibility to accompany migrants, to create a space where they feel safe, where they can come and talk. This is rooted in scriptural tradition: Jesus was from a migrant family and in the spread of Christianity, migration goes back to the Acts of the Apostles. Advocacy and advice are what the Church can offer today. We can point migrants towards the services available.

Bishop Lynch, Head of the Bishops' Conference Office for Migrants and Refugee Policy, 12 April 2008

How the Catholic Church in England and Wales helps asylum seekers and immigrant workers

▶ It has established The Office for Refugee Policy (ORP) which monitors information and prepares briefs on immigration to enable the bishops to develop policy and respond to debates. The ORP represents the bishops on the immigration issue nationally and internationally and helps ordinary Catholics to become engaged in refugee work.

▶ In April 2008, the Catholic Bishops' Conference launched 'Mission of the Church to Migrants in England and Wales' putting forward a range of ways in which local parishes can create 'a ministry of welcome' for immigrants worshipping in a local parish. These include:

  ▶ making leaflets on local healthcare, admissions policies of local Catholic schools, etc., available in appropriate languages
  ▶ providing English language classes
  ▶ organising collections of essential equipment to give to migrants to help them set up home.

▶ Parishes with substantial numbers of immigrants have set up legal advice clinics where lawyers with appropriate language skills help immigrants cope with the legal issues of settling in the UK.

▶ Some parishes are providing Masses in languages other than English so that immigrant workers can maintain their faith and worship until they learn English.

▶ Westminster Cathedral has an annual Migrants Mass.

▶ Parishes are being encouraged to elevate the status of immigrant workers and help British society to see that immigrants are not a drain on Britain's resources, but hard-working, dedicated people who have suffered much to reach a haven of peace and opportunity. Newsletters from the ORP point to the vital work being done by immigrant workers in low paid jobs for the NHS.

In a message, released in advance of the January 19, 2014, World Day of Migrants and Refugees, Pope Francis called for a 'change in attitude' toward migrants and refugees around the world, moving away from attitudes of 'defensiveness and fear, indifference and fear,' typical of a 'throwaway culture'. 'Migrants and refugees are not pawns on the chessboard of humanity,' the Holy Father wrote.

United States Conference of Catholic Bishops, 26 September 2013

Archbishop Nicholls celebrating the Migrants Mass at Westminster Cathedral, May 2013.

Why the Catholic Church helps asylum seekers and immigrant workers

▶ The Bible teaches that God is a God of justice who requires his followers to behave justly and seek justice for everyone. This is taught in the Old Testament book of Amos. So Catholics should be seeking justice for immigrants and asylum seekers.

▶ The Catholic Church teaches that no one should be oppressed and that Christians should seek justice for the oppressed.

▶ Through working for justice for the oppressed, Christians show that they love God and their neighbours.

▶ Christians should follow the Golden Rule – service to others is the way to treat others as you would like to be treated.

▶ Throughout his life, Jesus served others – he came 'not to be served but to serve others' (Mark 10:45) and Christians should follow the example of Jesus.

▶ It is the teaching of Jesus, for example in the Parable of the Good Samaritan (see page 88) and the Parable of the Sheep and the Goats (see page 53).

▶ Jesus himself was a refugee and asylum seeker when the holy family fled to Egypt to avoid Herod's slaughter of the innocents.

A Catholic priest and nun join migrant domestic workers demanding fair treatment.

Questions

b) Do you think it is important for the Catholic Church to help immigrant workers? Give two reasons for your point of view. **(4)**

c) Explain why Catholics should help immigrant workers and/or asylum seekers. **(8)**

d) 'Catholics should do more to help asylum seekers and immigrant workers.'

    (i) Do you agree? Give reasons for your opinion. **(3)**

    (ii) Give reasons why some people may disagree with you. **(3)**

Exam Tip

d) Use the answering evaluation questions advice from page 9. Arguments for could be the reasons for helping plus any ideas you may have of what more the Church could do. Arguments against would be the work the Catholic Church is already doing.

Summary

The Catholic Church helps refugees and immigrant workers through a special office which tells parishes how they can help and which deals with publicity. Parishes offer help with such things as legal problems and English classes.

The Church helps because of the teachings of Jesus such as the parables of the Good Samaritan and the Sheep and the Goats.

Topic 3.4.7 The United Kingdom as a multi-faith society

KEY WORDS

Religious freedom – the right to practise your religion and change your religion

Religious pluralism – accepting all religions as having an equal right to co-exist

Many societies were mono-faith (having only one religion) until the twentieth century. In some ways, Great Britain has been a multi-faith society ever since the Reformation in the sixteenth century. Although Queen Elizabeth I made the Church of England the state religion, there were other Churches: Protestants who were not Church of England (Nonconformists), Roman Catholics and, from 1657, Jews. So Britain had to have laws encouraging religious freedom (everyone being free to follow their chosen religion without discrimination). These were:

▶ 1688 Nonconformists were given freedom of worship.
▶ 1828 Nonconformists were given the same political rights as members of the Church of England.
▶ 1829 Roman Catholics were given the same political rights as members of the Church of England.
▶ 1858 Jews were given the same political rights as members of the Church of England.

These meant that members of any religion were free to worship in Great Britain and had equal political rights so that it became a religiously pluralist society.

However, it was in the twentieth century that Great Britain became truly multi-faith as members of religions other than Christianity and Judaism came to Britain as immigrants (although immigrants from the Caribbean and Africa were mainly Christian).

The census figures in the margin give the view for the whole of England and Wales, but the percentages of religions can change if you look at certain areas where some religions are more prevalent. For example:

▶ The London Borough of Tower Hamlets has the highest percentage of Muslims of any UK council area at 34.5 per cent.
▶ Harrow has the highest percentage of Hindus of any UK council area at 25.3 per cent.
▶ The London Borough of Barnet has the highest percentage of Jews of any UK council area at 15.2 per cent.
▶ Slough has highest percentage of Sikhs of any UK council area at 10.6 per cent.
▶ The Borough of Rushmoor has the highest percentage of Buddhists of any UK council area at 3.3 per cent.
▶ In Birmingham, 46.1 per cent of the population is Christian, 21.8 per cent Muslim, 3.0 per cent Sikh, 2.1 per cent Hindu.
▶ In Bradford, 45.9 per cent of the population is Christian, 24.7 per cent Muslim, 1.0 per cent Sikh, 0.9 per cent Hindu.
▶ In the London Borough of Hounslow, there are 106,660 Christians, 26,261 Hindus, 35,666 Muslims and 22,749 Sikhs. However, many

Statistics

Census facts on religion in England and Wales

Christians
33,200,000 = 59%

No religion
14,100,000 = 25.1%

No answer
4,037,465 = 7.2%

Muslim
2,700,000 = 4.8%

Hindu
817,000 = 1.6%

Sikh
423,000 = 0.8%

Jewish
263,000 = 0.5%

Buddhist
248,000 = 0.4%

Source: Census 2011, Office for National Statistics

of the non-Christians live in the area of Southall which is 31.0 per cent Sikh, 25.8 per cent Muslim, 23.4 per cent Hindu, 12.3 per cent Christian.

The benefits of living in a multi-faith society

A multi-faith society has many benefits:

▶ People can learn about other religions from their friends and neighbours, and this can help them to see what religions have in common.

▶ People from different religions may practise their religion more seriously (for example, Muslims praying five times a day) and this may make people think about how they practise their own religion.

▶ People may come to understand why different religions believe what they do and this may make people think more seriously about their own religion and consider why they believe what they do.

▶ People are likely to become a lot more understanding about each other's religions and realise that everyone is entitled to their own opinion about religion.

▶ Religious toleration and understanding will exist in a multi-faith society and this may help to stop religious conflicts such as those between Protestant and Catholic Christians in Northern Ireland or between Hindus, Muslims and Sikhs in India.

▶ A multi-faith society may even make some people think more about religion as they come across religious ideas they have never thought about before.

These new religious buildings show the multi-faith nature of British society. These pictures show the Shri Swaminarayan Mandir in Neasden, London, and the Tibetan Buddhist Temple of Samye Lings in Dumfriesshire, Scotland.

Exam Tip

c) 'Explain why' means give reasons. One way to answer this question would be to use the census facts and the facts from three different local councils and explain how each shows the UK to be a multi-faith society. Make sure you use some specialist vocabulary such as: Census 2011, non-Christian, Muslim, Hindu, Sikh, Jewish, Buddhist, no religion.

Questions

b) Do you think it is a good idea to have a lot of different religions in one place? Give two reasons for your point of view. **(4)**

c) Explain why the United Kingdom is often referred to as a multi-faith society. **(8)**

d) 'All societies should be multi-faith societies.'

   (i) Do you agree? Give reasons for your opinion. **(3)**

   (ii) Give reasons why some people may disagree with you. **(3)**

Summary

Britain is a multi-faith society because several religions are practised here and everyone is free to practise their religion. A multi-faith society has many benefits such as religious freedom and the opportunity to find out about, and think more deeply about, different religions.

93

Topic 3.4.8 Differences among Christians in their attitudes to other religions

> All nations form but one community. This is so because all stem from the one stock which God created to people the entire Earth, and also because all share a common destiny, namely God ... The Catholic Church recognises in other religions that search for the God who is unknown yet near since he gives life and breath and all things and wants all men to be saved.
>
> *Catechism of the Catholic Church 842–843*

> Although in ways known only to himself God can lead those who, through no fault of their own, are ignorant of the Gospel, to that faith without which it is impossible to please him, the Church still has the obligation and also the sacred right to evangelise all men.
>
> *Catechism of the Catholic Church 848*

> Christianity is the one true religion only because God decided so, only because the light of Christ falls on it ... No matter how good and true any other religion might seem, it is false, useless – because the light of Christ has not fallen on it.
>
> *Karl Barth (Evangelical Protestant theologian)*

All Christians believe in religious freedom. That is, they believe everyone has the right to follow, or not follow, any religion they wish. However, there are different Christian attitudes to other religions.

1. Catholics and many other Christians believe that non-Christian religions are searching for God and have some truth, but only Christianity has the whole truth (this is often known as inclusivism). They believe that other religions should be respected, and that their followers may get to heaven. However, they believe Christians have a duty to try to put across the Gospel message (evangelise) to people of other religions because they have the full truth. They have this attitude because:

   ▸ It is the teaching of the Church in the Catechism and papal encyclicals.
   ▸ They believe Jesus is the Son of God who shows the true nature of God.
   ▸ The Bible teaches that Christianity reveals the full truth about God. Only Christians are assured of salvation, depending on future conduct, but other religions such as Judaism can contact God and may have the possibility of eternal life.

Christian missionaries, like these at a Catholic Mission in Kenya, often proclaim the Gospel by helping people, so showing them God's love.

2. Some Evangelical Protestant Christians feel that, although members of other religions must be respected and given the freedom to practise their religion, everyone has the right to convert others. They believe Christianity is the only true religion and so they must try to convert everyone to Christianity (this is often called exclusivism). They have this attitude because:

- They believe that sayings of Jesus such as, 'I am the way and the truth and the life. No one comes to the Father except through me' (John 14:6) mean that only Christians will go to heaven.
- They think the command of Jesus for people to love their neighbour means that if people love their neighbour, they must want their neighbour to go to heaven and so they will want to convert them to Christianity.
- They believe that the final words of Jesus to his followers, 'Therefore go and make disciples of all nations' (Matthew 28:19), mean that everyone must be converted to Christianity.

Pope John Paul II meeting the Dalai Lama in 1982. How does this photo show the Catholic Church teaching that other religions should be respected?

3. Some Liberal Protestant Christians believe that all religions are equal and are just different ways of finding God (this is often called pluralism). So they feel that Christians should respect other religions and work with them to make Britain a more spiritual and holy country. They have this attitude because:

- They do not believe the Bible is the word of God.
- They see Muslims, Hindus, Jews, Sikhs and Buddhists living good and holy lives in Britain today.
- They believe God is a force, like gravity, who can be discovered by people in different ways.
- They feel that the words of Jesus such as 'In my Father's house are many rooms' (John 14:2), mean that there is room in heaven for a variety of religions.

> All religions have a common faith in a higher reality which demands brotherhood on Earth ... perhaps one day such names as Christianity, Buddhism, Islam, Hinduism will no longer be used to describe men's religious experience.
>
> *John Hick (Christian philosopher)*

Questions

b) Do you think all religions are the same? Give two reasons for your point of view. **(4)**

c) Explain why some Christians believe that all other religions are wrong, and some do not. **(8)**

d) 'All societies should be multi-faith societies.'
   (i) Do you agree? Give reasons for your opinion. **(3)**
   (ii) Give reasons why some people may disagree with you. **(3)**

Exam Tip

c) 'Explain why' means give reasons. One way to answer this question would be to use two reasons for the Evangelical Protestant view that all other religions are wrong and two reasons why Catholics think they are not all wrong. Make sure you use some specialist vocabulary such as: exclusivism, inclusivism, Catechism, Encyclicals, Bible, Jesus, commands, convert.

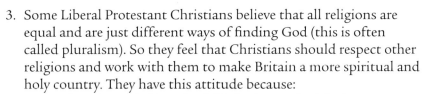

Summary

All Christians believe in religious freedom, but:

- some Christians believe there is some truth in other religions
- some Christians believe Christianity is the only true religion
- some Christians believe all religions are a path to God.

Topic 3.4.9 Issues raised for religion by a multi-faith society

KEY WORD

Interfaith marriage – marriage where the husband and wife are from different religions

Tolerance is so important, and never more so for Jews and Muslims. After September 11, the imam of the local mosque came to say a prayer for peace in Arabic, and I went to the mosque to say a prayer for peace in Hebrew.

Dr J. Romain, rabbi of Maidenhead (quoted in The Times, *31 March 2004)*

I'm a minister in the Church with roots in the Sikh faith. The idea that I could be both a Sikh and a Methodist at the same time is a nonsense. The way I would describe myself is as a follower of Jesus Christ with roots in the Sikh faith.

Rev Inderjit Bhogal, former President of the Methodist Conference

For a multi-faith society to work, people need to have the same rights regardless of the religion they do or do not belong to. A multi-faith society cannot accept any one religion as being the true one because it would mean that, ideally, that religion should be the only religion and so the society should be mono-faith.

Similarly a multi-faith society must have religious freedom. The people living in the society must be free to choose or reject any or all of the religions practised in the society. If all religions have equal rights, then all people must have the right to pick and choose between religions.

A society that is both religiously pluralist and has religious freedom can raise a number of issues for religion.

Conversion

Conversion is an issue because the teachings of religions and the facts of a multi-faith society conflict with each other.

1. Many religions see it as their right, and even their duty, to convert everyone to their religion because:
   ‣ They believe that their religion is the only true religion and that all other religions are mistaken.
   ‣ They believe that everyone should go to heaven and the only way for the followers of other religions to get to heaven is for them to be converted.
   ‣ Their holy books teach them that they should convert non-believers.

2. Trying to convert other religions in a multi-faith society can cause major problems because:
   ‣ Many people would say that trying to convert followers of other religions when living in a multi-faith society is a type of prejudice and discrimination. Treating people differently because of their religion and trying to convert other religions is discriminating against those who do not have the same faith as you.
   ‣ Many people would say that it is impossible to regard all other religions as wrong unless you have studied all of them and compared them to decide which one is true. No one who is trying to convert others has done this.
   ‣ It can lead to arguments and even violence within a multi-faith society when people are told their religion is wrong.

The Catholic Church, and many other religious groups, differentiate between 'proclamation' and 'proselytisation'. They believe they have a duty to tell people about their faith (proclamation or evangelisation), but not to try to make converts of people from other religions (proselytisation). This ensures religious harmony in a multi-faith society.

Bringing up children

A multi-faith society requires everyone (including children) to have religious freedom. When children reach an age where they can think for themselves about religion they must be able to choose which religion to follow, or to reject religion. It also requires that children should learn about the different religions in the society so that they can respect other religions and respect people's right to be religious or not religious as they wish. However, this causes problems for many religious believers because:

> He who knows one, knows none.
>
> *From* Introduction to the Science of Religion *by Max Muller, 1873*

▶ Most religions encourage parents to ensure that their children are brought up in their religion, and become members of it; consequently many parents do not want their children to learn about other religions or have the chance to choose a different religion, or reject religion.

▶ Most religions teach that only those who follow their religion will have a good life after death, so religious parents may worry that they will not see their children after death unless they stay in their religion.

▶ Social and peer pressures compel parents to exert pressure on their children to remain in the faith to preserve family and cultural traditions.

▶ Children educated in state schools experience the secular nature of British life and are tempted away from religious lifestyles.

Interfaith marriages

In a multi-faith society, young people of different faiths are going to meet, fall in love and want to marry (interfaith marriage). This can raise many problems for religious parents and religious leaders because:

▶ Often there can be no religious wedding ceremony because both couples must be members of the same religion for a religious wedding ceremony to be allowed.

▶ There is a question of which religion the children of the marriage will be brought up in. Some religions insist on a child being brought up in their religion, but how can a couple decide on this?

Is it easier to keep the faith in a faith school like this Church of England primary, or a non-faith school?

Twelve years ago, Mary and Daniel fell in love with each other. They shared everything – except religion. Mary's parents refused to let her marry a non-Catholic while Daniel's parents were equally adamant that he should not marry outside the Jewish faith. The couple split up. However, although Daniel went away and married someone of his own faith, it proved an unsuccessful match and ended in divorce. He returned to his home town and, to his surprise, found Mary still there. This time they allowed no external factors to impede their togetherness, and they now have two children. Both regard the marriage as blissfully happy, and only regret the twelve years they needlessly spent apart. Their story will be seen in some quarters as the triumph of love over tradition. Others will see it as a religious disaster.

Rabbi Jonathan Romain

▶ There is also the problem of what will happen after death? Will the couple have to be buried in separate parts of the cemetery according to their religion?

▶ For the parents and relatives of the couple there is often the feeling that they have betrayed their roots and family by falling in love with someone from a different religion.

Unless these issues are dealt with, then religion itself can work against community cohesion and promote conflict and hatred.

How can you tell this is an interfaith wedding?

Summary

A multi-faith society needs to have laws giving equal rights to all religions and to those who have no religion. However, a multi-faith society can raise problems for religious people in areas such as:

- conversion attempts by other faiths because it is like discrimination
- bringing up children because they may leave their parents' faith
- interfaith marriages because of having to decide which faith the children of such a marriage should be brought up in.

Questions

b) Do you think children should be free to choose their own religion? Give two reasons for your point of view. **(4)**

c) Explain why interfaith marriages may cause problems. **(8)**

d) 'In a multi-faith society, no religion should try to convert other people.'

    (i) Do you agree? Give reasons for your opinion. **(3)**

    (ii) Give reasons why some people may disagree with you. **(3)**

Exam Tip

b) You should already have thought about this, and you just have to give two reasons for your opinion. For example, if you disagree you could use two reasons from topic 3.1.1 on pages 2–3.

Topic 3.4.10 Ways in which religions work to promote community cohesion in the United Kingdom

The different religions in the United Kingdom are beginning to work to promote community cohesion in the following ways.

1. Different religions are beginning to work with each other to try to discover what is the same in their religions (for example, Judaism, Islam and Christianity believe in the prophets **Abraham** and **Moses**), and from this work out ways of living together without trying to convert each other.

   In September 2006, Pope Benedict XVI addressed a meeting with envoys from the Muslim world at the Pope's residence near Rome. 'I would like today to stress my total and profound respect for all Muslims,' the Pope said in the speech, adding that, 'Christians and Muslims alike must reject all forms of violence and respect religious liberty … The inter-religious and inter-cultural dialogue between Christians and Muslims is, in effect, a vital necessity, on which a large part of our future depends.'

2. Some religious groups are developing ways of helping interfaith marriages.
   - Many Protestant Churches and Liberal/Reform Jewish synagogues have developed special wedding services for mixed faith couples.
   - The Mission and Public Affairs Division of the Archbishops' Council of the Church of England has published Guidelines for the celebration of interfaith marriages in church.
   - Religious leaders who have married partners of another religion have set up the website www.interfaithmarriage.org.uk to offer help and advice to couples from different religions.

Catholic schools are always looking for opportunities to improve their contribution to social harmony in the different communities which they serve, whether on the local, national or global level. Oona Stannard, Catholic Education Service Chief Executive and Director of the CES, said: 'If we don't define ourselves, others will do it for us. We have to be transparent about what a Catholic education has to offer the whole community because if we don't make it apparent others will make presumptions. This simple document helps us to share what is good so that we can live up to the goal of learning about one another, learning from one another and learning with one another.'

Guidance document on community cohesion, 14 February 2008

Pope Francis met with the Christian, Jewish, Muslim, Buddhist, Hindu, Sikh and Jain delegations that had come to the Vatican for his inauguration in 2013. Do you think Catholics can accept other people's religions?

Religions are different roads converging to the same point. What does it matter which road we take as long as we reach the same goal? In reality, there are as many different religions as there are individuals.

Mohandas Gandhi

Let there be no compulsion in religion.

Surah 2:256

The lamps are different, but the light is the same.

Rumi, a medieval Iranian Sufi, speaking about religions

In a personal message to the world's Muslims to mark the end of Ramadan, the Pope said: 'Turning to mutual respect in inter-religious relations, especially between Christians and Muslims, we are called to respect the religion of the other, its teachings, its symbols, its values. Particular respect is due to religious leaders and to places of worship. How painful are attacks on one or other of these ... Regarding the education of Muslim and Christian youth, we have to bring up our young people to think and speak respectfully of other religions and their followers, and to avoid ridiculing or denigrating their convictions and practices.'

Report from the Catholic Herald, *2 August 2013*

3. As far as issues with the upbringing of children are concerned, religions are responding in different ways:
   ▸ Some Protestant Christian Churches and Liberal/Reform Jewish synagogues encourage mixed faith parents to bring up their children in both faiths, leaving it up to the children to choose which faith to follow when they are adults.
   ▸ Leaders from the Church of England, Hindu, Sikh, Catholic, Muslim, Jewish and Buddhist faiths have signed a joint statement to follow the principles for good religious education contained in the non-statutory National Framework on Religious Education so that children in faith schools (schools following a curriculum based on one faith) will now teach the main religions practised in the United Kingdom. In their statement, the faith leaders say religious education 'enables pupils to develop respect for and sensitivity to others, in particular those whose faith and beliefs are different from their own, and promotes discernment and enables pupils to combat prejudice'.

4. The main way in which religions are trying to promote community cohesion is through joining together in special groups to explore ways of helping community cohesion.
   ▸ There are national groups such as the Inter Faith Network for the UK, which was founded in 1987 to promote good relations between people of different faiths in this country. Its member organisations include representative bodies from the Baha'i, Buddhist, Christian, Hindu, Jain, Jewish, Muslim, Sikh and Zoroastrian communities; see www.interfaith.org.uk.
   ▸ There are also groups in most towns and cities that bring together the different religious groups in an area to promote community cohesion between them, for example, Cambridge Inter-faith Group, Concord the Leeds Interfaith Group and the Glasgow Forum of Faiths.

The St Mungo Museum is the only museum in the UK dedicated to promoting community cohesion through religion. It is in the grounds of Glasgow Cathedral.

- There are individual places of worship that work together, for example, 'What we are trying to do in Southall is to understand other traditions by living among them and conversing with them on their terms ... Our neighbours next door are Hindus. For the last three years at Diwali, we have gone there for a meal and then gone out into the garden to set off the fireworks.' Father Michael Barnes, parish priest, St Anselm's, Southall.

GLASGOW FORUM OF FAITHS DECLARATION

The current world situation has exposed the fragility of inter-faith relations and the need for an initiative that helps faith communities to listen and build relationships with each other. There is also an urgent need to show the general public that religion should not be a source of strife and that inter-faith activity is worthwhile.

The Forum of Faiths will bring together civic authorities (councillors and council officials) and the leaders of the main faith communities who have subscribed to this Declaration to work together for mutual understanding and the good of the City of Glasgow. We hope the Forum of Faiths will contribute to a better understanding of shared religious values.

The Declaration was signed by the Council leaders, the Strathclyde Police leaders and the Glasgow leaders of the Baha'i faith, the Buddhist faith, the Christian Church of Scotland (like the URC in England), the Christian Roman Catholic Church, the Christian Scottish Episcopal Church (like the Church of England), the Hindu faith, the Jewish faith, the Muslim faith and the Sikh faith.

All religions should stand side by side and go hand in hand. They are one family ... like windows in an endless tapestry of man's eternal search, they give visions of Truth and Reality. And the real truth of all religion is Harmony.

His Holiness Pramukh Swami Maharaj (BAPS)

To recognise the oneness of all humanity is an essential pillar of Sikhism. Some call themselves Hindus, others call themselves Muslims, but humanity worldwide is made up of one race.

Akal Ustal

Questions

b) Do you think different religions should work together in the United Kingdom? Give the reasons for your point of view. **(4)**

c) Explain how different religions are working together to promote community cohesion in the United Kingdom. **(8)**

d) 'It is easy for different religions to work together in the United Kingdom.'

   (i) Do you agree? Give reasons for your opinion. **(3)**

   (ii) Give reasons why some people may disagree with you. **(3)**

Exam Tip

c) To answer this question you could use the second bullet from point 3 on page 100 and the three bullets from point 4. Make sure you use some specialist vocabulary such as: Church of England, Hindu, Sikh, Catholic, Muslim, Jewish, Buddhist, National Framework on Religious Education, Inter Faith Network for the UK, Cambridge Inter-faith Group, Concord the Leeds Interfaith Group, Glasgow Forum of Faiths.

Summary

Religions are working for community cohesion in the United Kingdom by:

- working to discover what is the same about religions
- helping with mixed-faith marriages
- making sure that all children learn about different faiths
- joining local and national groups to promote community cohesion.

Topic 3.4.11 How an issue from religion and community cohesion has been presented in one form of the media

You have to study how **one** issue from religion and community cohesion has been presented in one form of the media.

Your issue could be connected with:

▶ equal rights for women in religion
▶ problems of discrimination and racism
▶ equal rights for ethnic minorities
▶ equal rights for religious minorities
▶ religion and racial harmony
▶ living in a multi-faith society
▶ religions working for community cohesion.

You can choose the form but it should only be one of the following:

▶ a television programme
▶ a radio programme
▶ a film
▶ an article in the national press.

You must choose both the issue and the type of media carefully to be able to answer questions on:

▶ why the issue is important
▶ how it is presented
▶ whether the presentation is fair to religious beliefs
▶ whether the presentation is fair to religious people.

To do this you must:

1. Select an issue and a form of media. It is very important that you select only one issue. Some films have several issues running through them. If you choose more than one issue, your answers are likely to be confused.
2. Decide why the issue is important (you may need to look at the views of different members of the particular religion and of the impact of the issue on society as a whole) and why you think the producers of the media decided to focus on this issue.
3. Write an outline of how the issue is presented, listing the main events and the way the events explore the issue.
4. Look closely at the way religious beliefs are treated in the presentation of the issue. Use this information to decide whether you think the presentation is fair to religious beliefs.

5. Look closely at the way religious people are treated in the presentation of the issue. Use this information to decide whether you think the presentation is fair to religious people.

In *Keeping the Faith*, Jake Schram and Brian Kilkenny Finn are single, successful, handsome, and confident young men living in New York who both fall in love with Anna Reilly. This is not the only problem, because Brian happens to be a Roman Catholic priest and Jake is a rabbi.
If you study this film you need to concentrate on the problems raised by living in a multi-faith society.

Questions

b) Do you think the media present religious people fairly? Give two reasons for your point of view. **(4)**

c) Choose an issue from religion and community cohesion presented in one form of the media and explain whether the presentation is fair to religious people. **(8)**

d) You are unlikely to be asked an evaluation question on this section as you only have to study one issue in one form of the media.

Exam Tip

c) Identify the issue, then briefly summarise the presentation. Decide whether you think the presentation is fair to religious people and give four reasons from the presentation to justify your opinion. Make sure you use specialist vocabulary from the presentation such as characters names.

Summary

When studying the presentation of an issue from religion and community cohesion in the media, you must be able to explain why the issue was chosen, how it is presented, whether the presentation treats religious people fairly and whether the presentation treats religious beliefs fairly.

How to answer exam questions

a) What is meant by interfaith marriage? (2)

An interfaith marriage is marriage where the husband and wife are from different religions.

b) Do you think religious people should try to convert other people to their religion? (4)

No I do not because trying to convert followers of other religions when living in a multi-faith society is a type of prejudice. Trying to convert other religions is discriminating against those who do not have the same faith as you.

Also trying to convert other people to your religion means you think their religion is wrong. But it is impossible to regard all other religions as wrong unless you have studied all of them and compared them.

c) Explain why the Roman Catholic Church works to help people who are asylum seekers and/or immigrant workers. (8)

The Catholic Church helps asylum seekers and migrant workers because the Bible teaches that God is a God of justice who requires his followers to behave justly and seek justice for everyone.

Also the Catholic Church teaches that no one should be oppressed and that Christians should seek justice for the oppressed. Christians should follow the Golden Rule – service to others is the way to treat others as you would like to be treated. Throughout his life Jesus served others – he came 'not to be served but to serve others'.

Finally, Jesus himself was a refugee and asylum seeker when the holy family fled to Egypt to avoid Herod's slaughter of the innocents, so Catholics remember this and feel they must help refugees and asylum seekers.

d) 'Religious people can achieve community cohesion.'
  In your answer you should refer to Roman Catholic Christianity.
  (i) Do you agree? Give reasons for your opinion. (3)
  (ii) Give reasons why some people may disagree with you. (3)

(i) As a Catholic, I agree with this statement because the Catholic Church and other Churches have begun to work with other religions to try to discover what is the same in their religions and from this work out ways of living together without conflict. Also religions have developed special groups to explore ways of helping community cohesion through national groups such as the Inter Faith Network for the UK. Also the teachings of the Catholic Church on racial harmony help different ethnic groups live together in harmony by condemning racism and encouraging equality.

(ii) Some people might disagree with me because they think that many religions see it as their right, and even their duty, to convert everyone to their religion but this can cause a lack of community cohesion within a multi-faith society. Also the Catholic Church, and most religions, encourages parents to ensure that their children are brought up in the faith. Consequently many parents do not want their children to learn about other religions which is essential for community cohesion. Finally they might feel that intermarriage is the best way to promote community cohesion and yet religions, including the Catholic Church, discourage members from marrying outside the faith.

Question a

A high mark answer because it gives a correct definition.

Question b

A high mark answer because an opinion is backed up by two developed reasons.

Question c

A high mark answer because it gives four reasons why the Roman Catholic Church helps asylum seekers and immigrant workers. There is good use of specialist vocabulary such as: Bible, God of justice, Old Testament, Amos, justice for the oppressed, love God and neighbour, Golden Rule, Jesus, service to others, Mark, the holy family, Herod's slaughter of the innocents.

Question d

A high mark answer because it states the candidate's own opinion and backs it up with three clear reasons for believing religious people can achieve community cohesion. It then gives three reasons for people disagreeing and believing that religion militates against community cohesion. One reason in part i) and two reasons in part ii) refer to the Catholic Church.

Section

8.1

Religion: Rights and responsibilities

Introduction

This section of the examination specification requires you to look at the issues surrounding religion and social responsibility based on the study of Christianity.

How Christians make moral decisions

You will need to understand the effects of, and give reasons for your own opinion about:

▶ why some Christians use only the Bible as a basis for making moral decisions
▶ the authority of the Church for Christians and why some Christians use only the Church's teachings as a basis for making moral decisions
▶ the role of conscience and why some Christians believe conscience is the most important guide in making moral decisions
▶ situation ethics and why some Christians use only situation ethics as a guide for making moral decisions
▶ why some Christians use a variety of authorities in making moral decisions.

Religion and human rights

You will need to understand the effects of, and give reasons for your own opinion about:

▶ human rights in the UK
▶ why human rights are important for Christians
▶ why it is important to take part in democratic and electoral processes
▶ Christian teachings on moral duties and responsibilities.

Religion and genetic engineering

You will need to understand the effects of, and give reasons for your own opinion about:

▶ the nature of genetic engineering, including cloning
▶ different Christian attitudes to genetic engineering and cloning.

Topic 8.1.1 The Bible as a basis for making moral decisions

KEY WORDS

Bible – the holy book of Christians

Decalogue – the Ten Commandments

The doctrinal standards of the Methodist Church are based upon the Divine revelation recorded in the Holy Scriptures which revelation Methodism acknowledges as the supreme rule of faith and practice.

From What the Churches Say, third edition

God is the author of Sacred Scripture because he has inspired its human authors; he acts in them and by means of them. He thus gives assurance that their writings teach without error his saving truth.

Catechism of the Catholic Church 136

Moral decisions are when you have to decide what is the right or wrong thing to do. Deciding whether to have a Mars bar or a Cadbury's Flake would not be a moral decision. But deciding whether to give 50p to save a child from polio, or spend 50p on sweets would be a moral decision. Most people need some help in making these kind of decisions.

The **Bible** is the holy book of Christians and is the basis of the Christian religion. Many Christians use only the Bible when making a moral decision because:

▶ They believe that the Bible is the word of God dictated by God to the writers of the Bible books. This means that the Bible is God's guidance to humans and so it has absolute authority for Christian decision-making.
▶ The Bible contains God's teachings on behaviour, which tell Christians how to behave. This can be seen in the **Decalogue**, which gives Christians very clear moral guidance: honour your parents, do not steal, do not kill, do not commit adultery, do not lie and do not desire other people's things.
▶ The Bible contains the teachings of Jesus on how to live. As Christians believe Jesus is the Son of God, they should follow his teachings about moral decision-making, for example in the Sermon on the Mount where Jesus explained the Ten Commandments.
▶ The Bible records events in the life of Jesus. This means many Christians ask themselves how Jesus would behave in this situation and then follow his example. As Christians believe Jesus is God's son, his example must be the best one to follow.
▶ The Bible contains letters from the leading disciples of Jesus (St Peter, St John and St James) and the Apostle St Paul. They wrote these letters to the early Christian Churches about how Christians should behave, and this guidance can also be used in making moral decisions today. Christians believe that the writers of the letters knew Jesus and were guided by the Holy Spirit so their guidance must be important for Christians today.

The Bible contains a whole set of stories, experiences, prayers and poems which reflect a pattern of God's dealings with a line of people that he got in touch with. Through these patterns we can come to know how God makes himself known, but I do not hold that the Bible is the word of God in any sense that guarantees its particular words.

David Jenkins, former Bishop of Durham, quoted in Christians in Britain Today by Denise Cush

The way the Bible is treated by some Christians shows its authority.

- They believe that only the Bible is definitely authenticated by God and so only by following the Bible can they be sure that their moral decisions will be approved of by God.

Although all Christians would accept that the Bible has some authority in making moral decisions, they do not all agree about how important it should be.

- Some Christians believe that the Bible was written by humans inspired by God. They believe that, although it has authority for moral decision-making, many of its attitudes reflect the social situation at the time of the writers (for example, St Paul's attitude to women and slaves) and it needs to be revised in the light of modern knowledge.
- Some Christians would use the Church to tell them what the Bible means for today, so they would put the authority of the Church over the Bible.
- Other Christians would use their own conscience or reason to decide whether to follow the Bible in making a moral decision in the twenty-first century.

Do you think God speaks through the Bible?

Questions

b) Do you think the Bible is all Christians need to make a moral decision? Give two reasons for your point of view. **(4)**

c) Explain why some Christians use only the Bible when making moral decisions. **(8)**

d) 'The Bible is the best guide we can have when making moral decisions.'

In your answer you should refer to Christianity.

    (i) Do you agree? Give reasons for your opinion. **(3)**

    (ii) Give reasons why some people may disagree with you. **(3)**

Exam Tip

c) 'Explain why' means give reasons. One way to answer this question would be to use four of the reasons why some Christians use only the Bible.

Remember you have four marks for spelling, punctuation and grammar in this section so try to use some specialist vocabulary such as: authority, Bible, Church, disciples, inspired, St Paul, St James, St John, St Peter, Sermon on the Mount, Ten Commandments.

Exam focus

Spelling, punctuation and grammar

Up to four marks will be awarded for your spelling, punctuation and grammar in your answer to Section 1 of both exam papers. This means you should take extra care with your spelling and make sure you use full stops and capital letters. You should use a wide range of specialist vocabulary, but don't let your use of specialist words confuse the meaning of your answer.

Summary

Some Christians would use only the Bible when making moral decisions because they believe that God speaks through the Bible. The Bible records God's teaching on how to behave and what Jesus taught about morality.

Topic 8.1.2 The authority of the Church as a basis for making moral decisions

KEY WORD

Church – the community of Christians (with a small c, it means a Christian place of worship)

The General Synod is the 'parliament' of the Church of England. It contains 560 members and consists of three 'houses' of bishops, clergy and laity, who meet together twice a year ... When preparing to make statements upon moral issues, the specialist department, or Board, will be asked to produce a theological rationale as guidance in the decision-making process.

From What the Churches Say, third edition

Interpreting Scripture is ultimately subject to the judgement of the Church which exercises the divinely conferred commission and ministry of watching over and interpreting the Word of God.

Catechism of the Catholic Church 119

Although the Bible is the basis of Christian decision-making, most Christians believe that the Bible needs to be explained to discover what it means for life today. Many Christians believe that only the Church has the right to explain what the Bible means, and what Christians should do about moral issues. This is because:

▶ They believe the Church is the Body of Christ. By this they mean that the Church is how Jesus Christ, the Son of God, works in the world. If the Church is the Body of Christ, then it must have the same authority as Christ.

▶ Most Christians believe that God did not stop speaking to people after the last book of the Bible was written. They believe that God speaks to the world today through the Church.

▶ The Church is the community of Christian believers. Therefore it must be guided by God and so be able to make decisions on moral issues.

▶ If individual Christians were to make their own decisions on everything, there could be lots of different opinions about how to behave, and no one would know which was the right thing for Christians to do. If people follow the guidance of the Church, they can be sure they are doing the right thing.

▶ Christians expect the Church to give them guidance on the Christian life, and making moral decisions is an important part of the Christian life.

▶ Catholic Christians believe that the authority of the Church comes from the Magisterium (the Pope and the bishops interpreting the Bible and tradition for Catholics today), which they believe gives infallible guidance on moral behaviour.

The General Synod of the Anglican Church. Many Anglican Christians believe that decisions of the General Synod on moral issues should be followed by all Christians.

Catholic cardinals congregating. Cardinals are chosen by the Pope from the bishops. The Cardinals elect the Pope. Catholic Christians believe that the teachings of the Church as decided by the Pope and bishops must be followed.

Questions

b) Do you think Christians should use only the teachings of the Church for making moral decisions? Give two reasons for your point of view. **(4)**

c) Explain why the Church has authority for Christians when making moral decisions. **(8)**

d) 'The Church gives Christians infallible guidance for making moral decisions.'

In your answer you should refer to Christianity.

    (i) Do you agree? Give reasons for your opinion. **(3)**

    (ii) Give reasons why some people may disagree with you. **(3)**

Exam Tip

b) You should already have thought about this, and you just have to give two reasons for your opinion. For example, if you think they should use only the Church's teachings, you could use two reasons from the bullet list on page 108. But your reasons must be developed, for example: most Christians believe that God did not stop speaking to people after the last book of the Bible was written (reason). They believe that God speaks to the world today through the Church (development).

> The ordinary and universal Magisterium of the Pope and the bishops in communion with him teaches the faithful the truth to believe, the charity to practise, the beatitude to hope for.
>
> *Catechism of the Catholic Church 2034*

Summary

The Church has authority because Church leaders are in the best position to say what the Bible means for today, and they always give guidance on moral issues. The Church is the final authority for Catholic Christians because the Pope and the bishops are believed to have special powers in interpreting the Bible.

Topic 8.1.3 The role of conscience as a guide in making moral decisions

KEY WORD

Conscience – an inner feeling of the rightness or wrongness of an action

All humans have a conscience which distinguishes between right and wrong and makes them feel guilty if they do things which they regard as wrong. Some Christians believe that a Christian should look at what the Bible and the Church say about a moral issue, but if they feel 'pangs of conscience' about doing it, they should follow their conscience.

Why some Christians believe they should follow their conscience

▶ Christians believe that God speaks to Christians. The conscience is like a voice in people's heads telling them what they should or should not do. The voice of conscience seems to be the same as the voice of God, therefore Christians should follow it.

▶ The Church says that Christians should follow their conscience as if it were the voice of God, and Christians are expected to follow the teachings of the Church.

▶ St Paul and St Thomas Aquinas taught that Christians should use their conscience as the final part of moral decision-making. Some Christians believe that if such great Christian thinkers say Christians should follow their conscience, then they also should follow their conscience if it tells them the Church is wrong (for example, on an issue like artificial contraception).

▶ The teachings of the Bible and the Church do not come directly from God. The Bible has been translated and often needs to be interpreted. The teachings of the Church come through the Pope, bishops, ministers, conferences, and so on. However, conscience is God speaking directly to individuals and so should be followed.

> Pray for us. We are sure that we have a clear conscience and desire to live honourably in every way.
>
> *Hebrews 13:18*

The Pope has the final responsibility for stating Roman Catholic views on moral issues, but should Catholics obey their conscience if it contradicts the Pope?

> A human being must always obey the certain judgement of his conscience. If he were deliberately to act against it, he would condemn himself. Yet it can happen that moral conscience remains in ignorance and makes erroneous judgements about acts to be performed or already committed.
>
> *Catechism of the Catholic Church 1790, 1794*

Why some Christians think they should not always follow their conscience

▶ People have been mistaken about the voice of God, for example, the Yorkshire Ripper claimed that God had told him to kill prostitutes. If you can be mistaken about the voice of God, you must also be able to be mistaken about the voice of conscience.

▶ If Christians follow the teachings of the Bible they are doing what all Christians agree is the Christian thing to do.

▶ If Christians follow the teachings of the Church, then they know other Christians will think that what they do is right.

▶ If everyone followed their conscience rather than laws, life would become chaotic and no one would know what sort of behaviour to expect from each other. Society needs to have agreement on what is right and wrong to work properly (see Topic 8.4.1).

Questions

b) Do you think your conscience is the voice of God? Give two reasons for your point of view. **(4)**

c) Explain why some Christians follow only their conscience when making moral decisions. **(8)**

d) 'Your conscience is the best guide for deciding what is right and what is wrong.'

In your answer you should refer to Christianity.

    (i) Do you agree? Give reasons for your opinion. **(3)**

    (ii) Give reasons why some people may disagree with you. **(3)**

Exam Tip

d) Use the technique for answering evaluation questions from this page. Arguments in favour of the quotation would come from reasons for obeying conscience in this topic plus any problems there might be with following the authority of the Bible and/or the Church. Arguments against would come from reasons against obeying your conscience in this topic and from the points in favour of following the authority of the Bible and the Church.

Exam focus

Evaluation questions

● Decide what you think about the statement.

● Give at least three brief reasons, or two longer reasons, or a paragraph reason, supporting your point of view.

● Look at the opposite point of view and give at least three brief reasons, or two longer reasons, or a paragraph reason, for why people have this view.

The evaluation questions mean that you must always be aware not only of your own point of view about a topic, but also about the opposite point of view.

Remember

Either your point of view, or the reasons for disagreeing with your point of view, should always be a Christian one in Unit 8, but you do not have to agree with the Christian view, just be able to give reasons for it.

Summary

Conscience is the inner feeling that makes people think something is right or wrong. Many Christians think conscience is the way God speaks to Christians today and so is the main guide for making moral decisions. Other Christians think it is safer to follow the Bible or the Church.

Topic 8.1.4 Situation ethics as a guide for making moral decisions

KEY WORD

Situation ethics – the idea that Christians should base moral decisions on what is the most loving thing to do

One of the teachers of the law came and heard them debating. Noticing that Jesus had given them a good answer, he asked him, 'Of all the commandments, which is the most important?'

'The most important one,' answered Jesus, 'is this: "Hear O Israel, the Lord our God, the Lord is one. Love the Lord your God with all your heart and with all your soul and with all your mind and with all your strength." The second is this: "Love your neighbour as yourself." There is no commandment greater than these.'

Mark 12:28–31

What is situation ethics?

Many of those Christians who believe that conscience is more important than the Bible or the Church believe that Christians should follow situation ethics. This is a Christian idea about making moral decisions which began with an American Christian thinker, Joseph Fletcher.

Accepting the authority of either the Bible or the Church means that things are either right or wrong regardless of the situation. For example, if the Bible says stealing is wrong, it cannot be allowed whatever the situation. So, if you find out that a madman has bought nuclear weapons, you would not be able to steal them from him to save the world, because stealing is wrong. Similarly, if the Church says abortion is wrong, it cannot be allowed whatever the circumstances. So, if a twelve-year-old girl was raped and became pregnant, she could not be allowed an abortion even if the pregnancy was affecting her mental health, because the Church has declared that abortion is wrong.

Fletcher felt that this was wrong and that Christians should base their moral decisions on Jesus' commandment to love your neighbour as yourself, and on the situation. So Fletcher said that Christians should only follow the Bible and/or the Church if it is the most loving thing to do. Therefore, a Christian would work out that the most loving thing to do in the situation of the madman would be to steal the nuclear weapons from him. The most loving thing to do in the situation of the twelve-year-old girl would be to allow her to have an abortion.

Why some Christians use situation ethics as a guide for making moral decisions

- ▶ Jesus seemed to follow situation ethics because he over-ruled what the Old Testament said when he thought it was unloving. For example, when a man with a paralysed arm asked to be healed on the **Sabbath Day**, Jesus healed him because he said it was more important to do good than to obey the law not to work on the Sabbath.
- ▶ They think it is wrong to ignore the consequences of your actions. You should only do what will produce good results. So they would steal the nuclear weapons from the madman and allow the twelve-year-old to have an abortion.
- ▶ They believe that Jesus' statement, that the most important laws are to love God and love your neighbour (see the margin), means that Christians should always do what will have the most loving results.

▶ They believe that Christianity is a religion of love and forgiveness (as shown in the life and death of Jesus) and so Christians should make their moral decisions based on love not laws.

Why some Christians think situation ethics is wrong

▶ They think God would not have given laws in the Bible if they were not to be followed. They believe the Bible is God's word to Christians about how to live, so it should be the basis for moral decision-making.

▶ They believe they should follow what all other Christians agree is the right way to behave (for example, the Ten Commandments and the Sermon on the Mount) rather than relying on their own ideas.

▶ They think the Church knows better what Christians should do than the individual and so they follow the guidance of the Church.

▶ They claim you can never know all the facts, and so don't know what the consequences might be. For example, what if a doctor in a remote area only has one unit of blood to save the lives of two people (an old alcoholic man and a mother with three young children). Following situation ethics he would use it for the mother, but what if he then discovered that the mother was a child abuser and the old man was about to discover a cure for cancer? The situation would be changed and he would have been better to follow Christian teaching and given them half each.

Can you run a modern business without working on a Saturday (Sabbath)?

In the present situation sinful man needs grace and revelation so moral and religious truths may be known by everyone with facility, with firm certainty and with no admixture of error.

Catechism of the Catholic Church 1960

Questions

b) Do you think situation ethics is a good way of making moral decisions? Give two reasons for your point of view. **(4)**

c) Explain why some Christians believe situation ethics is the most Christian way of making moral decisions. **(8)**

d) 'Christians should always do the most loving thing.'

In your answer you should refer to Christianity.

    (i) Do you agree? Give reasons for your opinion. **(3)**

    (ii) Give reasons why some people may disagree with you. **(3)**

Exam Tip

c) 'Explain why' means give reasons. One way to answer this question would be to use the four reasons on page 112 for why some Christians use Situation Ethics.

Remember you have four marks for spelling, punctuation and grammar in this section so try to use some specialist vocabulary such as: Jesus, Old Testament, Sabbath, consequences, love your neighbour, forgiveness.

Summary

Situation ethics is the idea that the only moral rule Christians need is to love your neighbour. Christians who follow this believe that all they need to do when faced with a moral decision is work out what is the most loving thing to do in that situation. Other Christians think this can cause problems because you never know all the facts or all the consequences of your actions.

Topic 8.1.5 Why some Christians use a variety of authorities in making moral decisions

There are problems with using the Bible as the only authority for moral teachings. Admittedly, Leviticus 18:22 says homosexuality is detestable, and so Christians might think this is the end of debate on homosexuality. However, Leviticus says many other things with which Christians may not agree:

Leviticus 11:10 says that shellfish are an abomination. Does this mean prawns, crabs, lobsters, etc., should be banned from all restaurants?

Leviticus 21:20 says that anyone with defective eyesight must not approach the altar of the Lord. Does this mean all Christians wearing glasses must be banned from taking communion?

Leviticus 19:27 bans men from cutting the hair at the sides of their heads. Should men really be punished for this?

Leviticus 20:10 says that anyone committing adultery must be put to death. Are modern Christians really prepared to follow this today?

What should happen to people who wear clothes made of two fibres (for example, cotton and polyester) as this is banned in Leviticus 19:19?

Although some Christians would use only one authority when making a moral decision, other Christians might use one authority usually, but refer to other authorities for complicated decisions. They would do this because:

▶ Protestants might usually use the Bible as their authority because it is straightforward to use teachings such as the Ten Commandments and the Sermon on the Mount when deciding on issues such as stealing, murder, adultery. However, when it comes to contemporary issues such as contraception, same sex weddings, or civil partnerships, it is difficult to use the Bible only. The Bible says nothing about contraception, so they would have to look elsewhere for guidance such as the teaching of the Church or their conscience. The Bible does not say anything about civil partnerships and same sex marriage, but it does condemn homosexuality – so would this mean a Protestant could not attend a friend's same sex wedding ceremony? Again they would have to look elsewhere.

▶ A Catholic would normally follow the authority of the Church, as the Magisterium applies the teachings of the Bible and the apostles to modern life. However, although the Church bans artificial methods of contraception, a Catholic may well apply situation ethics to the issue of supplying condoms to African states with high incidences of HIV/AIDS. They might find it difficult to make a decision about same sex wedding ceremonies because the Catholic Church is against same sex marriage. They may well turn to their conscience or situation ethics to make a decision.

Why might an invite to a same sex wedding cause problems for some Christians?

▶ A Christian who usually followed their conscience might turn to the authority of the Bible or the Church if what their conscience was telling them went against what they knew was accepted Christian teaching. A good example would be if a Christian heard the voice of God telling them to kill all doctors who perform abortions. The Bible and the Church say that it is wrong to murder whatever the reasons. So they would use the authority of the Bible or the Church to reject the voice of their conscience because, although they might feel the purpose of stopping abortions may be a good one, that does not justify killing people to achieve it.

▶ A Christian who usually used situation ethics might decide that the issue was so complicated and the effects of a choice so uncertain that the safest thing would be to follow either the authority of the Bible or the authority of the Church because they are more likely to give the right choice than an individual trying to work it all out for themselves.

Why, according to the Bible, might Johnny Depp have problems becoming a priest?

Questions

b) Do you think the Bible tells you all you need to know when making moral decisions? Give two reasons for your point of view. **(4)**

c) Explain why some Christians use a variety of authorities when making moral decisions. **(8)**

d) 'You need more guidance than the Bible when you have to make a moral decision.'

In your answer you should refer to Christianity.

(i) Do you agree? Give reasons for your opinion. **(3)**

(ii) Give reasons why some people may disagree with you. **(3)**

Exam Tip

d) Use the technique for answering evaluation questions on page 111. Arguments in favour of the quotation would come from the first paragraph on page 108, the final bullet point on page 110, the first bullet on page 114. Arguments against would come from page 106.

Summary

When Christians have to decide what to do about an issue they can:

● use what the Bible says about it
● use what Church leaders say about it
● use what they feel is right (their conscience)
● work out what is the most loving thing to do (situation ethics).

Most Christians would use more than one of these.

In 1997 Cardinal Hume wrote that love between two persons, whether of the same sex, or of a different sex, is to be treasured and respected. This respect demands that such loving relationships be afforded social recognition according to social justice principles. He proposed three criteria for considering issues of social policy: are there reasonable grounds for judging that the institution of marriage and the family could, and would be undermined by a change in law? Would society's rejection of a proposed change be more harmful to the common good than the acceptance of such a change? Does a person's sexual orientation or activity constitute, in specific circumstances, a sufficient reason for treating that person in any way differently from other citizens? We suggest that it is perfectly proper for Catholics, using fully informed consciences, to support the legal extension of civil marriage to same-sex couples.

Letter to The Times *from 27 prominent British Catholics (quoted in* New Ways Ministry)

Topic 8.1.6 Human rights in the United Kingdom

KEY WORD

Human rights – the rights and freedoms to which everyone is entitled

According to the UK Human Trafficking Centre (UKHTC) 1000 victims of trafficking for forced labour had been referred to the centre since 2009, but the Centre thinks this is just the tip of the iceberg since forced labour in the UK is very much a hidden crime. It can range from a 15-year-old being made to work in a field to a middle-aged man who has fallen on hard times working in a kitchen. The UKHTC said forced labour victims worked in low-paid jobs in private houses and the hospitality, farming and manufacturing sectors. The workers live in very difficult conditions quite often being made to share a bed with someone they don't know in very poor-quality housing. They have no possessions and no freedom and little downtime as they are made to work such long hours. The NSPCC is among charities offering training to workers such as GPs, social workers and midwives to spot victims of trafficking for forced labour.

Collated from news reports, March 2013

In 1998, the Government passed the Human Rights Act to give UK citizens the fundamental rights and freedoms contained in the European Union Charter of Fundamental Rights.

Your human rights include:

- The right to life – this means that the law must protect you from being killed. This right is claimed by asylum seekers who will be killed if they return to their native country.
- Freedom from torture and degrading treatment – this means that no one can be tortured in the UK or by anyone acting on behalf of UK authorities, for example, British soldiers.
- Freedom from slavery and forced labour.
- The right to liberty – this means that people are free to do anything that is not against the law and cannot be detained without being charged and brought before the courts.
- The right to a fair trial – this means the trial is held in public, the judgement is made by an impartial person(s), you must: know what you are accused of, have access to legal representation, be able to put your side of the case and question the prosecution.
- The right not to be punished for something that wasn't a crime when you did it.

Police outside a South London block of flats where three women were allegedly held captive as slaves for 30 years. Which of the women's human rights had been abused?

- The right to respect for private and family life – meaning no one has the right to enter your home without the law's permission or publish information about your private life unless it is 'in the public interest'.
- Freedom of thought, conscience and religion – this means that no one can be prosecuted for their ideas and beliefs.
- Freedom of expression – means people can say what they think and publish their ideas but only as long as they do not break other laws (respect for privacy, national security, racial and religious tolerance and so on).
- Freedom of assembly and association – this means people have the right to meet with others to discuss their views and to organise public demonstrations to publicise their views.
- The right to marry or form a civil partnership and start a family.
- The right not to be discriminated against in respect of these rights and freedoms.
- The right to own property.
- The right to an education.
- The right to participate in free elections – this includes the right to vote, the right to stand as a candidate, the right to a secret ballot.

If any of these rights and freedoms are abused, you have a right to go to court to restore your right or receive compensation, even if the abuse was by someone in authority, for example, a police officer.

Clearly, the possession of such rights gives all citizens of the UK a duty to respect the rights of other people, which might involve restricting your own rights.

Questions

b) Do you think human rights need more protection in the United Kingdom? Give two reasons for your point of view. **(4)**

c) Explain why it is important for the UK to have human rights laws. **(8)**

d) 'Human rights laws are only useful for people who break the law.'
   In your answer you should refer to Christianity.

    (i) Do you agree? Give reasons for your opinion. **(3)**

    (ii) Give reasons why some people may disagree with you. **(3)**

Exam Tip

c) 'Explain why' means give reasons. One way to answer this question would be to look at four important human rights, for example, the right to life, right to liberty, right to a fair trial, right to participate in free elections. You should then explain what it would be like if those laws were not there and therefore why they are important.

Remember you have four marks for spelling, punctuation and grammar in this section so try to use some specialist vocabulary such as: asylum seekers, detention, charged, courts.

Summary

Citizens of the UK have certain basic rights such as the right to life, the right to liberty, the right to a fair trial, the right to freedom of conscience and religion, the right to marry and start a family, the right to an education, the right to take part in free elections. These rights are meant to make sure that all UK citizens are treated fairly and equally by the state.

Topic 8.1.7 Why human rights are important for Christians

The Archbishop of Canterbury and the Archbishop of Cape Town demanded ... to know what the UN Security Council and regional leaders in the SADC (Southern Africa Development Community) were doing to protect worshipping Anglicans from being intimidated and beaten in police-force attacks on churches across Harare.

A joint statement, issued by the Archbishops ... said that the continuing failure to enforce court orders permitting Anglicans to worship in their cathedral church in Harare and other parishes was 'a clear violation of Article 18 of the UN Charter on Human Rights which expressly gives people the right to worship and freedom of thought'.

The Church Times, 6 June 2008

What do you think this cartoon means?

Christians believe that human rights are important because:

▶ The right to life is a basic Christian belief because of the belief in the sanctity of life – life is holy and belongs to God and should only be taken by God.
▶ Christians believe that all people are made in the image of God and so are one human family. The equality and dignity of the human family is shown in the teachings of Jesus and the Church. Also, teachings such as the Parable of the Sheep and the Goats (see page 122) encourage Christians to treat everyone as if they were Jesus. Therefore it is important to Christians that everyone is treated fairly and equally and so they have the right to:
  ▶ not be tortured
  ▶ freedom from slavery and forced labour
  ▶ liberty
  ▶ a fair trial
  ▶ not be punished for something that wasn't a crime when they did it
  ▶ own property
  ▶ an education
  ▶ participate in free elections.
▶ Freedom of thought, conscience and religion, freedom of expression, freedom of assembly and association are an essential part of being Christian. Christians must have the legal right to believe in Christianity, to share their beliefs with others and to meet together for worship. Many Christians would also want the right to have processions (legally the same as a demonstration) to celebrate festivals such as **Easter** and **Pentecost**.
▶ The right to not be discriminated against in respect of these rights and freedoms is another essential human right for Christians because it ensures that Christians will not be disadvantaged compared to others. Employers cannot discriminate against Christians over jobs and pay. For example, employers cannot refuse to employ Christians because they themselves are non-religious and don't want religious people in the workplace.

Human rights are also important to Christians because Christians believe in justice and many human rights are a fundamental part of justice and a just society (see Topic 8.4.3).

Why some human rights can cause problems for Christians

Although human rights are important to Christians, some Christians do not approve of all human rights.

▶ Many Christians are against the right to form civil partnerships because they believe that homosexuality is against God's will as shown in the Bible. They also believe that they have the right to discriminate against homosexuals by refusing to allow them the same sort of Church blessings they give to divorced couples who have had a civil wedding.

▶ Some Christians are against the right to marry a person from a different faith. They believe that Christians should only marry Christians so that the children are brought up as Christians. They would also discriminate against inter-faith couples by refusing to allow them to marry in church.

▶ Some Christians are against the right of homosexuals to raise a family. They believe that children should be brought up by a mother and a father. Some Churches have opposed the adoption laws which make it illegal for adoption agencies (including Christian ones) to discriminate against homosexual couples when approving couples for adoption.

▶ There might also be problems for the Church if a Catholic woman who wanted to be a priest used human rights laws against the Catholic Church, or if a Catholic priest used human rights laws to demand the right to marry.

An American archbishop has defended a Catholic school's decision to sack a teacher after it learned of his same-sex marriage. Archbishop Peter Sartain of Seattle, said the school's decision was not discriminatory but held to Church teaching and the school's Catholic mission .... Archbishop Sartain said that 'leaders of Catholic schools are charged with the responsibility of both imparting and modeling' the Catholic Church's teaching, adding that the decision by the board and administrators of Eastside, an independent Catholic school, asking Mr Zmuda to resign 'was made after a great deal of prayer and consultation. In no way was their goal to be discriminatory to anyone but to be faithful to their mission as a Catholic school.'

Catholic Herald, *17 March 2014*

Questions

b) Do you think Christians should accept all human rights laws? Give two reasons for your point of view. **(4)**

c) Explain why human rights laws are important for Christians. **(8)**

d) 'If Christians believed in human rights, they would let women be priests.'

In your answer you should refer to Christianity.

(i) Do you agree? Give reasons for your opinion. **(3)**

(ii) Give reasons why some people may disagree with you. **(3)**

Exam Tip

b) You should already have thought about this, and you just have to give two reasons for your opinion. For example, if you think they should accept all human rights laws, you could use these two reasons:

• If Christians want the protection of human rights laws for their Church and beliefs, they must accept that everyone should have those rights.

• Christians believe that everyone is made in the image of God and so everyone should have the same rights.

Summary

All human rights are important to Christians because they believe that all people are made in the image of God and so should have the same rights. They are also important because Christians believe in the sanctity of life and so all life belongs to God. However, some rights can cause problems for Christians, for example when homosexuals and women want to have equal rights in religion.

Topic 8.1.8 Why it is important to take part in democratic and electoral processes

KEY WORDS

Democratic processes – the ways in which all citizens can take part in government (usually through elections)

Electoral processes – the ways in which voting is organised

Political party – a group which tries to be elected into power on its policies (for example, Labour, Conservative)

Pressure group – a group formed to influence government policy on a particular issue

What are electoral and democratic processes?

The UK is a democracy. This means that the government is 'by the people, of the people and for the people' (US President Abraham Lincoln in his Gettysburg Address, 1863).

Being a democracy means every UK citizen over the age of eighteen is entitled to vote for:

▶ MPs who sit in the House of Commons (the Prime Minister and the Cabinet – the national government – must have a majority in the House of Commons)
▶ local councillors
▶ MEPs (members of the European Parliament).

At elections, the candidates, or their political party, set out a manifesto of what they intend to do if they are elected.

Every UK citizen over the age of eighteen is entitled to be a candidate in any of these elections as long as they can find ten electors to nominate them and put down a financial deposit.

In addition, every citizen has the right to try to change the policies of the government, local council or EU by:

▶ joining or forming a political party
▶ joining or forming a pressure group
▶ having a meeting with their MP, councillor or MEP (all of these run local 'surgeries' to deal with individual voter's concerns).

Chancellor George Osborne delivering his budget to the House of Commons. Does it matter who you elect as your MP?

Why is it important to take part in electoral and democratic processes?

◗ The national government sets the rates of tax and collects the taxes (you pay income tax on your earnings and VAT on what you buy, the government sets the rates for these), so voting gives you some control over this.

◗ Local councils set the level of the council tax which all residents have to pay according to the value of their home, so voting gives you some control over this.

◗ The European Parliament has some control over EU spending, which affects how much tax the UK government needs to collect, so it is important to vote in European elections.

◗ The national government can pass new laws which will affect your life (for example, compulsory identity cards). Taking part in **electoral** and **democratic processes** gives you a chance to affect these laws.

◗ The national government is responsible for many important things (for example, the police, the prison service, immigration, the armed forces, schools, the NHS, benefits and pensions) and taking part in electoral and democratic processes gives you a say in how these are run.

◗ Local councils are responsible for such things as: refuse disposal, leisure and cultural services, trading standards, social services, housing services, maintaining the roads, footpaths and street lighting in the area, and so on. These are important areas that you need to have a say in.

◗ Your ancestors fought to have these electoral and democratic rights (in 1832 only five per cent of the adult population had them) and so you should use them.

◗ Countries where people do not have these rights often treat their citizens badly, and if people in the UK do not use their rights, a small number of people could elect a government which took away our rights so that they could treat us badly.

In the Catholic Tradition, responsible citizenship is a virtue, and participation in political life is a moral obligation. This obligation is rooted in our baptismal commitment to follow Jesus Christ and to bear Christian witness in all we do.

United States Conference of Catholic Bishops: Forming Consciences for Faithful Citizenship: A Call to Political Responsibility (2007)

Questions

b) Do you think it is important to vote in elections? Give two reasons for your point of view. **(4)**

c) Explain why it is important to take part in democratic and electoral processes. **(8)**

d) 'It doesn't matter whether or not you vote.'
   In your answer you should refer to Christianity.

   (i) Do you agree? Give reasons for your opinion. **(3)**

   (ii) Give reasons why some people may disagree with you. **(3)**

Exam Tip

d) Use the technique for answering evaluation questions from page 111. Arguments in favour of the quotation would come from your class discussions, but are likely to include such reasons as: one vote makes no difference to the outcome as there are over 60 million people in the UK; all politicians make promises they don't keep so they aren't worth voting for; whoever is voted in will just have to do what the EU says. Arguments against would come from the reasons why it is important to vote on this page.

Summary

It is important for people to vote in elections and be involved in politics because it gives people a chance to choose and affect governments and councils. These can have a big influence because they set taxes, pass new laws and run organisations like the NHS, and people should have a say in how this is done.

Topic 8.1.9 Christian teachings on moral duties and responsibilities

KEY WORDS

Golden Rule – the teaching of Jesus that you should treat others as you would like them to treat you

Social change – the way in which society has changed and is changing (and also the possibilities for future change)

As Catholics, we should be guided more by our moral convictions than by our attachment to a political party or interest group. When necessary, our participation should help transform the party to which we belong; we should not let the party transform us in such a way that we neglect or deny fundamental moral truths. We are called to bring together our principles and our political choices, our values and our votes, to help build a better world.

United States Conference of Catholic Bishops: Forming Consciences for Faithful Citizenship: A Call to Political Responsibility (2007)

Most Christians believe that they should take part in electoral and democratic processes, but that how they take part should be determined by Christian teachings on the moral duties and responsibilities of Christians. Many believe that it is the moral duty of Christians to bring about social change so that society becomes truly Christian. The main teachings which are likely to guide Christians in this are:

1. The Golden Rule

Jesus said that the Golden Rule of the Christian life is to treat other people as you would want them to treat you. 'So in everything, do to others what you would have them do to you, for this sums up the Law and the Prophets.' (Matthew 7:12).

So when Christians vote they should look at the policies of the candidates and try to work out whether the policies will affect other people in the way the Christian would want to be affected if they were in that situation. For example, if a party wants to change the law to send all asylum seekers back to their home country, the Christian would have to think, 'If I were a member of an ethnic group being slaughtered by the army in my own country, would I want to be sent back to be slaughtered?'

2. The Parable of the Sheep and the Goats

When the Son of Man comes in his glory ... All the nations will be gathered before him, and he will separate the people from one another as a shepherd separates the sheep from the goats. He will put the sheep on his right and the goats on his left.

Then the King will say to those on his right, "Come you who are blessed by my Father ... For I was hungry and you gave me something to eat, I was thirsty and you gave me something to drink, I was a stranger and you invited me in, I needed clothes and you clothed me, I was sick and you looked after me, I was in prison and you came to visit me."

... Then he will say to those on his left ... "I tell you the truth, whatever you did not do for one of the least of these, you did not do for me." Then they will go away to eternal punishment, but the righteous to eternal life.

Adapted from Matthew 25:31–46

In the Parable of the Sheep and the Goats, Jesus showed that it is the duty of Christians to feed the hungry, clothe the naked, give drink to the thirsty, look after the sick and help those in prison. These teachings should affect the way a Christian votes and participates in politics. For example, if a party's policy was to cut off benefits to people who refused to work, the Christian would accept this using the Golden Rule because they would want to work if they were in that position, but they would have to think again about the effects on the children of the jobless who could starve.

3. Am I my brother's keeper?

In Genesis 4, Adam's son Cain is jealous of his brother Abel and murders him. When God asks Cain where his brother is, Cain replies, 'I don't know. Am I my brother's keeper?' God then punishes Cain by putting a mark on his forehead so that everyone knows what he has done and he is forced to become a homeless wanderer. This shows that God created humans to be their brothers' keepers, in other words, to look after each other.

This is explained more fully by St John who says:

> We should love one another. Do not be like Cain who ... murdered his brother ... Because his own actions were evil and his brother's were righteous ... Anyone who hates his brother is a murderer, and you know that no murderer has eternal life in him ... If anyone had material possessions and sees his brother in need but has no pity on him, how can the love of God be in him? Dear children, let us not love with words or tongue but with actions and in truth.

1 John 3:11–18

Should being your brother's keeper make you work for community cohesion?

These Christian teachings on being our brother's keeper show Christians that they have a duty to look after everyone in need as the main principle in human rights and political processes.

Questions

b) Do you think you are your brother's keeper? Give two reasons for your point of view. **(4)**

c) Explain why the Parable of the Sheep and the Goats leads some Christians to bring about social change. **(8)**

d) 'Christians should always treat other people in the way they would like to be treated.'

In your answer you should refer to Christianity.

(i) Do you agree? Give reasons for your opinion. **(3)**

(ii) Give reasons why some people may disagree with you. **(3)**

Exam Tip

c) 'Explain why' means give reasons. One way to answer this question would be to use four of the points made in the parable (for example, poor people might be Jesus himself and Christians should feed the hungry, visit those in prison and clothe the naked) and explain how each point could lead Christians to work for social change.

Remember you have four marks for spelling, punctuation and grammar in this section so try to use some specialist vocabulary such as: hungry, naked, thirsty, sick, prison, blessed by my Father, eternal punishment, Son of Man/Jesus.

Summary

Most Christians believe that they should take part in electoral and democratic processes to make society more Christian. They are guided by Christian teachings such as:

- the Golden Rule, which says Christians should treat other people in the way they would like to be treated
- the Parable of the Sheep and the Goats, which says that Christians should help the homeless, the sick and the hungry
- the story of Cain and Abel, which tells Christians that they are responsible for the rights of others.

Topic 8.1.10 The nature of genetic engineering, including cloning

The UK is likely to be the first country in the world to legalise a new fertilisation procedure involving three parents after the government set out new draft regulations. The technique allows DNA from a second woman to be implanted into a mother's egg before IVF fertilisation with the father's sperm. Experts hope the technique will prevent mitochondrial diseases such as muscular dystrophy. One in 6,500 babies suffers from mitochondrial conditions, and disorders are passed down from the mother. Defective mitochondria lead to conditions that can cause weakness, sight problems, heart failure and even death in severe cases.

However, the technique is controversial with opponents claiming it is unethical for babies to have three parents and suggesting the procedure could lead to 'designer babies'. They argue that affected couples could find other routes to having children such as adoption or egg donation.

Adapted from various news sources

Genetic engineering is 'the deliberate modification of the characters of an organism by the manipulation of the genetic material' (Oxford English Dictionary). In connection with medical issues (which is all you have to study), it is using techniques of gene development and manipulation to find cures or prevention for disease and disabilities in humans.

Genetic diseases affect large numbers of people. Defective inherited genes can cause mental disability, physical deformity or early death. Scientists are involved in genetic research into: cystic fibrosis, muscular dystrophy, sickle-cell anaemia, Tay-Sachs disease and Huntington's chorea. They have been helped by the **Human Genome Project**, which is mapping all the genes in the human body.

Most genetic research has been based on:

- germline gene therapy, which enables genetic changes to be made to those cells that transmit information from one generation to the next, enabling permanent changes to be made
- pre-implantation genetic diagnosis (PGD), which removes defective genes from embryos so that women at risk of producing babies with diseases such as cystic fibrosis produce healthy babies.

Stem cell research

More recently, cloning processes have been used to grow healthy cells to replace the malfunctioning ones and so cure disease. This process involves creating **stem cells** either from embryos produced for in-vitro fertilisation (IVF) but not used, or from adult bone marrow or blood. These stem cells are then cultivated and kept alive so that they can multiply and be transplanted into diseased cells to produce a cure.

Legislation permitting stem cell research in the United Kingdom was passed by Parliament in February 2001.

Even more recently (May 2008), the UK Parliament made it possible for scientists to use human–animal embryos for medical research. Most of these embryos are likely to be cybrids (a human nucleus in an empty animal egg making an embryo which is 99.9 per cent human). Cybrids could carry the DNA of patients with genetic diseases, which could then be used for stem cell research into the causes of and cures for the disease.

Non-religious arguments in favour of genetic engineering

- It offers the prospect of cures for currently incurable diseases.
- It is being done in other countries and so is available to those rich enough to travel and pay for treatments.

▶ Cloning processes have been used to grow healthy cells to replace the malfunctioning ones and so cure disease.

▶ Cloning using animal eggs, as in cybrids, does not involve any loss of human life.

▶ Genetic research is an integral part of medical research and is bound to include some genetic engineering.

▶ Genetic research is closely monitored by the law, but has vast potential benefits.

Non-religious arguments against genetic engineering

▶ There is too little information about the long-term consequences.

▶ It has effects which would be irreversible, so if anything went wrong it would be permanent.

▶ It places too much power in the hands of scientists who could use genetic engineering to act like Dr Frankenstein to produce scientifically created human beings.

▶ It treats the human body as a commodity no different from plants.

▶ It offers the possibility of people having to be genetically screened before getting life insurance, senior jobs, etc., with anyone likely to develop illness or die young losing out.

All seven of Sharon Bernardi's children died from a rare genetic disease caused by a defect in Sharon's mitochondria. Only her fourth child, Edward lived beyond childhood, thanks to drugs and blood transfusions, but his health deteriorated and he died in 2011 aged 21. Now Sharon is supporting medical research that would allow defective mitochondria to be replaced by DNA from another woman.

Questions

b) Do you think cloning should be allowed for medical research? Give two reasons for your point of view. **(4)**

c) Explain why some people think genetic engineering and cloning for medical research are wrong. **(8)**

d) 'Only God has the right to interfere with our genes.'

In your answer you should refer to Christianity.

(i) Do you agree? Give reasons for your opinion. **(3)**

(ii) Give reasons why some people may disagree with you. **(3)**

Exam Tip

b) You should already have thought about this, and you just have to give two reasons for your opinion. For example, if you think cloning should be allowed, you could use these two reasons:

- Cloning processes have been used to grow healthy cells to replace the malfunctioning ones and so cure disease.
- Cloning is not like creating human life and could give cures for many diseases.

Summary

Genetic engineering is finding out which genes cause diseases, such as muscular dystrophy, and then working out how the genes can be changed (often by cloning) so that the disease does not develop. Genetic research in the UK is controlled by the law and by the Human Fertilisation and Embryology Authority. Some people are in favour because it can lead to cures for dreadful diseases, some people are against because they think the likely effects are not really known.

Topic 8.1.11 Different attitudes to genetic engineering and cloning in Christianity

> When you enter a town and are welcomed, eat what is set before you. Heal the sick who are there and tell them, 'The kingdom of God is near you.'
>
> *Luke 10:8–9*

> Jesus of Nazareth was a healer. He cured diseases, and showed that God's purposes include overcoming 'those things in His creation that spoil it and that diminish the life of His children.' Clearly, where genetic manipulation is the means of healing diseases – in animals or humans – it is to be welcomed.
>
> *Statement from the Methodist Church*

Do humans have the right to interfere with God's design of DNA and genes?

There are several attitudes to genetic engineering amongst Christians.

Some Christians, mainly Liberal Protestants, believe that genetic engineering is a good thing which should be supported by the Church as long as it is done for the cure of disease and not to produce 'perfect humans'. Such Christians support the work of the Human Fertilisation and Embryology Authority which supervises genetic engineering using human embryos. They support genetic engineering because:

▶ Jesus was a healer who showed that Christians should do all they can to cure disease.

Discovering the genetic make-up of humans and using those discoveries to improve human life is part of what God wants humans to do as stewards of his creation. It is no different from researching into drugs which can be used to improve human life.

▶ There is a difference between creating cells and creating people. Creating people by science rather than sex would be wrong because it would be taking over God's role in the creation of life, but creating cells is working with God.
▶ As far as using embryos for genetic research is concerned, embryos cannot be regarded as potential human life until they are fourteen days old (the time limit set by the Human Fertilisation and Embryology Authority for genetic research).
▶ They accept most of the non-religious arguments in favour of genetic engineering.

Some Christians, mainly Catholics, believe that genetic engineering is permissible as long as it is only for curing diseases and does not use human embryos. They agree with genetic research for the same first three reasons as Liberal Protestants, but disagree with the use of embryos because:

▶ Life begins at the moment of conception whether in a womb or a glass dish.
▶ Killing an embryo is killing human life, which is banned by the Bible and the Church.
▶ Embryos for research have been produced by methods with which the Catholic Church disagrees (see Topic 8.2.7).

Some Christians are opposed to any form of genetic research at all. They have this attitude because:

▶ They believe that God has created the genetic make-up of each human being at the moment of conception and people have no right to interfere with God's will.
▶ They believe that genetic engineering is 'playing God', and that is a great sin.

- They believe that it is wrong to try to make the Earth perfect, as only heaven is perfect. This life is a preparation for heaven and should not be used to try to make heaven on Earth.
- They accept the non-religious arguments against genetic engineering.

What does this cartoon make you think about genetic research?

Questions

b) Do you think cloning for medical research is against God's will? Give two reasons for your point of view. **(4)**

c) Explain why some Christians are in favour of genetic engineering, but some are not. **(8)**

d) 'Christians should agree with cloning.'

In your answer you should refer to Christianity.

    (i) Do you agree? Give reasons for your opinion. **(3)**

    (ii) Give reasons why some people may disagree with you. **(3)**

Exam Tip

d) Use the technique for answering evaluation questions from page 111. Reasons for supporting this statement could be: Liberal Protestant reasons for supporting genetic research on page 126. Reasons for not supporting this statement could be Christian reasons for opposing genetic research on this page.

The Congregation for the Doctrine of Faith (CDF) today released Dignitas Personae, a document which addresses a range of issues including stem cell therapies, embryo experimentation and infertility treatments. 'Methods which do not cause serious harm to the subject from whom the stem cells are taken are to be considered licit. This is generally the case when tissues are taken from: a) an adult organism; b) the blood of the umbilical cord at the time of birth; c) fetuses who have died of natural causes. The obtaining of stem cells from a living human embryo, on the other hand, invariably causes the death of the embryo and is consequently gravely illicit ...' (Dignitas Personae, n. 32) 'Research initiatives involving the use of adult stem cells, since they do not present ethical problems, should be encouraged and supported.' (Dignitas Personae, n. 32) The Most Reverend Peter Smith, Archbishop of Cardiff commented, 'We hope to see more research focusing on adult stem cells, as their use raises none of the problems created by embryonic stem cells which require the destruction of human embryos.'

The Catholic Church in England and Wales Bishops' Conference 12 December 2008

Summary

Some Christians allow all genetic research, as long as it is to find cures for diseases, because Jesus was a healer.

Some Christians allow genetic research which does not involve the destruction of embryos, which they believe to be human life.

Some Christians oppose all genetic research because they believe it is 'playing God'.

How to answer exam questions

a) What are human rights? (2)

Human rights are the rights and freedoms to which everyone is entitled.

b) Do you think you are your brother's keeper? Give two reasons for your point of view. (4)

Yes I do think I am my brother's keeper because of the story of Cain and Abel when God punished Cain for not looking after Abel. God created us to look after each other. Also in his letter to Christians, St John said that Christians should not be like Cain who murdered his brother. As a Christian, I believe I should look after everyone in need.

c) Explain why some Christians use only the teachings of the Church to make moral decisions. (8)

Catholic Christians believe that only the Church has the right to explain what the Bible means, and what Christians should do about moral issues because they believe the Church is the Body of Christ.

Catholic Christians believe that the authority of the Church comes from the Magisterium (the Pope and the bishops interpreting the Bible and tradition for Catholics today), which they believe gives infallible guidance on moral behaviour.

They believe that God did not stop speaking to people after the last book of the Bible was written. They believe that God speaks to the world today through the Church.

They also believe that if individual Christians were to make their own decisions on everything, there could be lots of different opinions about how to behave, and no one would know which was the right thing for Christians to do.

d) 'Your conscience should always be your guide.'
   In your answer you should refer to Christianity.
   (i)   Do you agree? Give reasons for your opinion. (3)
   (ii) Give reasons why some people may disagree with you. (3)

(i) I disagree with this because as a Catholic I believe I am better following the teachings of the Church because the Church knows better than I do what are the right things to do. Also people have been mistaken about the voice of God, for example, the Yorkshire Ripper claimed that God had told him to kill prostitutes, and if you can be mistaken about the voice of God, you must also be able to be mistaken about the voice of conscience. Also, if everyone followed their conscience rather than laws, life would become chaotic and no one would know what sort of behaviour to expect from each other.

(ii) I can see why some people would disagree with me because the voice of conscience seems to be the same as the voice of God, therefore Christians should follow it. Also the Church says that Christians should follow their conscience as if it were the voice of God, and Christians are expected to follow the teachings of the Church. Finally, St Paul and St Thomas Aquinas taught that Christians should use their conscience as the final part of moral decision-making. Some Christians believe that if such great Christian thinkers say Christians should follow their conscience, then they should follow their conscience.

Question a

High marks because it is a correct definition.

Question b

A high mark answer because an opinion is backed up by two developed reasons.

Question c

A high mark answer because it gives four clear reasons why some Christians use only the guidance of the Church. There is also good use of specialist vocabulary such as Body of Christ, Son of God, authority, Magisterium, Pope, bishops, infallible, Bible, opinion.

Question d

A high mark answer because it states the candidate's own opinion and backs it up with three clear Christian reasons for thinking that you should not always follow your conscience. It then gives three reasons for people disagreeing and believing that conscience is the voice of God.

SPaG

A high mark answer because the answer spells, punctuates and uses the rules of grammar with consistent accuracy and effective control of meaning. A wide range of specialist terms is used adeptly and with precision.

Section 8.2

Religion: Environmental and medical issues

Introduction

This section of the examination specification requires you to look at the issues surrounding the impact of religion on environmental and medical issues.

Religion and environmental issues

You will need to understand the effects of, and give reasons for your own opinion about:

▶ global warming – its causes and possible solutions
▶ forms of pollution and their possible solutions
▶ the scarcity of natural resources and how this poses a threat to the future of the planet, with possible solutions
▶ Christian teachings on stewardship and their effects on Christian attitudes to the environment
▶ the teachings of one religion other than Christianity on stewardship and their effects on its followers in their attitudes to the environment.

Religion and infertility treatments

You will need to understand the effects of, and give reasons for your own opinion about:

▶ the nature and importance of medical treatments for infertility
▶ different attitudes to infertility treatments among Christians and the reasons for them
▶ attitudes to infertility treatments in one religion other than Christianity and the reasons for them.

Religion and transplant surgery

You will need to understand the effects of, and give reasons for your own opinion about:

▶ the nature and importance of transplant surgery
▶ different attitudes to transplant surgery in Christianity and the reasons for them
▶ different attitudes to transplant surgery in one religion other than Christianity and the reasons for them.

Topic 8.2.1 Global warming

KEY WORD

Global warming – the increase in the temperature of the Earth's atmosphere (thought to be caused by the greenhouse effect)

The Met Office has supported a report by its Chief Scientist, Dame Julia Slingo, on the extreme storms and flooding that battered Britain this winter, after she was criticised by climate change sceptics. The Met Office said Dame Julia was supported by all the evidence when she stated in her report, 'It is clear that global warming has led to an increase in moisture in the atmosphere, which means that when conditions are favourable to the formation of storms there is a greater risk of intense rainfall.'

Adapted from various news sources, February 2014

Global warming (now often referred to as 'climate change') is the fact that the Earth is warmer than it has been for over a thousand years. Global average temperatures rose by about 0.8 degrees Celsius between 1901 and 2010 and by 0.5 degrees Celsius between 1979 and 2010. Many scientists believe that the Earth has probably never warmed as fast as it has in the past 30 years – a period when natural influences on global temperatures, such as solar cycles and volcanoes, should have cooled the Earth down.

The UK Climate Impacts Programme assumes that if this trend continues, it would lead to average temperatures in the south east of England rising by 1.3 degrees Celsius by 2020 and by 2 degrees Celsius by 2050. There would be rainfall increase of 15–20 per cent in the north of England and Scotland by 2050. Other scientists have claimed that such rises in temperature will lead to a rise in the level of the sea (because water expands as it gets warmer), which means some coastal areas could disappear. Other studies have predicted that southern Mediterranean countries, such as Spain, could become deserts.

Scientists are agreed that the net effects of climate change up to the year 2025 will prove to be beneficial with increased agricultural yields, fewer deaths from the cold, lower energy use and possibly increased biodiversity. However, the benefits are likely to start decreasing after 2025, and by 2070 the cost of climate change will outweigh the benefits globally.

Adapted from various news sources, October 2013

The causes of global warming

1. The greenhouse effect

The United Nations Intergovernmental Panel on Climate Change and most scientists believe that global warming is caused by human activity in what is known as 'the greenhouse effect'. The burning of fossil fuels (gas, coal and oil) produces carbon dioxide. This produces a barrier in the atmosphere rather like the glass in a greenhouse so that the heat from the Sun can get through, but cannot get back out again, thus causing the Earth's temperature to rise.

In one sense the greenhouse effect has always been there and indeed is necessary for life to exist on Earth. If it weren't for these gases, Earth would be too cold for life. However, most scientists claim that global warming is happening because people are producing far more greenhouse gases through burning fossil fuels in power stations, cars, planes, and so on. As countries such as China and India become more developed, it is likely that by 2050 people will be creating twice the amount of carbon gases (our carbon footprint) as in 2010, causing more and more global warming.

Many people think the storms that destroyed the railway line at Dawlish in 2014 were caused by climate change.

British children are deeply concerned about the impact of climate change on their own lives and those of children in poorer nations, according to a new poll for Unicef. Three-quarters of 11 to 16-year-olds were worried about how global warming will change the world and wanted the government to do more to tackle the threat. But the results come as the row increased over the dropping of debate over climate change from the national curriculum for under-14s' geography classes, with the delivery of a 65,000-strong petition to the Department for Education.

The Unicef poll, conducted by Ipsos-Mori, found that two-thirds of young people were worried about how climate change will affect other children and families in developing countries and that only one per cent said they knew nothing about climate change.

'The results of this survey offer a timely reminder to politicians that climate change is an issue of tremendous concern to Britons and casts a long shadow over young people's view of their future,' said David Bull, Unicef UK's executive director. 'Young people are not only concerned about their own future [but also] the impact climate change is having on children in less developed countries where climate change is a key driver of hunger and malnutrition.'

David Carrington, The Guardian, *17 April 2013*

2. Natural climate change

The Earth's climate has always been changing. Those few scientists who think that recent global warming is a natural process point to the fact that, in the last 10,000 years, the warmest periods happened well before humans started to produce large amounts of carbon dioxide. They also claim that if the greenhouse effect was happening, then the troposphere (the layer of the Earth's atmosphere roughly 10–15 km above us) should heat up faster than the Earth's surface, but it does not seem to be.

Furthermore, they claim that nature produces far more carbon gases from volcanic emissions, animals, bacteria, decaying vegetation and the ocean than humans are ever likely to.

3. Solar activity

Some scientists claim that changes in the Earth's temperature are caused by the amount of radiation coming from the Sun.

These scientists believe that the heating effects of the Sun's rays are normally kept from the Earth by clouds, but when solar activity is high, solar winds cause fewer clouds to form so that more of the Sun's heat reaches the Earth and it warms up.

Are young people more worried about the environment because it's their future?

131

These scientists claim that the evidence does not fit the theory that global warming is caused by carbon emissions because, for example, the Earth grew cooler after the Second World War when global carbon dioxide levels were rising rapidly.

Although there are arguments about its causes, there is no argument about the fact that the Earth's surface is getting warmer and that the results could be disastrous.

Possible solutions

Most of the world's scientists believe that climate change is mainly caused by the carbon emissions produced by human activity. There are several ways by which these could be reduced:

▶ We could use energy efficiency technologies (such as building insulation, more efficient light bulbs and energy efficient electrical appliances) to allow us to use less energy to get the same (or higher) levels of production, service, and comfort. For example: modern refrigerators use 40 per cent less energy than those built ten years ago, it would take 50 new cars to produce the same quantity of air quality pollutant emissions per kilometre as a vehicle made in 1970.
▶ Using renewable energy sources such as solar, wind, geothermal, hydro and bioenergy could produce electricity without producing any carbon emissions after the facilities had been built.
▶ Building cheaper and more easily available methods of public transport could greatly reduce carbon emissions. The greenest forms of transport are electric trains and trams, the least green are planes and diesel buses.
▶ If costs mean that some countries still need to use coal-fired power stations, new technology exists to capture and store carbon emissions from power plants.
▶ Car manufacturers could use ethanol, biodiesel, electric batteries and hydrogen to power cars without carbon emissions.

There are problems, however, with some of these solutions. Biofuels (ethanol and biodiesel are both produced from crops grown on land which could otherwise be used to grow food) could lead to world starvation. Electric batteries can cause as many carbon emissions in their production and re-charging, as can trains and trams if they rely on electricity produced by power stations using oil or coal. Solutions also need to be worldwide: China, the USA and India are responsible for over 50 per cent of the world's carbon emissions while the UK is only responsible for 1.57 per cent.

Exam Tip

b) You should already have thought about this, and you just have to give two reasons for your opinion. For example, if you think it is a problem, you could use these two reasons:
- It will lead to the ice-caps melting, which would flood coastal areas.
- It could lead to countries like Spain becoming deserts.

Summary

Global warming means that the atmosphere of the Earth is getting warmer and this could mean that some towns and cities near the sea could disappear under water.

Most scientists think global warming is caused by people putting too much carbon into the atmosphere, but some think it is caused by an increase in radiation from the Sun or by the changing nature of Earth's climate.

Most scientists think global warming could be reduced by increasing the use of non-fossil fuels to produce electricity and power, such as wind, water, waves, etc., and by employing more energy efficiencies.

Questions

b) Do you think global warming is a problem? Give two reasons for your point of view. (4)
c) Explain why global warming is happening. (8)
d) 'Global warming will make the UK a nicer place to live.'
In your answer you should refer to at least one religion.
    (i) Do you agree? Give reasons for your opinion. (3)
    (ii) Give reasons why some people may disagree with you. (3)

Topic 8.2.2 Forms of pollution and their possible solutions

The main forms of pollution other than carbon emissions are:

1. Acid rain

Buildings and forests in Scandinavian countries are being destroyed by the **acid rain** coming from the United Kingdom (90 per cent of acid rain in Norway comes from other countries). Burning fossil fuels releases sulphuric and nitric acids which go into the atmosphere and change the pH of the rainwater in clouds from pH5/6 to pH3 making it so acidic that it can burn things when it reaches the ground.

The effects of acid rain on a Scandinavian forest

2. Human waste

The waste produced by humans in the form of sewage, refuse (rubbish put into bins) and litter (rubbish left on the streets and elsewhere) is not only a major form of pollution, but also a major threat to the future of the planet. As the world economy grows so does its production of waste. For example, Europe produces more than 2.5 billion tons of solid waste a year, and every day the inhabitants of New York throw away approximately 26,000 tons. Traditional waste management strategies include reusing materials, recovering materials through recycling, incineration and landfills.

Human excreta and other waterborne waste products from houses, streets and factories are transported through sewers to sewage works where the raw sewage has to undergo a series of treatments to make it safe for discharge into rivers or the sea. Solid sewage has to be pasteurised to make it safe to use as fertiliser on farmers' fields. Raw sewage, or sewage that has not been treated adequately, is one serious source of water pollution and a cause of eutrophication (see page 134).

Apart from being unsightly and degrading, litter has helped cause an increase in the rat population to 70 million in the UK. The 2006 National Rodent Survey highlighted compost bins, discarded fast-food containers, bird feeders, litter and poor maintenance of sewage pipes as some of the main causes of the rat boom. Rats bring many diseases to humans such as the deadly Weil's disease. Litter also chokes many animals, causes thousands of bike and car accidents when it is on roads, and it is estimated that a fire breaks out every twelve minutes because of litter.

Walking through British towns and cities, it's often hard to avoid the litter strewn across the pavements, roads and green spaces – anything from food wrappers, cigarette butts and dog mess to bottles, cans and plastic bags. A staggering 30 million tonnes of litter are removed from England's streets every year.

Despite numerous anti-litter campaigns over the last decade, the amount of litter being dropped is not decreasing. The latest data, from the Encams (Keep Britain Tidy) local environmental quality survey of England for 2007/08, shows that while there has been a modest reduction of 3 per cent in the amount of litter compared to the previous year, levels have risen since 2004/05.

Since the 1960s, littering has increased by 500 per cent, according to Litterbugs, a recent Policy Exchange and Campaign to Protect Rural England (CPRE) report. It is an unwelcome consequence of the increasingly throwaway society we now live in.

Flemmich Webb, The Guardian, 20 May 2009

3. Eutrophication

An excess of nitrates, nitrites and phosphates in rivers is leading to a lack of oxygen and an increase in aquatic plants which are causing fish to die and poisons to enter water supplies. This is called eutrophication and is caused by fertilisers being washed into streams, sewage pollution and a lack of trees to soak up the nitrogen. This could lead to major health problems for humans, such as septicaemia.

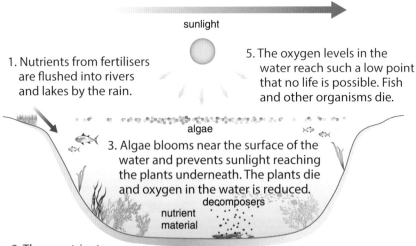

sunlight

1. Nutrients from fertilisers are flushed into rivers and lakes by the rain.

5. The oxygen levels in the water reach such a low point that no life is possible. Fish and other organisms die.

algae

3. Algae blooms near the surface of the water and prevents sunlight reaching the plants underneath. The plants die and oxygen in the water is reduced.

decomposers

nutrient material

2. These nutrients cause plants in the water to grow excessively.

4. As the plants die, they are broken down by decomposers, which uses up even more oxygen in the water.

The process of eutrophication.

4. Radioactive pollution

Nuclear power stations do not produce carbon dioxide, but do produce nuclear waste which will take thousands, if not millions, of years to be safe. This waste is being buried and no one knows whether the containers it is buried in will be able to contain it safely for this length of time. When humans come into contact with too much radiation they can be killed, get cancer and have genetically mutated children, as seen in the Chernobyl nuclear power station disaster of 1986.

On 11 March 2011, a large tsunami hit the east coast of Japan. The Fukushima Nuclear Power Plant was flooded and began releasing substantial amounts of radioactive materials. It was the largest nuclear incident since the 1986 Chernobyl disaster and the clean-up process is expected to take decades.

Possible solutions

1. Acid rain

The solution to acid rain is closely connected with the solution to the greenhouse effect. If society stops burning fossil fuels in power stations, acid rain will not be produced, so the solution is to use alternative sources of energy such as the wind, Sun, tides and nuclear energy.

2. Human waste

The problems of waste could be solved by a combination of recycling, using incinerators to produce electricity, anaerobic digestion and Multiple Solid Waste (MSW) methods to produce fuel. Each method of waste disposal has its drawbacks. Reusing glass bottles can require more energy than their initial manufacture as they have to be sterilised. Incineration produces greenhouse gases and toxic chemicals like dioxins and lead.

Litter is a problem which can only be solved by the people who cause it. Basically, if people stopped dropping litter, the problem would go away! The UK has passed laws to try to solve the problem. Firstly, those who throw down, drop or deposit and leave litter in any place, even if it is just a cigarette end or chewing gum, can be given an on-the-spot fine or face a court prosecution. Secondly, if you see an area that is badly littered and report it to your local council, the council must clear all the litter within a fixed period (six hours in places like a high street).

Is litter always the fault of humans?

3. Eutrophication

Eutrophication is already being cut down through improved sewage treatment, less use of phosphates in detergents and less use of nitrates in farming fertilisers. However, an increase in organic farming methods could reverse this as the use of manure in fields leads to an increase in nitrates in streams and rivers.

4. Radioactive pollution

Some nuclear waste can be reprocessed (a chemical operation which separates the useful fuel for recycling from the waste). The UK's Sellafield plant in Cumbria is one of the world's two nuclear reprocessing plants. Reprocessing means that 97 per cent of the waste can be re-used. However, the remaining 3 per cent of waste has to be stored. The safest method of treating long-term nuclear waste is geological disposal (isolating the waste deep inside a suitable rock formation to ensure that no significant quantities of radioactivity ever reach the surface environment). The UK government is working on a project for this.

Remember: carbon emissions are also a form of pollution.

Questions

b) Do you think litter is a problem? Give two reasons for your point of view. **(4)**

c) Explain how the problems of pollution can be solved. **(8)**

d) 'Science and the Government have pollution under control.'

In your answer you should refer to at least one religion.

   (i) Do you agree? Give reasons for your opinion. **(3)**

   (ii) Give reasons why some people may disagree with you. **(3)**

Exam Tip

c) One way to answer this question would be to identify four types of pollution and use the solutions on these pages to explain how they can be solved. You should try to use some specialist vocabulary such as: greenhouse effect, fossil fuels, recycling, incinerators, anaerobic digestion, prosecution, legislation, reprocessing, geological disposal.

Summary

Pollution takes several forms. Acid rain is caused by high level carbon emissions (as global warming could be) and damages buildings and plants. Human waste (refuse and sewage) can cause major health problems if not dealt with properly as can radioactive waste from nuclear power plants. Eutrophication caused by nitrates and sewage kills fish in streams and rivers, and litter dropped by humans leads to an increase in rats.

Possible solutions are:

- producing electricity from alternative sources
- more efficient means of waste disposal, recycling, nuclear reprocessing and geological storage
- people being made to stop dropping litter.

Topic 8.2.3 The scarcity of natural resources

KEY WORD

Natural resources – naturally occurring materials, such as oil and fertile land, which can be used by humans

Natural resources are naturally occurring materials, such as oil and fertile land, which can be used by humans.

They can be divided into two types:

1. **Renewable resources** These are resources which humans can use over and over again because they renew themselves. Examples of renewable resources are: wind power, solar power, water power, fertile land producing food, oil seed rape and sugar cane (which can provide energy for cars), soft woods (which grow very quickly and can be used for paper, furniture, etc.). Human use of such renewable resources causes no problems. However, using renewable resources to produce electricity is often expensive.

2. **Finite or non-renewable resources** These are resources which disappear once they are used. Examples are: oil, coal, iron, tin, copper, uranium, natural gas and hard woods. Human use of finite resources causes major problems because as the resource is used it becomes more scarce and so can be used less.

This power station in Stockton-on-Tees runs on household waste. It therefore provides a solution to both the scarcity of oil and gas and waste disposal.

The problem is most obvious in the case of oil. It is usually thought that a decline in the availability of oil would have the most effect on people's use of cars, but it is not only petrol and diesel that come from oil. All plastics and road surfaces, most candles, polishes and chemical foodstuffs come from oil. Clearly, if the oil begins to dry up, there will be major effects on people's lives. Similarly, all the metals used in everyday living from car panels and railway tracks to pans and kitchen appliances come from finite ores such as iron, aluminium and tin.

> David Cameron is losing the battle for public opinion over fracking for shale gas because of high-profile public protests against the controversial technique, polling suggests.
>
> The latest results of a long-running survey on British attitudes towards shale gas, undertaken by YouGov and commissioned by the University of Nottingham, show an increase in the number of people opposed to fracking and a decrease in those in favour for the second time since protests at Balcombe in West Sussex last August.
>
> The slide in support comes despite several major speeches by the prime minister in support of shale gas over the same period, including last week's address to the World Economic Forum in Davos where he said the UK needed to 'embrace the opportunities of shale gas' even though he understood 'the concerns some people have'.
>
> *Adam Vaughan, The Guardian, 28 January 2014*

Many scientists feel that unless we stop using these finite resources as we are, they will soon run out. This would mean no cars, no televisions, stereos, and so on. In other words, the problem of resources could have as severe consequences as the problems of global warming and pollution.

Possible solutions

- There are now several alternative ways of making electricity which do not use non-renewable resources. For example: nuclear power, wind power, sea power (using either the waves or the tides), hydroelectric power (using the water in a dam) and solar power (using the Sun's heat).
- Oil and gas reserves can be greatly increased by fracking (the process of drilling down into the earth before a high-pressure water mixture is directed at the rock to release the gas inside). The US and Canada now have at least an extra hundred years of oil and gas, as could the UK.
- Car manufacturers are looking at water, sugar cane and electric batteries as ways of powering cars. There are already a few fuel-cell cars on the market powered by the hydrogen from water.
- Recycling will enable the lifetime of many finite resources to be extended. For example, some cars are now made of almost 75 per cent recycled materials.
- Scientists are working on using chemicals from plants rather than oil to produce such things as plastics.

Will people be prepared to make the effort to recycle?

Questions

b) Do you think we should be worried about natural resources running out? Give two reasons for your point of view. **(4)**

c) Explain why natural resources raise problems for humanity. **(8)**

d) 'Governments will make sure that natural resources do not run out.'

In your answer you should refer to at least one religion.

   (i) Do you agree? Give reasons for your opinion. **(3)**

   (ii) Give reasons why some people may disagree with you. **(3)**

Exam Tip

d) Use the technique for answering evaluation questions from page 111. Arguments in favour of the quotation would come from possible solutions (above). Arguments against could come from the problems of governments working together on resources and the opposition of people to techniques like fracking.

Natural resources often play a role in fuelling conflicts, undermining peacebuilding efforts and contributing to a relapse in conflict if they are not properly managed. Indeed, over the past 60 years, at least 40 per cent of internal conflicts had a link to natural resources and since 1990 there have been at least 18 violent conflicts fuelled by the exploitation of natural resources …. To support the UN's peace and security architecture, UNEP is providing technical expertise on how natural resources and the environmental can contribute to more effective conflict prevention, resolution and peacebuilding.

United Nations Environment Programme

Summary

Resources are a problem because those which cannot be grown again (non-renewable resources) such as oil, natural gas and metals will disappear. This will lead to major problems in maintaining our lifestyles.

However, alternative energy supplies, recycling and techniques such as fracking could help solve the problems.

Topic 8.2.4 Christian teachings on stewardship

KEY WORDS

Conservation – protecting and preserving natural resources and the environment

Creation – the act of creating the universe, or the universe which has been created

Environment – the surroundings in which plants and animals live and on which they depend to live

Stewardship – looking after something so it can be passed on to the next generation

Use of the mineral, vegetable and animal resources of the universe cannot be divorced from moral imperatives. Man's dominion over inanimate and other living beings granted by the Creator is not absolute; it is limited by concern for the quality of life of his neighbour, including generations to come; it requires a religious respect for the integrity of nature.

Catechism of the Catholic Church 2415

It is a basic belief of Christianity that God gave humans the stewardship of the Earth and its resources. Stewardship means looking after something so that it can be passed on to the next generation.

In the Genesis accounts of creation, God gave humans the right to rule over the Earth. This gives humans control of animals, all other living creatures and plants. However, the rest of the Bible makes clear that the right to rule gives humans many responsibilities.

The Old Testament teaches that humans have a responsibility to treat animals humanely and to treat the land kindly by not growing crops every fiftieth year.

In the Parable of the Talents or Minas (Luke 19:11–26), Jesus taught that God expects humans to pass on to the next generation more than they have been given. Many Christians believe that this means Christians have a responsibility to leave the Earth a better place than they found it.

In many of his teachings, especially the Sermon on the Mount, Jesus taught that Christians have a responsibility to ensure a fair sharing of the Earth's resources.

The Bible also makes clear that there will be a judgement day at the end of the world when people will be judged on their beliefs and behaviour. Most Christians believe that part of this judgement will be on how they have fulfilled their duty as stewards of God's Earth.

Why do you think Catholic Christians launched a climate justice campaign?

How beliefs about stewardship affect Christian attitudes to the environment

- The responsibility to be God's stewards and to leave the Earth a better place than they found it means that Christians should try to reduce pollution, practise conservation and preserve resources for future generations.
- The belief that stewardship means a fair sharing of the Earth's resources means that Christians should try to improve the quality of life of the less fortunate by sharing the Earth's resources more fairly and improving the standard of living in LEDCs (Less Economically Developed Countries) without causing more pollution.
- The belief that, after death, they will be judged by God on their behaviour as stewards means that many Christians feel they have a duty to share in and support the work of groups which try to reduce pollution and conserve resources. This is a way of living as God wants them to.
- Belief in stewardship also means that every Christian should be judging what they are doing in their life as an individual by the standards of Christian stewardship. It is only by being a good steward, and conserving the environment and scarce resources that a Christian can become a good Christian.

However, Christians believe humans have been placed in control and so, in tackling environmental issues, human concerns cannot be ignored – for example, shutting down a factory which causes pollution but employs 3000 people would not be a Christian solution.

Questions

b) Do you think Christians should do more to care for the environment? Give two reasons for your point of view. **(4)**

c) Explain why Christians have a duty to care for the environment. **(8)**

d) 'If Christians followed their teachings on stewardship, there would be no environmental problems.'

In your answer, you should refer to at least one religion.

(i) Do you agree? Give reasons for your opinion. **(3)**

(ii) Give reasons why some people may disagree with you. **(3)**

Exam Tip

b) You should already have thought about this, and you just have to give two reasons for your opinion. For example, if you think they should take more care of the environment, you could use two of the bullet points from how beliefs about stewardship affect attitudes towards the environment.

I wish to mention another threat to peace, which arises from the greedy exploitation of environmental resources. Even if 'nature is at our disposition', all too often we do not 'respect it or consider it a gracious gift which we must care for and set at the service of our brothers and sisters, including future generations'. Here too what is crucial is responsibility on the part of all in pursuing, in a spirit of fraternity, policies respectful of this earth which is our common home. I recall a popular saying: 'God always forgives, we sometimes forgive, but when nature – creation – is mistreated, she never forgives!'. We have also witnessed the devastating effects of several recent natural disasters. In particular, I would mention once more the numerous victims and the great devastation caused in the Philippines and other countries of South-East Asia as a result of typhoon Haiyan.

Statement by Pope Francis to the Diplomatic Corps, 14 January 2014

Summary

Christians believe that God made humans to look after the world as his stewards – to have authority over animals and plants. However, the Bible also teaches that Christians should care for the environment and leave the Earth a better place than they found it.

Topic 8.2.5a The teachings of Islam on stewardship

> Behold thy Lord said to the angels, 'I will create a vicegerent on earth.' ... And He taught Adam the nature of all things ... And behold, We said to the angels: 'Bow down to Adam.' And they bowed down: Not so Iblis: he refused and was haughty: He was of those who reject the faith.
>
> *The Qur'an 2:30–34*

Islam teaches that God created Adam as his **khalifah** (vice-regent or vice-gerent – someone who looks after things for you). This means that all Muslims are God's khalifahs who have to keep the balance of creation and look after the Earth for God by following the way of life set out for Muslims in the Qur'an and the Shari'ah. This involves being part of the **ummah**.

Islam also teaches that there will be a **Day of Judgement** when people will be questioned by God on the way they have looked after the Earth and the life on Earth. Those who have polluted or misused God's gifts will not be allowed into heaven.

According to Islam, this life is a test from God on which they will be judged at the end of the world. A major part of the test is looking after the environment in the way of Islam and those who fail the test will be punished.

How Islamic teachings about stewardship affect attitudes to the environment

> It is important, therefore, for Muslims to play a leading part in the efforts to protect our environment. Life on earth is set up with natural balance and this is the key to our survival here.
>
> *From* What Does Islam Say *by Ibrahim Hewitt*

◗ The responsibility to be God's khalifah means that Muslims should try to reduce pollution and preserve resources by following the Shari'ah.
◗ The Shari'ah and the ummah make many Muslims believe that stewardship means a fair sharing of the Earth's resources, so Muslims should try to improve the quality of life of the less fortunate by sharing the Earth's resources more fairly and improving the standard of living in LEDCs without causing more pollution.

Why might Muslims support wind farms like this off-shore one at Redcar?

▶ The belief in life as a test with judgement on their behaviour as khalifahs means that many Muslims feel they have a duty to share in and support the work of groups that try to reduce pollution and conserve resources. It also means that every Muslim should be judging what they are doing in their life as an individual by the standards of Islamic stewardship.

▶ There is a unity and balance in creation, therefore Muslims have a duty to preserve the environment and make sure that it continues to be what God intended it to be.

However, Muslims believe that human interests come first so the effects of environmental projects on humans cannot be ignored.

Ramadan Mubarak! By the grace of God, we've made it to another Ramadan! With that comes yet another opportunity to reduce our wastefulness and green our lifestyle. Green Muslims is excited to share a few resources we hope will help you Green your Ramadan!

Green Ramadan – Daily Tips

Check out the Green Muslims Facebook page or our blog for simple daily tips on how to take one step towards greening your Ramadan. We'll also be posting reflections from members!

Ramadan Toolkit

Our Ramadan toolkit includes all the inspirational ayahs, quotes, and hadith covered in the daily tips.

Rent our Zero-trash Plate Set for your next Iftar

Are you planning an event or workshop for your organization in DC Metro area? Having a big potluck or picnic? Renting the Green Muslims Zero Trash Party Set is not only a way to save the costs of buying disposable plates, but a great contribution to protect our planet, reduce the size of our land fills, and inspire your friends to environmental stewardship.

Ramadan advice from www.greenmuslims.org

Exam Tip

c) 'Explain why' means give reasons. One way to answer this question would be to use four reasons from how Islamic teachings on stewardship affect attitudes to the environment. Make sure to use some specialist vocabulary such as: khalifah, Qur'an, Shari'ah, ummah, judgement, creation, LEDC.

Questions

b) Do you think religious people do enough for the environment? Give two reasons for your point of view. **(4)**

c) Choose one religion other than Christianity and explain why its followers have a duty to take care of the Earth. **(8)**

d) 'The environment is the government's responsibility not religion's.'

In your answer, you should refer to at least one religion.

    (i) Do you agree? Give reasons for your opinion. **(3)**

    (ii) Give reasons why some people may disagree with you. **(3)**

Summary

Islam teaches that God created humans as his stewards of the Earth. He showed people how to look after the Earth in the Qur'an. Life is a test and God will judge Muslims on how well they have looked after the world.

Topic 8.2.5b The teachings of Judaism on stewardship

Judaism teaches that God made humans as stewards of his Earth. In Genesis 1:28, God gave humans control of the Earth and all its creatures. However, this does not mean that humans can do what they want with the Earth. As God's stewards, Jewish people must look after the Earth in the way God intended.

This way is shown in the mitzvot which tell Jewish people:

- that around every town there must be an area of open land which cannot be used in any way, not even for growing crops
- never to destroy things of the Earth which are useful
- to celebrate the festival of Tu B'Shevat (New Year for Trees) by planting trees in areas where they are needed or by paying someone to plant a tree for them in another country
- to not plant or harvest crops every 50 years to give the land a chance to recharge its batteries.

> God blessed them and said to them, 'Be fruitful and increase in number; fill the Earth and subdue it. Rule over the fish ... and the birds ... and over every living creature ...'
>
> *Genesis 1:28*

> Jewish tradition teaches us to care for our planet in order to preserve that which God has created. Psalm 24 notes, 'The Earth is the Lord's and the fullness thereof,' a dramatic assertion of God's ownership of the land. It follows, then, that any act that damages our Earth is an offense against the property of God.
>
> *Statement on the environment from Reform Judaism.org*

Should every town have big green spaces such as Hampstead Heath in London?

How Jewish teachings about stewardship affect attitudes to the environment

- The responsibility to be God's stewards means that Jewish people should try to reduce pollution and preserve resources by following the teachings of the Torah.
- The Tenakh and Talmud lead many Jewish people to believe that stewardship means a fair sharing of the Earth's resources, so Jewish people should try to improve the quality of life of the less fortunate by sharing the Earth's resources more fairly and improving the standard of living in LEDCs without causing more pollution.

- The belief in life as a test with judgement on how well they have followed the mitzvot means that many Jewish people feel they have a duty to share in and support the work of groups which try to reduce pollution and conserve resources.
- God created the environment as something which is good, therefore Jewish people have a duty to preserve the environment and make sure that it continues to be what God intended it to be.
- Orthodox Jewish people must obey the mitzvot on caring for the environment because they believe they must obey all of the mitzvot.

Although Jewish people must be concerned about environmental issues and support the work of groups which are trying to stop pollution, end waste and use resources responsibly, Judaism teaches that human interests come first, and that environmental issues cannot ignore the human issues.

People are beginning to regard themselves as just another part of the ecosystem. In Jewish thinking, such a view is misguided and dangerous. It leads to denying the supreme value of human beings ... For Jews, environmental concerns have to take into account the special place of humanity in creation. In other words, they have to have a moral dimension.

From Judaism by Arye Forta

The signing of the Coalition on the Environment and Jewish Life's Energy Covenant Campaign Declaration in 2012. 'As Jews: God, we are taught, declares to us, "Look at My works! See how beautiful they are, how excellent! For your sake I created them all. See to it that you do not spoil and destroy My world, for if you do, there will be no one after you to repair it." (Ecclesiastes Rabbah 7:13).' An extract from the Declaration.

Exam Tip

c) 'Explain why' means give reasons. One way to answer this question would be to use four reasons from how Jewish teachings on stewardship affect attitudes to the environment. Make sure to use some specialist vocabulary such as: mitzvot, Torah, Tenakh, Talmud, judgement, creation, LEDC.

Questions

b) Do you think religious people do enough for the environment? Give two reasons for your point of view. **(4)**

c) Choose one religion other than Christianity and explain why its followers have a duty to take care of the Earth. **(8)**

d) 'The environment is the government's responsibility not religion's.' In your answer, you should refer to at least one religion.

    (i) Do you agree? Give reasons for your opinion. **(3)**

    (ii) Give reasons why some people may disagree with you. **(3)**

Summary

Judaism teaches that God created humans as his stewards of the Earth to have authority over animals and plants. He showed people how to look after the Earth in the mitzvot. Life is a test and God will judge Jewish people on how well they have looked after the world.

Topic 8.2.5c The teachings of Hinduism on stewardship

The waters are the body of breath, and the moon up there is its luminous appearance. So, the extent of the waters and of that moon is the same as the extent of breath. Now, all of these are of equal extent, all are without limit. So those who venerate them as finite win only a limited world, whereas those who venerate them as infinite win a world without limit.

Upanishad 1:5:13

Why might Vishnu appearing as a tortoise affect Hindu attitudes to stewardship and the environment?

Although many Hindus would not necessarily talk about being stewards of the Earth, they do feel that they have a duty to look after the Earth and that Hindus have certain duties towards the Earth. Hindu beliefs about stewardship include:

1. Respect for animal life. In his avatars, Vishnu appeared as a fish, a tortoise, a boar and a lion. Krishna was a cowherd. Many Hindus believe that they may have been animals in previous incarnations so animals are respected. Many think that the teachings on **ahimsa** (non-violence) mean that they should be vegetarians refusing to take any form of life because they have respect for all life. Almost all Hindus regard the cow as sacred because of its connections with Krishna.

2. Respect for nature. Forests are very special to Hindus. The third **ashrama** after the **householder** is the forest dweller (vanaprastha). The forests are pure nature untouched by humans and it is in living here that Hindus can find union with God. According to Hindu stories, Krishna spent much of his time in the forest, which also makes them very special places. Certain trees are thought to be especially holy, for example, the banyan tree is thought to be holy because it is connected with religious experiences of **swamis**. This is perhaps why the major Hindu green group, the Chipko, began with tree hugging.

How Hindu teachings about stewardship affect attitudes to the environment

▶ The need to respect the eternal law of nature means that Hindus should try to reduce pollution and preserve resources.

▶ The avatars of the gods make many Hindus believe that stewardship means protecting animals and being vegetarian.

▶ Many Hindus believe that respect for life means a fair sharing of the Earth's resources, so Hindus should try to improve the quality of life of the less fortunate by sharing the Earth's resources more fairly and improving the standard of living in LEDCs without causing more pollution.

▶ The belief in respect for life and nature means that many Hindus feel they have a duty to share in and support the work of groups which try to reduce pollution and conserve resources.

Although Hindus should have a great respect for the environment, some Hindus feel that as humans are the most advanced life-form, they have been given the right to use the Earth's resources in any way they think is right. There is a lot of conflict in India today between those Hindus who want industrial progress regardless of the environment and those who think the environment must be protected from industry.

May men and oxen both plough in contentment, in contentment the plough cleave the furrow. Auspicious furrow, we venerate you. We pray you, bless us and bring us abundant harvests.

Rig Veda IV.57

Sanatana Dharma envisions the vastness of God's manifestation and the immense cycles of time in which it is perfectly created, preserved and destroyed, again and again, every dissolution being the preamble to the next creative impulse. Notwithstanding this spiritual reassurance, Hindus still know we must do all that is humanly possible to protect the Earth and her resources for the present as well as future generations.

Conclusion to the Hindu declaration on climate change at the Parliament of the World's Religions, December 2009

Questions

b) Do you think religious people do enough for the environment? Give two reasons for your point of view. **(4)**

c) Choose one religion other than Christianity and explain why its followers have a duty to take care of the Earth. **(8)**

d) 'The environment is the government's responsibility not religion's.'

In your answer, you should refer to at least one religion.

    (i) Do you agree? Give reasons for your opinion. **(3)**

    (ii) Give reasons why some people may disagree with you. **(3)**

Exam Tip

c) 'Explain why' means give reasons. One way to answer this question would be to use four reasons from how Hindu teachings on stewardship affect attitudes to the environment. Make sure to use some specialist vocabulary such as: respect, eternal law, Krishna, avatar, ahimsa, creation, LEDC.

Summary

Hindus believe they have a duty to show stewardship towards the Earth. The avatars of the gods as animals mean that Hindus should respect and look after animals. The law of nature and respect for life mean that Hindus should reduce pollution and try for a fair sharing of resources. However, some Hindus believe the interests of humans should come first.

Topic 8.2.5d The teachings of Sikhism on stewardship

First God Created His Light; and from it were all men made.

Yes, from God's Light comes the whole universe ... The One True God is within all, and it is He alone who creates all. And whosoever realises His will, knows the One alone, Yes, he alone is the Servant of God.

Guru Granth Sahib

In 2014 Sikhs worldwide will be celebrating the fourth annual worldwide Sikh Vatavaran Diwas (Sikh Environment Day). This day marks the New Year in the Sikh calendar and the Gurgaddi Diwas of Sri Guru Har Rai Ji who is remembered for his deep sensitivity to nature and its preservation. This is the fourth celebration planned by EcoSikh an organisation that was created as the Sikh community's contribution to the Plans for Generational Change project initiated by the Alliance of Religions and Conservation (ARC)with the United Nations Development Programme. The project works with the major world religions to improve their relationship with the environment.

www.ecosikh.org

Although Sikhs do not always talk about being stewards of the Earth, they do feel that they have a duty to look after the Earth. There are many stories of the **Gurus** acting as stewards of the Earth such as the following:

1. Blessed by Guru Nanak, Baba Buddha had the unique distinction of anointing five succeeding Gurus. After doing active service he retired to a bir (forest) where he created such an environment that tigers, goats, peacocks and snakes all existed in harmony amidst lakes and greenery.

2. When Guru Amar Das realised that the Beas River water was not fit for human consumption, he constructed a baoli, covering the entire area with trees. This not only provided safe drinking water for the people but also helped to create an eco-friendly environment. This has now become a place of worship, the Baoli Sahib.

3. Guru Har Rai developed Kiratpur Sahib as a town of parks and gardens. Located on the banks of a tributary of the Sutlej, he planted flowers and fruit-bearing trees all over the area. This created a salubrious environment, attracting beautiful birds to the town and turning it into an idyllic place to live. So Guru Har Rai acted as a steward.

Sikhs should follow the examples of the Gurus, and so if the Gurus acted as stewards of the Earth, all Sikhs should also act as stewards of the Earth.

Sikh beliefs about stewardship include: respect for nature, keeping sound ecosystems, reducing pollution, and respect for animal life.

How Sikh teachings about stewardship affect attitudes to the environment

▶ The need to respect the light of God in the universe means that Sikhs should try to reduce pollution and preserve resources.
▶ The examples of the Gurus make most Sikhs believe that they should protect animals and create and preserve ecosystems.
▶ Many Sikhs believe that respect for God's light in the Earth's people means a fair sharing of the Earth's resources, so Sikhs

should try to improve the quality of life of the less fortunate by sharing the Earth's resources more fairly and improving the standard of living in LEDCs without causing more pollution.

▶ The belief in respect for God's light in life and nature means that many Sikhs feel they have a duty to share in and support the work of groups which try to reduce pollution and conserve resources.

Although Sikhs should have a great respect for the environment, some Sikhs feel that, as humans are the most advanced life-form, they have been given the right to use the Earth's resources in any way they think is right. Such Sikhs would feel that in arguments between environmental protection and human jobs and living standards, the rights of humans should come first.

Questions

b) Do you think religious people do enough for the environment? Give two reasons for your point of view. **(4)**

c) Choose one religion other than Christianity and explain why its followers have a duty to take care of the Earth. **(8)**

d) 'The environment is the government's responsibility not religion's.'

In your answer, you should refer to at least one religion.

(i) Do you agree? Give reasons for your opinion. **(3)**

(ii) Give reasons why some people may disagree with you. **(3)**

Exam Tip

c) 'Explain why' means give reasons. One way to answer this question would be to use four reasons from how Sikh teachings on stewardship affect attitudes to the environment. Make sure to use some specialist vocabulary such as: Guru, light of God, ecosystems, quality of life, respect, Guru Nanak, creation, LEDC.

> The Universe is not an illusion. It is reality, not final and permanent but a reality on account of the presence of God in it. This world is the abode of the Almighty and yet He transcends it.
>
> *Guru Gobind Singh*

Summary

Sikhs believe they have a duty to show stewardship towards the Earth. The examples of the Gurus mean that Sikhs should respect and look after animals. Respect for God's light in life and nature means that Sikhs should reduce pollution and try for a fair sharing of resources. However, most Sikhs believe the interests of humans should come first.

Topic 8.2.6 The nature and importance of medical treatments for infertility

KEY WORDS

Artificial insemination – injecting semen into the uterus by artificial means

Embryo – a fertilised egg in the first eight weeks after conception

Infertility – not being able to have children

In-vitro fertilisation (IVF) – the method of fertilising a human egg in a test tube

Surrogacy – an arrangement whereby a woman bears a child on behalf of another woman; or where an egg is donated and fertilised by the man through IVF and then implanted into the woman's uterus

The Human Fertilisation and Embryology Act 2008 ensures that the creation and use of embryos outside the human body is regulated by the HFEA; bans selecting the sex of offspring; requires clinics to take account of the child's welfare when providing fertility treatment; allows both parents in same-sex relationships to be regarded as the legal parents of a child born using a surrogate or donated sperm or eggs or embryos. In 2009, 1756 children were born from donor conception.

Medical treatments for infertility are often referred to as 'assisted conception' and include:

In-vitro fertilisation (IVF) When an egg from the woman is fertilised outside the womb using either the husband's/partner's or a donor's sperm and then replaced in the womb.

Artificial insemination by husband (AIH) When the husband's/partner's sperm is inserted into his wife/partner by mechanical means.

Artificial insemination by donor (AID) When an anonymous man donates sperm which is inserted mechanically into the mother.

Egg donation When an egg is donated by another woman, fertilised by IVF using the husband's/partner's sperm and then placed in the wife's/partner's womb by mechanical means.

Embryo donation When both egg and sperm come from donors, are fertilised using IVF and then inserted into the woman's womb mechanically.

Surrogacy Either when the egg and sperm of male and female partners are fertilised by IVF and then placed into another woman's womb; or when another woman is artificially inseminated by the male partner's sperm. In both cases, after the birth the woman hands the baby to the husband and wife/partners.

Is test-tube conception the right way to begin life?

All the medical treatments now being used by couples in Britain are supervised by the Human Fertilisation and Embryology Authority (HFEA), though there have been many arguments about the morality of these treatments. Since 1 April 2005, children born from donated sperm, eggs or embryos (donor insemination – DI) have the right to discover their genetic parents when they are eighteen. It is estimated that about 50,000 children have been born from donations, but only about 10 per cent of those have been told that they have other genetic parents. Only DI children born after 1 April 2005 have the right to know about their genetic origins.

Why infertility treatments are important

- Infertility has become much more of a problem in the western world in recent years with as many as 12.5 per cent of couples in the UK estimated to have fertility problems.
- Male infertility is a particular problem in western developed nations. According to the HFEA, up to 1.5 million men in the UK alone have fertility problems.
- In 2007, 12 per cent of all births in the UK were as a result of fertility treatments, showing how important these treatments are to large numbers of couples.
- It is a part of human nature to want to have children and raise a family, after all this is the way the species survives. If treatments are available to ensure that people have a family, they must be important because having a family is important.
- Psychological problems are caused if couples are desperate to have children but cannot. Infertility treatments can prevent their problems becoming mental illnesses.

There are several techniques of medically assisted conception available today. Most of these techniques raise important moral questions. In some cases babies are being conceived outside marriage, because couples are offered sperm or ova which have been donated by a third party. Often, the procedures involved mean that babies are conceived not through sexual intercourse but as the result of purely technical procedures. Lastly, a number of the techniques involve, directly or indirectly, the destruction of unborn human life. However, in Catholic morality: life is a gift from God; each person is created in the image of God; each person, therefore possesses the same fundamental rights: the right to life and physical integrity from the moment of conception; the right to be conceived and reared by parents who have entered a marital commitment.

The Catholic Bishops' Joint Committee on Bio-Ethical Issues

Questions

b) Do you think all couples should have a right to infertility treatments? Give two reasons for your point of view. **(4)**

c) Explain why infertility treatments are important. **(8)**

d) 'Everyone has the right to have children.'
   In your answer, you should refer to at least one religion.
   (i) Do you agree? Give reasons for your opinion. **(3)**
   (ii) Give reasons why some people may disagree with you. **(3)**

Exam Tip

d) Use the technique for answering evaluation questions from page 111. Arguments in favour of the quotation could come from the teachings of Christianity and one other religion on the importance of raising a family plus the biological argument of continuing the species. Arguments against could come from Christian teachings against the use of some infertility treatments (see page 150) plus the expense involved.

Summary

Infertility is when a couple cannot have a baby. There are now several medical treatments that can help infertile couples to have babies such as IVF, artificial insemination, egg and embryo donation.

Infertility treatments are important because a lot of people in developed societies have fertility problems.

Topic 8.2.7 Different attitudes to infertility treatments among Christians

Techniques that entail the disassociation of husband and wife, by the intrusion of a person other than the couple ... are gravely immoral. These techniques infringe the child's right to be born of a father and mother known to him and bound to each other by marriage ... Techniques involving only the married couple ... are perhaps less reprehensible yet remain morally unacceptable. They dissociate the sexual act from the procreative act.

Catechism of the Catholic Church 2376, 2377

'Lisa Jardine is in her element. The new chair of the Human Fertilisation and Embryology Authority ... Jardine, professor of renaissance studies at Queen Mary, University of London, finds to her evident joy that she is embroiled in questions of life and death, at the moral meeting point of science and religious conviction.' *The Guardian*, 28 May 2008. Should a Catholic have this job?

There are two very different Christian views on infertility.

The Catholic view is that life is given by God and that no one has a right to children. Although the Catholic Church feels great sympathy for the childless who want children, it only allows methods which do not threaten the sacredness of life and in which sex acts are natural. This means that all fertility treatments involving medical technology are banned for Catholics. The reasons for this attitude are:

▶ IVF involves fertilising several eggs, some of which are thrown away or used for experimentation. The Catholic Church believes that treating embryos in this way is no different from abortion, which is banned by the Church.
▶ All forms of artificial insemination or surrogacy involve masturbation by the male, which is a sin for Catholics.
▶ All forms of embryo technology involve fertilisation taking place apart from the sex act. Catholics believe that God intended procreation to be a part of the sex act.

The Division of the Methodist Church responsible for advising the Church on medical ethics has accepted for the time being the scientific judgement that remedies for human infertility, and for certain genetic diseases and handicaps, would be greatly assisted if research on embryos not required for artificial insemination continues to be carried out ... that investigation ... is permissible up to fourteen days.

Statement of the Methodist Church in What the Churches Say

The other Christian Churches allow IVF and AIH because:

▶ It is good to use technology to provide couples with the joy of children as having children is one of the purposes of Christian marriage.
▶ The egg and sperm are from the husband and wife and so the baby will be the biological offspring of its mother and father.
▶ The discarded embryos are not foetuses and their destruction can be justified by the doctrine of double effect (the intention is to produce children for childless couples not to kill embryos).

They have major concerns about all other embryo technology, though none have actually been banned by the Churches. They feel that all the other methods involve problems of who the parent is and could lead to problems for the children in terms of their identity and also legal problems about exactly who the parents are.

All Christians would encourage childless couples to adopt.

Hugh Jackman and his wife Deborra-Lee Furness decided to adopt after failed IVF and now have a happy family.

Questions

b) Do you think Christians should be able to have all types of infertility treatments if they can't have a baby? Give two reasons for your point of view. **(4)**

c) Explain why some Christians agree with many infertility treatments, but other Christians are against all infertility treatments. **(8)**

d) 'All Christians should raise a family.'

In your answer, you should refer to Christianity.

    (i) Do you agree? Give reasons for your opinion. **(3)**

    (ii) Give reasons why some people may disagree with you. **(3)**

Exam Tip

b) You should already have thought about this, and you just have to give two reasons for your opinion. For example, if you think they should not, you could use two of the bullet points from why Catholics are against infertility treatments.

Some developing countries now market ART (assisted reproductive technology) in ways that exploit women with little income so that they make themselves available to donate eggs and act as surrogate mothers just for the money, at great risk to themselves, as rich Westerners go for cheaper options to treatment than they can get at home. And as the use of these technologies continues to increase, so does the acceptance that makes it more difficult for Christians to express concerns. Regulation around the world of these technologies varies enormously, the United States is among the least regulated in the developed world. This makes it even harder for Christians to work out what is ethically okay and what is not. As more extreme practices are introduced, the less extreme ones can look relatively harmless.

The Gospel Coalition (an American Evangelical Christian organisation)

Summary

Some Christians, mainly Catholics, do not allow any of the fertility treatments because they involve either immoral sex or taking the life of unwanted embryos.

Other Christians allow IVF and AIH, but are suspicious of all other methods even though they do not ban them.

Topic 8.2.8a Islam and infertility treatments

In Islam, family life is governed by laws taken directly from the Qur'an and the Sunnah ... No Muslim man is allowed to donate sperm to a woman who is not his legal wife and no woman is allowed to donate an egg to another woman ... If a married woman conceives using sperm from a third party because her husband is infertile, this is adultery ... If a woman carries an embryo fertilised with the sperm and egg of another couple, the child legally belongs to the surrogate mother.

From What Does Islam Say?
by Ibrahim Hewitt

Most Muslims accept IVF and AIH when couples are having fertility problems because:

▶ It is simply the use of medicine to bring about the family life, which all Muslims are expected to have.
▶ The egg and sperm are from the husband and wife and so the baby will be the biological offspring of its mother and father.
▶ The discarded embryos are not foetuses and their destruction can be justified because it is not taking life and the intention is to produce children for childless couples, not to kill embryos.

However, Islamic lawyers have banned all the other types of embryo technology because:

▶ They deny a child's right to know its natural parents, which is essential in Islam.
▶ Any form of egg or sperm donation is regarded as a form of adultery.
▶ Egg and sperm donation is very similar to adoption, which is banned in Islam.

Questions

b) Do you think children born from sperm or egg donation have a right to know the donors? Give two reasons for your point of view. **(4)**

c) Choose one religion other than Christianity and explain why its followers agree with some infertility treatments but not others. **(8)**

d) 'Religious people have no greater right to have children than non-religious people.'

In your answer, you should refer to at least one religion.

    (i) Do you agree? Give reasons for your opinion. **(3)**

    (ii) Give reasons why some people may disagree with you. **(3)**

Exam Tip

c) 'Explain why' means give reasons. One way to answer this question would be to give two reasons for why Muslims accept IVF and AIH, and two reasons for why they do not agree with donation and surrogacy.

Make sure you use some specialist vocabulary such as: IVF, AIH, discarded embryos, embryo technology, natural parents, adoption.

Is it really wrong to conceive children by AID, as this child was?

Summary

Islam allows IVF and AIH because they only involve the husband and wife. Islam does not allow any other forms of fertility treatment because they cause problems concerning the identity of the parents.

Topic 8.2.8b Judaism and infertility treatments

IVF and AIH are accepted by all Jewish people because:

- Having children is extremely important in the Jewish faith and for the preservation of Judaism.
- Rabbis are very supportive of couples who are having fertility problems and feel that God intends humans to use the benefits of technology as long as it is within the mitzvot.
- The discarded embryos are not regarded as foetuses and their destruction can be justified by the double effect theory because it is not taking life and the intention is to produce children for childless couples, not to kill embryos.

Most Orthodox Jews do not allow AID as it is seen as a form of adultery. Surrogacy is not allowed as it is felt that whoever gives birth to a child is the mother and Jewishness is passed on by the mother.

Many Orthodox Jews accept egg donation as long as the egg is donated by a Jewish woman to make the baby Jewish.

Most **Reform Jews** accept AID, egg donation and surrogacy as they believe that upbringing is what makes a child Jewish.

> One day Elisha went to Shunem. And a well-to-do woman was there, who urged him to stay for a meal. So whenever he came by, he stopped there to eat … 'What can be done for her?' Elisha asked. Gehazi said, 'Well, she has no son and her husband is old.'
>
> Then Elisha said, 'Call her.' So he called her, and she stood in the doorway. 'About this time next year,' Elisha said, 'you will hold a son in your arms.'
>
> *2 Kings 4:8–16*

Questions

b) Do you think children born from sperm or egg donation have a right to know the donors? Give two reasons for your point of view. **(4)**

c) Choose one religion other than Christianity and explain why its followers agree with some infertility treatments but not others. **(8)**

d) 'Religious people have no greater right to have children than non-religious people.'

In your answer, you should refer to at least one religion.

   (i) Do you agree? Give reasons for your opinion. **(3)**

   (ii) Give reasons why some people may disagree with you. **(3)**

Exam Tip

c) 'Explain why' means give reasons. One way to answer this question would be to give two reasons for why some Jewish people accept IVF and AIH, and two reasons for why some do not agree with AID and surrogacy.

Make sure you use some specialist vocabulary such as: IVF, AIH, discarded embryos, embryo technology, natural parents, surrogacy, Orthodox, Reform, egg donation.

An embryologist carrying out a sample preparation.

Summary

All Jewish people accept IVF and AIH because having children is very important in Judaism. Some Jewish people accept all forms of fertility treatment, but some do not accept AID or surrogacy because of problems concerning the identity of parents.

Topic 8.2.8c Hinduism and infertility treatments

Many Hindus accept IVF, AIH, AID and egg donation because:

▶ It is simply the use of medicine to bring about the family life that all Hindus are expected to have to fulfil the householder stage of life.
▶ The egg and sperm are from either the husband or the wife and so the baby will be the biological offspring of one of the parents.
▶ The **Laws of Manu** encourage infertile couples to adopt from a relative and they take this to mean that if infertility treatments had been available when the laws were written, they would have been approved.
▶ The discarded embryos are not foetuses as no soul has been transferred to them and their destruction can be justified because it is not taking life and the intention is to produce children for childless couples, not to kill embryos.

Some Hindus do not allow AID, egg donation or surrogacy because:

▶ They believe **caste** is passed down through the parents and so the child could be a different caste from the parents.
▶ IVF involves fertilising several eggs, some of which are thrown away or used for experimentation. Some Hindus believe that once an embryo has been created, it is alive and so cannot then be deliberately killed, in just the same way that such Hindus would not approve of abortion.
▶ They see AID and egg donation as a form of adultery, which is banned by Hinduism.

> The one who rules over both knowledge and ignorance … alone presides over womb after womb, and thus over all visible forms and all the sources of birth.
>
> *Svetasvatara Upanishad 5:1–2*

Questions

b) Do you think children born from sperm or egg donation have a right to know the donors? Give two reasons for your point of view. **(4)**

c) Choose one religion other than Christianity and explain why its followers agree with some infertility treatments but not others. **(8)**

d) 'Religious people have no greater right to have children than non-religious people.'

In your answer, you should refer to at least one religion.

    (i) Do you agree? Give reasons for your opinion. **(3)**

    (ii) Give reasons why some people may disagree with you. **(3)**

Exam Tip

c) 'Explain why' means give reasons. One way to answer this question would be to give two reasons for why some Hindus accept IVF and AIH, and two reasons for why some Hindus do not agree with AID and egg donation.

Make sure you use some specialist vocabulary such as: IVF, AIH, discarded embryos, embryo technology, natural parents, caste, Laws of Manu, surrogacy.

Summary

Many Hindus allow IVF, AIH, AID and egg donation because Hindus need to have a family.

Some Hindus do not allow AID, egg donation or surrogacy because caste is passed on by the parents.

Topic 8.2.8d Sikhism and infertility treatments

Some Sikhs reject all forms of infertility treatments which involve technology. The reasons for this attitude are:

▶ IVF involves fertilising several eggs, some of which are thrown away or used for experimentation. Such Sikhs believe that once an embryo has been created, it is alive and so cannot then be deliberately killed, in just the same way that such Sikhs would not approve of abortion.

▶ They see AID and egg donation as a form of adultery, which is banned by Sikhism.

Many Sikhs would accept AIH and IVF for a Sikh family, however they have major concerns about AID, egg donation and surrogacy (though they would not ban them). The reasons for this attitude are:

▶ It is good to use technology to provide couples with the joy of children. Nine of the Gurus had families and so Sikhs should have children.

▶ The egg and sperm in AIH and IVF are from the husband and wife and so the baby will be the biological offspring of its mother and father.

▶ The discarded embryos are not foetuses as no soul has been transferred to them and their destruction can be justified because it is not taking life, and the intention is to produce children for childless couples, not to kill embryos.

▶ In AID, egg donation and surrogacy, there are concerns about the identity of the child.

> A child is born when it pleases God.
>
> *Guru Granth Sahib 921*

> Cursed is he who kills a daughter.
>
> *Guru Granth Sahib 1413*

Questions

b) Do you think children born from sperm or egg donation have a right to know the donors? Give two reasons for your point of view. **(4)**

c) Choose one religion other than Christianity and explain why its followers agree with some infertility treatments but not others. **(8)**

d) 'Religious people have no greater right to have children than non-religious people.'

In your answer, you should refer to at least one religion.

(i) Do you agree? Give reasons for your opinion. **(3)**

(ii) Give reasons why some people may disagree with you. **(3)**

Exam Tip

c) 'Explain why' means give reasons. One way to answer this question would be to give two reasons why some Sikhs accept IVF and AIH, and two reasons for why most Sikhs do not agree with donation and surrogacy.

Make sure you use some specialist vocabulary such as: IVF, AIH, discarded embryos, embryo technology, natural parents, Gurus, egg donation, surrogacy.

Summary

Some Sikhs do not allow any of the infertility treatments because they involve taking the life of unwanted embryos.

Other Sikhs allow IVF and AIH, but are suspicious of all other methods even though they do not ban them.

Topic 8.2.9 The nature and importance of transplant surgery

KEY WORD

Organ donation – giving organs to be used in transplant surgery

90 per cent of the public are in favour of transplant surgery, but less than 50 per cent of the adult population is on the NHS Organ Donor Register.

One-third of families refuses to give permission for organs of a family member to be used for transplant surgery even though the victim has signed a donor card.

UKTSSA (United Kingdom Transplant Support Service Authority)

Evel Knievel, a stunt motor cyclist who made the Guinness Book of Records for the most broken bones, was in need of a life-saving liver transplant as a result of suffering the long-term effects of Hepatitis C contracted after one of the numerous blood transfusions he needed for his injuries. After the transplant he said, 'Before I had it my doctors told me that it would be the biggest thing that I ever had to face and believe me, when they take your liver out of ya and put another one in it's like replacing a football in your stomach'.

Transplant surgery is the use of organs taken from one person and put into another person to replace an organ that is malfunctioning or diseased. A wide range of organs can now be transplanted successfully (from hearts to eye corneas), but there are problems in that the organs have to be compatible, and drugs usually have to be used to prevent the donated organ being rejected by the host. However, transplant surgery is very effective and gives life and hope to people for whom there is otherwise no hope.

Evel Knievel on one of his famous jumps.

There are two types of transplant surgery – one uses organs from a dead person, the other uses organs from a living person which they can live without (for example, bone-marrow, single kidneys). In the UK, the Health Secretary set up ULTRA (Unrelated Live Transplant Regulatory Authority) to regulate live transplants with the aim of preventing commercial organ dealings, so that people cannot sell their organs.

The first heart transplant was carried out by Dr Christiaan Barnard in December 1967 and the patient survived for 18 days. His second heart transplant patient survived for 19 months. He said of the operation, 'It is infinitely better to transplant a heart than to bury it to be devoured by worms'. Nowadays over 90 per cent of heart transplant patients survive for for a year and over 75 per cent survive for over three years.

Why transplant surgery is important

- It is an effective and proven method of curing life-threatening diseases (for example, heart or kidney malfunction) and improving people's lives (for example, cornea grafting giving sight to the blind).
- In March 2007, 7234 people were waiting for vital organ transplants (in other words, their lives were at risk without a transplant and they needed organs from a dead donor), but in the previous year only 3000 transplants were carried out. So transplants could save over 4000 extra lives a year.
- The number of people needing transplant surgery rises by 8 per cent each year so transplants are an important part of health provision.
- Transplant surgery is a proven and efficient way of bringing life out of death. It gives people a chance to help others after their death by using organs which would otherwise be buried or burned.
- It is pioneering surgical methods which could be used to cure diseases by the use of artificial organs (spare part surgery).

Organ donor rates appear to be linked to the number of fatal road crashes. According to the Department of Health, Spain has the highest rate of organ donation, but it also has the highest rate of deaths from road accidents. Most organ donations come from victims of fatal road accidents. So the safer the roads, the fewer organ donors there will be. Does this make you think again about transplant surgery?

Questions

b) Do you think transplant surgery is worth the expense? Give two reasons for your point of view. **(4)**

c) Explain why many people believe transplant surgery is important. **(8)**

d) 'People should be able to sell their organs for transplant.'

In your answer, you should refer to at least one religion.

   (i) Do you agree? Give reasons for your opinion. **(3)**

   (ii) Give reasons why some people may disagree with you. **(3)**

Exam Tip

d) Use the technique for answering evaluation questions from page 111. Arguments in favour of the quotation could come from lesson discussions on why poor people may find it useful to sell their organs. Arguments against could come from the teachings of Christianity and one other religion on why allowing the sale of organs is wrong (see pages 158–163).

Summary

Transplant surgery is using healthy organs from a donor to replace a dying organ in a patient. It is important because it can give life to dying people and it brings life out of death.

Topic 8.2.10 Different attitudes to transplant surgery in Christianity

One of the strongest arguments for organ donation is the love and compassion such an act exhibits toward others. We all are familiar with the biblical premises of 'loving our neighbors' and 'doing unto others as we would have them do unto us' as we try to emulate Christ's unconditional love … As Jesus was trying to convey this message of unconditional love for others, He spoke of caring for the hungry, thirsty, homeless, naked, sick, and imprisoned (Matthew 25:35-46). Should we not use the best medical technology available to prolong the life of those in dire need?

Protestant Christian view in apologeticspress.org

Most Christians agree with transplant surgery, but would object to rich people or surgeons in the developed world paying for organs from the poor. The reasons for this attitude are:

▶ Christians who believe in the immortality of the soul believe that the body is not needed after death and therefore its organs can be used to help the living.
▶ Christians who believe in resurrection believe St Paul's words that the body will be transformed and that the resurrected body will not need the physical organs.
▶ Jesus told Christians that they should love their neighbours and leaving your organs to save lives after your death is a way of loving your neighbour.
▶ Jesus also said that Christians should treat others as they would wish to be treated by them – and most Christians would want a transplant if they needed it.
▶ Christians object to paying for organs because it is likely to lead to exploiting the poor (for example, fathers selling a kidney to feed their family) and the Bible is full of statements about not exploiting the poor.

Some Christians are opposed to transplant surgery using organs from dead people, but accept transplants using organs donated by living relatives. They would not allow such organs to be paid for. This attitude is based on:

▶ the Christian belief that organs such as the heart are an intrinsic part of the individual who has been created by God
▶ transplanting organs from the dead into the living is usurping the role of God, and humans do not have the right to act as God
▶ organs that can be used from the living are not vital and so can be used to obey Jesus' command to love your neighbour
▶ organs cannot be paid for because that is exploiting the poor, which is banned in the Bible.

Some Christians do not agree with transplants at all and will not carry a donor card. They have this attitude because:

▶ They believe that transplants could disregard the sanctity of life. Will surgeons who have a patient desperate for a transplant work to the best of their ability to save the life of a potential donor?
▶ They believe that transplanting organs is usurping God's role and it is wrong to 'play God'.
▶ It raises the problem of when someone is dead, as such things as heart transplants require the heart to be removed before it has stopped beating.
▶ It raises the moral/emotional problem: does a surgeon save the life of an unknown accident victim or the patient they know who needs a transplant?

◗ It diverts resources from prevention or less expensive cures which could improve the lives of far more people than a single transplant.

Once doctors develop techniques through transplant surgery moral problems are bound to arise. The issue for Christians is whether issues around transplant surgery are simply medical issues, or whether they are religious issues which need to be determined by Church leaders. When surgeons were going to separate conjoined twins Jodie and Mary in November 2000 because Mary was using her sister's heart after hers failed, the Roman Catholic Church made a court submission to have the operation banned because the surgeons were going to murder Mary and use some of her organs to save Jodie. The courts decided the operation should go ahead and Jodie survived.

The funeral of Mary, the conjoined twin whose life was sacrificed to save her sister.

In his address to the XVIII International Congress of the Transplantation Society, Pope John Paul II clearly emphasises the evil of intentionally causing death to the donor in disposing of his organs. Therefore, to sacrifice the life of a donor in order to obtain an organ for someone else violates the fifth commandment: 'Thou shalt not kill.' ... The Holy Father is emphasising that vital organs can be removed from the body only when the person is certainly dead. However, the medical community knows that unpaired vital organs taken from a 'certainly dead' donor are unsuitable for transplantation. Therefore, we maintain that only one of paired vital organs or a part of an unpaired vital organ may be removed from a living human person for transplantation. This ethical principle should be self-evident, since to violate it would mean intentionally to cause the death of the donor.

Catholic World News, *March 2001*

Questions

b) Do you think Christians should agree with transplant surgery? Give two reasons for your point of view. **(4)**

c) Explain why there are different attitudes to transplant surgery in Christianity. **(8)**

d) 'Transplant surgery is a gift from God so Christians should agree with it.'

In your answer, you should refer to Christianity.

    (i) Do you agree? Give reasons for your opinion. **(3)**

    (ii) Give reasons why some people may disagree with you. **(3)**

Exam Tip

b) You should already have thought about this, and you just have to give two reasons for your opinion. For example, if you think they should, you could use two of the bullet points from why some Christians agree with transplants.

Summary

Some Christians agree with both types of transplant surgery, but not with buying organs from poor people, because they believe the body is not needed after death.

Some Christians only agree with living transplants because using dead people is 'playing God'.

Some Christians believe that all forms of transplant surgery are wrong because it is 'playing God'.

Topic 8.2.11a Islam and transplant surgery

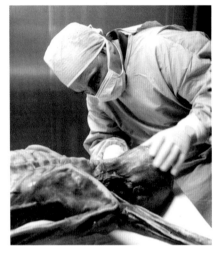

If people die unexpectedly, a post-mortem is carried out where the dead person is opened up by a pathologist to determine the cause of death. Why do post-mortems as well as transplants cause problems for Muslims?

Most Muslims are opposed to transplant surgery and will not carry donor cards because:

▶ The Shari'ah teaches that nothing should be removed from the body after death and opposes post-mortems. Therefore organs should not be removed from dead Muslims.
▶ The Qur'an says that God has created the body of a person and so to take parts from one body and put them into another is to act as God (shirk), which is the greatest sin of Islam.
▶ The Muslim belief in the sanctity of life means that all life belongs to God and only God has the right to give and take life.
▶ Many Muslims believe that they will need all their bodily organs if they are to be resurrected on the Last Day.

Some Muslims allow transplant surgery using organs from a living donor because:

▶ some Muslim lawyers have said that it is permissible
▶ a ruling, **fatwa**, was issued by the Muslim Law Council of the United Kingdom in 1995 saying that Muslims could carry donor cards and have transplants
▶ Islam aims to do good and is not intended to put burdens on people that they cannot bear. If a close relative is dying and a transplant would save them, then it should be given, just as pork can be eaten if a Muslim would otherwise starve to death.

Questions

b) Do you think transplant surgery is wrong? Give two reasons for your point of view. **(4)**

c) Choose one religion other than Christianity and explain why some of its followers agree with transplant surgery and some do not. **(8)**

d) 'All religious people should carry a donor card.'

In your answer, you should refer to at least one religion.

   (i) Do you agree? Give reasons for your opinion. **(3)**

   (ii) Give reasons why some people may disagree with you. **(3)**

Exam Tip

c) 'Explain why' means give reasons. One way to answer this question would be to give two reasons why some Muslims agree with transplant surgery, and two reasons why some Muslims think transplant surgery is wrong.

Remember to use some specialist vocabulary such as: Shari'ah, post-mortem, Qur'an, shirk, sanctity of life, fatwa, Muslim Law Council, donor card.

Summary

Most Muslims do not agree with transplant surgery because they believe they need all their organs for the Last Day.

Some Muslims allow transplants from close relatives because it is allowed by some Muslim lawyers.

Topic 8.2.11b Judaism and transplant surgery

Many Jewish people allow transplant surgery using organs from a living donor as long as the donor is Jewish because:

- They believe that organs such as the heart are an intrinsic part of the individual who has been created by God.
- Organs from non-Jews might affect one's Jewishness (being a Jew is passed on by the blood of the mother).
- Transplanting organs from the dead into the living is usurping the role of God, and humans do not have the right to act as God.
- Organs which can be used from the living are not vital and so can be used to obey the mitzvah to preserve life.
- Organs cannot be paid for because that is exploiting the poor, which is banned in the Torah and Tenakh.

Some Jewish people are completely opposed to transplant surgery and will not carry donor cards. They believe that transplanting organs from one person to another is against God's will. They have this attitude because:

- They believe that transplanting organs is breaking the mitzvot on the sanctity of life.
- They believe that the organs have been created by God for a specific individual and cannot be put into someone else. They are particularly concerned that transplants may affect people's Jewishness.

Some Jewish people agree with transplant surgery, but would object to rich people or surgeons in the developed world paying for organs from the poor. They have this attitude because:

- They believe God wants people to use medical technology to save lives.
- They believe that organ donation is a way of obeying the mitzvot to love your neighbour.
- They believe the Tenakh forbids exploiting the poor.

Kidney donor Rabbi Boruch Wolf (left) and recipient Leonard Burger (centre) meet before their kidney transplant surgeries.

Exam Tip

c) 'Explain why' means give reasons. One way to answer this question would be to give two reasons why some Jewish people agree with transplant surgery, and two reasons why some Jewish people think transplant surgery is wrong. Remember to use some specialist vocabulary such as: Jewishness, mitzvah, Torah, Tenakh, sanctity of life, donor card, organ donation.

Questions

b) Do you think transplant surgery is wrong? Give two reasons for your point of view. **(4)**

c) Choose one religion other than Christianity and explain why some of its followers agree with transplant surgery and some do not. **(8)**

d) 'All religious people should carry a donor card.'

In your answer, you should refer to at least one religion.

    (i) Do you agree? Give reasons for your opinion. **(3)**

    (ii) Give reasons why some people may disagree with you. **(3)**

Summary

Most Jewish people agree with transplants from living donors, but not from the dead because organs from non-Jews would alter a person's Jewishness.

Some Jewish people are against all transplants because they think they are breaking the laws on the sanctity of life.

Some Jewish people agree with transplants because they save lives and show love of one's neighbour.

Topic 8.2.11c Hinduism and transplant surgery

Most Hindus allow transplant surgery and would carry donor cards. They have this attitude because:

▶ They believe that the body is not important, it is the soul that matters. When someone dies, it is their body that dies, their soul will be reborn into another body. As the dead body will be burned, its organs can be used to help others.

▶ As the soul is the immortal part of a person, it does not matter which bits are added to or taken away from the body.

▶ They believe that donating your organs to save lives will result in good **karma** and an increased chance of moksha.

Some Hindus are opposed to any form of transplant surgery and will not carry donor cards. They have this attitude because:

▶ They believe that transplants are trying to break the law of karma. If a person is intended to suffer from a bad heart because of their previous bad deeds, they should not try to avoid this by having a transplant.

▶ They believe in ahimsa and transplant surgery is doing violence to the person from whom the organ is taken.

▶ They are worried that poor people may be tempted to sell their organs or even die to provide money for their family.

Questions

b) Do you think transplant surgery is wrong? Give two reasons for your point of view. **(4)**

c) Choose one religion other than Christianity and explain why some of its followers agree with transplant surgery and some do not. **(8)**

d) 'All religious people should carry a donor card.'

In your answer, you should refer to at least one religion.

(i) Do you agree? Give reasons for your opinion. **(3)**

(ii) Give reasons why some people may disagree with you. **(3)**

Exam Tip

c) 'Explain why' means give reasons. One way to answer this question would be to give two reasons why some Hindus agree with transplant surgery, and two reasons why some Hindus think transplant surgery is wrong. Remember to use some specialist vocabulary such as: immortal, karma, moksha, law of karma, ahimsa, sanctity of life, donor card.

Summary

Most Hindus allow transplant surgery because they believe that the soul leaves the body at death, so the organs are not needed.

Some Hindus do not allow transplant surgery because they think it is breaking the law of karma.

Topic 8.2.11d Sikhism and transplant surgery

The vast majority of Sikhs are in favour of transplant surgery from both dead and living donors. However, they are opposed to the idea of selling organs for transplants. They have this attitude because:

▶ The Sikh faith stresses the importance of **sewa** and noble deeds. Organ donation is a form of sewa.
▶ Guru Nanak encouraged trying to leave a legacy which would ensure your good deeds continuing after your death.
▶ Sikhs believe life after death is a continuous cycle of rebirth – the physical body is not needed in this cycle.
▶ There are many examples of selfless giving and sacrifice in Sikh teachings by the ten Gurus and other Sikhs.
▶ Sikhism endorses organ and tissue donation as the ultimate act of charity or benevolence.

A few Sikhs do not agree with transplant surgery in any form, but especially donations from dead people. They have this attitude because:

▶ It raises the problem of when someone is dead as such things as heart transplants require the heart to be removed before it has stopped beating.
▶ It raises the moral/emotional problem: will surgeons who have a patient desperate for a transplant work to the best of their ability to save the life of a potential donor?
▶ It causes a trade in organs from people in the less-developed world to rich people in the developed world.

> The dead sustain their bond with the living through virtuous deeds.
>
> *Guru Nanak, Guru Granth Sahib*

> The Sikh religion teaches that life continues after death in the soul, and not the physical body. The last act of giving and helping others through organ donation is both consistent with, and in the spirit of, Sikh teachings.
>
> *Dr Indarjit Singh OBE*

Questions

b) Do you think transplant surgery is wrong? Give two reasons for your point of view. **(4)**

c) Choose one religion other than Christianity and explain why some of its followers agree with transplant surgery and some do not. **(8)**

d) 'All religious people should carry a donor card.'

In your answer, you should refer to at least one religion.

    (i) Do you agree? Give reasons for your opinion. **(3)**

    (ii) Give reasons why some people may disagree with you. **(3)**

Exam Tip

c) 'Explain why' means give reasons. One way to answer this question would be to give two reasons why some Sikhs agree with transplant surgery, and two reasons why some Sikhs think transplant surgery is wrong. Remember to use some specialist vocabulary such as: sewa, noble deeds, Guru Nanak, cycle of rebirth, Ten Gurus, developed and less-developed world, sanctity of life, donor card.

Summary

Most Sikhs agree with all transplant surgery because the body is not needed after death and donation is a form of sewa.

A few Sikhs do not agree with any transplant surgery because of concerns about when someone is dead and pressures on the living to donate their organs.

How to answer exam questions

a) What is global warming? (2)

Global warming is the increase in the temperature of the Earth thought to be caused by the greenhouse effect.

b) Do you think natural resources will run out? Give two reasons for your point of view. (4)

Yes I do think they will run out because a resource like oil is a finite non-renewable resource which means that when once we use it, it cannot be replaced. We use oil for many things, not only for producing electricity and powering cars but also plastics, so we will use it up. Resources like metals are also non-renewable and we will use them up for things like cars, machinery and domestic appliances.

c) Choose one religion other than Christianity and explain why some of its followers are against transplant surgery. (8)

I am going to write about Islam. Most Muslims are opposed to transplant surgery because the Shari'ah teaches that nothing should be removed from the body after death. Also the Qur'an says that God has created the body of a person and so to take parts from one body and put them into another is to act as God (shirk), which is the greatest sin of Islam. The Muslim belief in the sanctity of life means that all life belongs to God and only God has the right to give and take life. Finally, many Muslims believe that they will need all their bodily organs if they are to be resurrected on the Last Day.

d) 'All religious people should live lifestyles which do not harm the environment.'

In your answer you should refer to at least one religion.

   (i)   Do you agree? Give reasons for your opinion. (3)

   (ii) Give reasons why some people may disagree with you. (3)

(i) I agree with this because I'm a Catholic and we believe we have a responsibility to be God's stewards and to leave the Earth a better place than we found it. The Church teaches that stewardship means a fair sharing of the Earth's resources without causing more pollution. We are also taught that we will be judged by God on our behaviour when we die, so we feel we need to reduce pollution and conserve resources as this is the type of life God wants us to live.

(ii) I can see why some Christians would disagree with me because they believe humans have been placed in control of the Earth by God and so, in tackling environmental issues, human concerns cannot be ignored. In the same way, some Muslims might disagree because they believe that human interests come first so the effects of environmental projects on humans cannot be ignored. Also although Hindus should have a great respect for the environment, some Hindus feel that as humans are the most advanced life-form, they have been given the right to use the Earth's resources in any way they think is right.

Question a

High marks because it is a correct definition.

Question b

A high mark answer because an opinion is backed up by two developed reasons.

Question c

A high mark answer because it identifies the religion the candidate has chosen and then gives four clear reasons why some Muslims are against transplant surgery. There is also a good use of specialist vocabulary such as Shari'ah, Qur'an, shirk, sin, sanctity of life, right to give and take life, vital organs, resurrected, Last Day.

Question d

A high mark answer because it states the candidate's own opinion and backs it up with three clear Catholic Christian reasons for thinking that religious people should have lifestyles that do not damage the environment. It is followed by a clear reason why some Christians might disagree, a clear reason why some Muslims might disagree and a clear reason why some Hindus might disagree.

Section
8.3

Religion: Peace and conflict

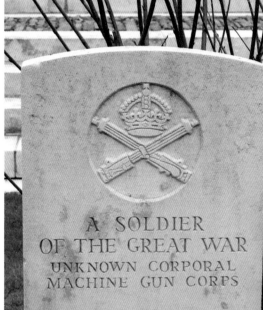

A SOLDIER
OF THE GREAT WAR
UNKNOWN CORPORAL
MACHINE GUN CORPS

Introduction

This section of the examination specification requires you to look at issues surrounding peace and conflict.

Religion and issues of war and peace

You will need to understand the effects of, and give reasons for your own opinion about:

▶ the United Nations and world peace
▶ how religious organisations try to promote world peace
▶ why wars occur
▶ the nature and importance of the theory of just war
▶ differences among Christians in their attitudes to war and the reasons for them
▶ the attitudes to war of one religion other than Christianity and the reasons for them.

Religion and bullying

You will need to understand the effects of, and give reasons for your own opinion about:

▶ Christian attitudes to bullying and the reasons for them
▶ the attitudes to bullying in one religion other than Christianity and the reasons for them.

Conflict and reconciliation

You will need to understand the effects of, and give reasons for your own opinion about:

▶ religious conflicts within families
▶ Christian teachings on forgiveness and reconciliation
▶ the teachings on forgiveness and reconciliation of one religion other than Christianity.

Topic 8.3.1 The United Nations and world peace

KEY WORDS

Conflict resolution – bringing a fight or struggle to a peaceful conclusion

The United Nations – an international body set up to promote world peace and co-operation

World peace – the ending of war throughout the whole world (the basic aim of the United Nations)

The United Nations (UN) was formed in 1945 after the end of the Second World War. The aim of the UN was to preserve world peace and to remove the causes of conflict by encouraging economic, social, educational and cultural progress throughout the world, especially in underdeveloped countries.

All the countries of the world can apply to be members of the UN and have a vote in the General Assembly which meets once a year to debate issues and to supervise the UN's work. Leadership and administration of the UN is by the Secretariat headed by the Secretary General (currently Ban Ki-moon) who has the power to bring any issue threatening world peace before the Security Council.

The Security Council has five permanent members (the USA, Russia, China, France and the United Kingdom) and ten non-permanent members who are elected by the General Assembly for a two-year term.

United Nations Security Council meeting.

Why the United Nations is important for world peace

Through the Security Council, the UN can recommend action to stop any threats to world peace by:

The judges of the International Criminal Court.

▶ imposing sanctions (for example, banning trade, banning cultural links, banning communications) on countries threatening world peace
▶ authorising the use of force by member states to stop an aggressor
▶ sending a UN peacekeeping force to:
  ▶ prevent the outbreak of conflict or the spill-over of conflict across borders
  ▶ stabilise conflict situations after a ceasefire and create an environment for the parties to reach a lasting peace agreement
  ▶ assist in conflict resolution through putting peace agreements into practice
  ▶ lead states or territories to stable government based on democratic principles and economic development, after they have been in conflict.

The United Nations also tries to keep world peace by running the International Criminal Court (ICC) in the Hague which ensures that international laws are upheld and prosecutes anyone committing war crimes. War crimes are defined as 'violations of the laws or customs of war', including 'murder, the ill-treatment or deportation of civilian residents of an occupied territory to slave labor camps, the murder or ill-treatment of prisoners of war, the killing of hostages, the wanton destruction of cities, towns and villages, and any devastation not justified by military necessity'. (Source: United Nations website)

One example of the UN's work for peace – Democratic Republic of Congo

UN peacekeeping forces are made up of soldiers, administrators and police officers from a number of countries so that no one nation has to pay all the funding or take all the risks. The forces wear blue helmets and UN insignia so that they can be clearly identified as peacekeepers. Since 1948 there have been 68 UN field missions and almost 200 UN organised peace settlements. In 2014 there were 15 peacekeeping operations and one special political mission – the United Nations Assistance Mission in Afghanistan (UNAMA), in operation. One recent UN field mission was to the Democratic Republic of Congo in central Africa.

We the peoples of the United Nations are determined

● to save succeeding generations from the scourge of war, which twice in our lifetime has brought untold sorrow to mankind, and
● to reaffirm faith in fundamental human rights, in the dignity and worth of the human person, in the equal rights of men and women and of nations large and small ... and for these ends
● to practise tolerance and live together in peace with one another as good neighbours, and to unite our strength to maintain international peace and security.

The Charter of the United Nations

UN peacekeepers in the Democratic Republic of Congo – note the blue helmets and white armoured vehicles.

Why the UN became involved in the Democratic Republic of Congo

The Democratic Republic of the Congo (DRC) was formed in 1998 after a civil war in what was then known as Zaire. However, the civil war continued with one side (including elements from those involved in the 1997 **genocide** in Rwanda) supported by one group of central African states and the other supported by Rwanda and Uganda. The UN was called in to stop the fighting and organised a ceasefire in 1999, and sent in a UN peacekeeping force to supervise the implementation of the ceasefire.

How the UN dealt with the situation

The peacekeeping force organised the first free and fair elections ever held in the area in 2006 which established a national assembly and a democratically elected president. The peacekeeping force remained to maintain the rule of law and support the Congolese government in stabilisation and peace consolidation. Although this worked in the west of the country, cycles of violence continued in the east, including gender and religion based violence carried out by both Congolese rebel armed groups and foreign intervention.

To counter these, the UN organised a conference of all the surrounding states in 2013 and persuaded them to sign a Peace Security and Cooperation Framework to guarantee peace in the DRC. In order to back this up, the UN agreed to strengthen the peacekeeping force so it had the military capacity to bring peace so that it now has three infantry battalions and one artillery battalion in the country.

Summary

The United Nations was formed at the end of the Second World War to preserve world peace. It is important because it brings all the countries of the world together and can send peacekeeping forces to stop conflicts.

The UN sent a peacekeeping force to the Democratic Republic of Congo to protect civilians and human rights and establish a democratic government.

Questions

b) Do you think the United Nations is important? Give two reasons for your point of view. **(4)**

c) Explain why there are different agencies in the United Nations. **(8)**

d) 'The United Nations is the best chance for world peace.'

In your answer, you should refer to at least one religion.

    (i) Do you agree? Give reasons for your opinion. **(3)**

    (ii) Give reasons why some people may disagree with you. **(3)**

Exam Tip

b) You should already have thought about this, and you just have to give two reasons for your opinion. For example, if you think it is, you could use two reasons from why the UN is important (you only need fairly short reasons for these questions and so any two of the bullet points on actions will be sufficient).

Topic 8.3.2 How religious organisations try to promote world peace

All religions believe in world peace, but still religious people fight in wars. However, there are groups in all religions which are anti-war and work for world peace. Some examples include Christian Peacemaker teams, Pax Christi International, the Fellowship of Reconciliation, the Muslim Peace Fellowship, the Jewish Peace Fellowship, Mahatma Gandhi Center for Global Nonviolence and the Sikh Khudai Khidmatgar.

How religious organisations work for world peace

Religious organisations do this by:

- organising public debates on the horrors of wars and conflicts and encouraging their followers to support political parties opposed to war. This could bring about world peace because the more people learn about the horrors of war, the more likely they are to vote for peace
- making public statements and organising protests about war such as condemning the use of drones in Afghanistan and Pakistan, the conflicts in Syria and the Democratic Republic of Congo. This could bring about peace because public opinion could be changed and governments take notice of public opinion
- organising and attending inter-faith conferences to help all religions work together to promote world peace. Many conflicts are caused by religious differences and if religions work together for peace, it is more likely to happen
- working for economic justice and global recognition of human rights to remove the causes of war. If groups like Christian Aid, CAFOD and Muslim Aid can help to give the poor of the world a decent standard of living, this could remove some of the major causes of war. If religious organisations could persuade the governments of the world to respect human rights, this could stop wars that are started because one country feels its fellow ethnic group in another country is being badly treated.

Questions

b) Do you think religious organisations can stop wars? Give two reasons for your point of view. **(4)**

c) Explain how religious organisations work for world peace. **(8)**

d) 'Religious organisations can stop wars.'

In your answer, you should refer to at least one religion.

(i) Do you agree? Give reasons for your opinion. **(3)**

(ii) Give reasons why some people may disagree with you. **(3)**

Exam Tip

c) One way to answer this question would be to use four of the ways in which religious organisations promote world peace and explain how each one might help to bring about world peace.

Make sure you use some specialist vocabulary such as: public debates, horrors of war, public opinion, drones, Afghanistan, Pakistan, Syrian conflict, Democratic Republic of Congo, inter-faith conferences, economic justice, CAFOD, Christian Aid, Muslim Aid.

Summary

There are organisations working for world peace in all the world's religions. They try to promote world peace by:

- going to war zones and supporting efforts to stop the war
- organising demonstrations against wars
- educating people about the need for world peace, for example.

Topic 8.3.3 Why wars occur

KEY WORDS

Aggression – attacking without being provoked

Exploitation – taking advantage of a weaker group

There is hardly a conflict in the world today – Iraq, Russia, Indonesia, the Holy Land – without a religious dimension. And that, says Archbishop Michael Fitzgerald, president of the Vatican's Pontifical Council for Inter-religious Dialogue, is why finding common ground between different faiths is crucial for world peace ... He emphasises that it is important not to see all Muslims as supporting terrorism. 'This is like linking the Irish to terrorism because of the IRA. It doesn't work that way. Many Muslims in the world don't agree with terrorism. We can't condemn them all. I think religious differences are used to set people against each other. Religion isn't usually the cause of the conflict, but it's an added factor. The underlying problems are usually social or political.

The Times, 9 October 2004

Although the last world war ended over 60 years ago, wars are still occurring all over the world. The most generally accepted reasons for wars occurring are the following.

1. Religion

Wars of aggression can occur because of religious differences.

▶ There may be two religious groups each of which wants to be dominant and each of which feels it has been badly treated by the other. For example, the war between Christians and Muslims in the Central African Republic.

▶ The majority of an area is one religion, but the country as a whole is a different religion. For example, the majority of Kashmir is Muslim (but a substantial minority is Hindu), but Kashmir is part of India which is Hindu. The Muslims of Kashmir are fighting to become part of the neighbouring Muslim state of Pakistan.

▶ There are differences within a religion and one religious group attacks the other for having different beliefs, for example, the war in Syria where the government forces are Shi'a Muslims and the rebel forces are Sunni Muslims.

Refugees from the conflict in the Central African Republic.

2. Nationalism and ethnicity

A major cause of wars is connected with issues of **nationalism** and **ethnicity**:

▶ One form of nationalism is the belief that each separate ethnic group should have its own country because it has a different culture. This leads minority ethnic groups to fight civil wars to establish an independent state, for example, the Tutsi rebels in the Democratic Republic of Congo and the ethnic Albanians in Kosovo.

▶ Another form of nationalism is to insist that any minority ethnic groups should be removed from the country so that the nation is only one ethnic group. This can lead to the genocide of an ethnic group such as the Tutsis in Rwanda in 1994.

▶ Tensions between ethnic groups often arise in countries which have been artificially created as a result of **colonialism**. This has happened a lot in Africa where countries such as Sudan and Kenya were created artificially by European conquerors, leading to the current civil war in South Sudan.

3. Economics

Wars of **exploitation** can occur if a country has resources that another country wants or needs.

▶ Some people think that Iraq was invaded because the West wanted to make sure it would have access to its enormous oil reserves.

▶ Economic problems in one country can lead to conflict in another country. For example, the economic crisis in Zimbabwe has led to mass migration of refugees looking for food and work into South Africa. Some South Africans have objected and begun to attack the refugees.

4. Ideological and political differences

Wars can sometimes occur because of **ideological** or political differences between countries or people within countries:

▶ In the Democratic Republic of Congo where ethnicity was used by two different political groups to gain power – one group supported by Uganda and Rwanda, the other supported by Zimbabwe, Angola and Namibia. The UN had to bring the two political groups together before it could begin to end the conflict.

▶ The Korean War began in 1949 when communist North Korea invaded South Korea with the aim of uniting the country under communism. A truce was declared in 1953 after the UN fought a war against North Korea and China, but there is still no peace and there are still outbreaks of conflict.

> At his Nuremberg trial, the Nazi war criminal Hermann Goering described how easy it is to organise a war: 'Why, of course the people don't want war. That is understood. But, after all, it is the leaders of a country who determine the policy and it is always a simple matter to drag the people along, whether it is a democracy, or a fascist dictatorship, or a parliament, or a communist dictatorship. Voice or no voice, the people can always be brought to the bidding of the leaders. That is easy. All you have to do is tell them they are being attacked, and denounce the peacemakers for lack of patriotism and exposing the country to danger.'
>
> *Hermann Goering, Nazi leader, at his trial for war crimes, 1945*

Many fear that the diamond trade funds war in the Congo.

Exam Tip

d) Use the technique for answering evaluation questions from page 111. Arguments in favour of the quotation would come from religious causes of war in this topic. Arguments against would come from the other causes of war in this topic.

Summary

Wars can occur for a number of reasons including: religion (for example, if followers of a religion are being badly treated in another country), nationalism and ethnicity (for example, if an ethnic group wants to set up its own country), economics (for example, if a country has oil but the country next door does not) and political reasons (for example, if one country is communist and wants to make other countries communist).

Questions

b) Do you think war is ever necessary? Give two reasons for your point of view. **(4)**

c) Explain why wars occur. **(8)**

d) 'Religion is the main cause of wars.'

In your answer, you should refer to at least one religion.

  (i) Do you agree? Give reasons for your opinion. **(3)**

  (ii) Give reasons why some people may disagree with you. **(3)**

Topic 8.3.4 The nature and importance of the theory of just war

KEY WORD

Just war – a war that is fought for the right reasons and in a right way

In a 45-minute speech, Lord Williams, honorary doctor of pastoral theology at Anglia Ruskin, and Master of Cambridge University's Magdalene College, asked whether there is a new 'ethic for warfare' in the modern world. Lord Williams explained that the traditional criteria for a 'just war' – such as sparing the innocent, knowing when you have won, and that violence is a last resort – are increasingly at odds with modern-day conflicts.

Cambridge News, *26 March 2014*

Although it is generally agreed that wars are bad because of their effects, it is also generally agreed that, in certain circumstances, wars are unavoidable and so can be justified. The theory used to decide whether a war is justified is known as the just war theory.

Although Christians associate this theory with St Thomas Aquinas (c. 1225–74) it was developed in Hinduism, Islam, Judaism and Buddhism long before Aquinas. Today it is generally agreed that a war is just if:

- the cause of the war is just (for example, it is fought in self-defence when another country attacks, or it is trying to remove a great injustice such as genocide)
- it is being fought by the authority of the United Nations
- it is being fought with the intention of restoring peace
- it is begun as a last resort – that is, all non-violent methods of trying to end the conflict have been tried and failed
- there is a reasonable chance of success. It would be wrong to waste lives in a war if there is no chance of achieving its aims
- the methods used avoid killing civilians. Although this would not ban such things as bombs aimed at armaments factories hitting hospitals accidentally, it would ban any methods which deliberately try to destroy civilian targets to make the civilian population afraid and sue for peace
- the methods used are proportional to the cause. For example, it would not be just to destroy a country with nuclear weapons because it had invaded a small island.

Questions

b) Do you think wars can ever be justified? Give two reasons for your point of view. **(4)**

c) Explain what would make a war a just war. **(8)**

d) 'War can never be right.'

In your answer, you should refer to at least one religion.

    (i) Do you agree? Give reasons for your opinion. **(3)**

    (ii) Give reasons why some people may disagree with you. **(3)**

Exam Tip

b) You should already have thought about this, and you just have to give two reasons for your opinion. For example, if you think wars can sometimes be justified, you could use two bullet points from the just war theory.

Summary

The just war theory is the idea that it is right to go to war if the reasons are just. For example, it has been agreed to by the UN, or it is being fought in self-defence.

Topic 8.3.5 Differences among Christians in their attitudes to war

Although all Christians believe in world peace and working to bring about peace, there are two very different Christian attitudes to war:

1. Christian pacifism

Pacifism means refusing to fight in wars. In the twentieth century many Christians have become pacifists. They feel that the way modern warfare affects so many innocent people means that war can never be justified. There are many Christian pacifist groups, the largest being the Catholic group Pax Christi. The Quakers, Plymouth **Brethren** and Christadelphians are completely pacifist Churches. Some Christian pacifists refuse to be involved in any kind of violence and would not resist anyone who attacked them.

A large crowd of anti-arms trade activists gather in the UK, September 2011.

The reasons for some Christians being pacifist are:

▶ Jesus taught in his Sermon on the Mount that Christians should not resist evil and that if they are hit on the right cheek they should turn and offer the left. Christian pacifists take this to mean that Christians should not fight and so cannot take part in wars.
▶ In the Sermon, Jesus also taught that Christians should love their enemies. It seems impossible to love someone you are trying to destroy and so this teaching of Jesus also seems to mean that Christians should not be involved in wars.
▶ Jesus stopped Peter from using violence when the soldiers came to arrest him with the words, 'Put your sword back in its place for all who draw the sword will die by the sword.' This again seems to show Jesus telling Christians not to be involved in wars.

KEY WORDS

Pacifism – the belief that all disputes should be settled by peaceful means

Weapons of mass destruction – weapons which can destroy large areas and numbers of people

---

Blessed are the peacemakers, for they will be called sons of God.

Matthew 5:9

I tell you, do not resist an evil person. If someone strikes you on the right cheek, turn to him the other also.

Matthew 5:39

On September 13 2002, the US Catholic Bishops entered the debate on US involvement in Iraq, by sending a letter to President Bush urging him not to enter into war with Iraq. They claimed that 'any pre-emptive, unilateral use of military force to overthrow the government of Iraq' would not meet the criteria of a 'just war' as defined by the Catholic Church.

Adapted from various news sources September 2002

> Everyone must submit himself to the governing authorities, for there is no authority except that which God has established. The authorities that exist have been established by God.
>
> *Romans 13:1*

> To the Christian serving in the armed forces of the 'Western democracies' there is the added assurance and comfort that their purpose is for defence and to maintain peace, not for selfish wars of aggression. The role of the Forces is almost entirely analogous to that of a police force ... Therefore a Christian can regard it as an honour, and as a duty to be faithfully followed, should God call him to serve in these armed forces.
>
> *From Christians and War published by the Armed Forces' Christian Union*

- The fifth commandment says that you should not kill. Christians should obey the teaching of the Ten Commandments and so should not be involved in killing people in wars.
- For the first 300 years of Christianity, Christians refused to fight in wars. The great Christian leaders (for example, Origen, Tertullian and Cyprian) all argued that Christians must not be involved in war and must be pacifists.
- So many horrible things have happened to civilians in modern wars because of the terrifying effects of weapons of mass destruction (for example, the effects of the Hiroshima and Nagasaki nuclear bombs) that they believe no modern war can be just and therefore Christians should not be involved in them.

2. The attitude that Christians can fight in just wars

Although all Christians believe that they are called to bring peace to the world, not all Christians think that pacifism is the only way to bring this about. The Christian Churches all make regular statements opposing war and encouraging their members to work for peace. However, they also realise that it is not always possible to avoid war. Many Christians believe that the way to work for peace is to be prepared to fight a just war (as explained in Topic 8.3.4).

British troops, including Prince Harry, in Afghanistan. Should Christian troops be used to keep the peace in Muslim countries?

The reasons for many Christians believing they can fight in just wars are:

- It is the teaching of all the main Churches (Catholic, Anglican, Methodist, Baptist, United Reform Church) that Christians have the right to fight in wars that fulfil the criteria for just wars.
- St Paul said in Romans 13 and Titus 3 that Christians have to obey the orders of the government because governments are authorised

by God. Therefore if the government authorises a war, Christians should fight in it.

▶ Jesus never condemned the soldiers he met and actually commended the faith of the Roman Centurion in Luke 7. This seems to mean that Jesus accepted the right of Christians to be soldiers.

▶ When Jesus was asked about paying taxes he said, 'Give to Caesar what is Caesar's', which must mean that it is acceptable for Christians to fight in a just war ordered by the government (Caesar).

▶ Everyone agrees that a police force is needed to protect innocent people from criminals, in the same way an army ready to fight just wars is needed to protect innocent countries from criminal ones.

Would pacifists agree that we need a police force?

Questions

b) Do you think Christians should fight in wars? Give two reasons for your point of view. **(4)**

c) Explain why some Christians are against fighting in wars, but some are not. **(8)**

d) 'Christians should support wars if they are fought for just reasons.'
In your answer, you should refer to Christianity.

    (i) Do you agree? Give reasons for your opinion. **(3)**

    (ii) Give reasons why some people may disagree with you. **(3)**

Exam Tip

c) 'Explain why' means give reasons. One way to answer this question would be to use at least two reasons for Christian pacifism, and at least two reasons for Christians supporting just wars. Remember to use some specialist vocabulary such as: pacifist, Pax Christi, Jesus, Sermon on Mount, love enemies, commandment, just war, Churches, St Paul, Romans, government authorities, Roman centurion, Caesar.

Summary

Some Christians believe that they should work for peace by refusing to fight in wars. They believe Christians should be pacifists because Jesus taught Christians to love their enemies.

Some Christians believe that the way to bring peace is to be prepared to fight in just wars. They will fight to defend the weak and to bring peace to the world because this has always been the Church's teaching.

Topic 8.3.6a Islam and attitudes to war

> Fight in the cause of God those who fight you, but do not transgress the limits; for God loveth not the transgressors.
>
> *Surah 2:190*

> Jaber reported that the Messenger of Allah said, 'War is a deception'.
>
> *Hadith quoted by Bukhari and Muslim*

Why do you think Muslims protest against wars they think are unjust?

There is no idea of pacifism or turning the other cheek in Islam. The Qur'an encourages all Muslims to 'struggle in the way of Islam'. The Arabic word for struggle is jihad which is often translated as holy war. However, Muslims believe in two forms of jihad, the greater and the lesser. The greater jihad is the struggle to make yourself and your society perfectly Muslim. This involves struggling with yourself and your desires, and not fighting. Lesser jihad is the struggle with forces outside yourself by means of war.

Most Muslims believe that if a war is just (the Muslims' criteria for a just war are very similar to those in Topic 8.3.4) then a Muslim must fight in it. The reasons for this view are:

- The Qur'an says that Muslims must fight if they are attacked and Muslims believe the Qur'an is the word of God.
- Muhammad is the great example for Muslims of how to live their lives (the perfect exemplar) and he fought in just wars, therefore so must Muslims.
- Muhammad made many statements (hadith) about war, which say that Muslims must fight in just wars. Muslims believe they must follow the teachings of Muhammad as he is the final prophet of God.
- The Qur'an says that anyone who dies fighting in a just war will go straight to heaven. This gives Muslims the assurance that they are fighting for God if they fight in a just war.

Some Muslims who follow the mystical Sufi tradition are pacifists and believe any form of fighting is wrong. Some Muslims, such as the Muslim Peace Fellowship, believe that the nature of modern weapons means that no war can be a just war, and so they oppose wars.

Summary

Muslims believe in peace, but Islam teaches that if the faith is attacked, Muslims must defend their faith by fighting jihad (a just war fought in a just way). They believe this because it is taught in the Qur'an, which they believe is the word of God.

Questions

b) Do you think religious people should fight in wars? Give two reasons for your point of view. **(4)**

c) Choose one religion other than Christianity and explain why its followers support just wars. **(8)**

d) 'Religious people should never fight in wars.'

   In your answer, you should refer to at least one religion.

   (i) Do you agree? Give reasons for your opinion. **(3)**

   (ii) Give reasons why some people may disagree with you. **(3)**

Exam Tip

d) Use the technique for answering evaluation questions from page 111. Arguments in favour of the quotation could come from the reasons why some Christians are pacifists (see Topic 8.3.5). Arguments against could come from why Muslims support just wars.

Topic 8.3.6b Judaism and attitudes to war

Peace is the ideal for all Jewish people. The perfect society, which Jews call the **Messianic Age**, is thought of as a time of peace when all weapons of war will be turned into instruments of peace.

However, although Jews should seek peace, Judaism teaches that Jewish people should fight in just wars because:

▶ The Talmud says that wars must be fought if they are milchemet mitzvah – that is if God has commanded it, if Jewish people are attacked by an enemy, if a pre-emptive strike will stop an enemy from attacking or if the war is going to the aid of a country that has been attacked.

▶ Jewish people can fight in other types of just wars because the Tenakh is full of accounts of wars in which God has been involved. If God ordered heroes like Joshua and David to fight in wars, then modern Jewish people must be able to fight in wars.

▶ The Tenakh accounts show how Israel was able to keep her independence by defending herself when attacked and so modern Israel should do the same.

▶ Jewish people also believe they should fight in wars because of their experience in the Holocaust when 6 million Jews were murdered. Some think this may not have happened if they had had a Jewish army to defend them.

However, some Jewish people (such as the Jewish Peace Fellowship) feel that the nature of modern weapons means that no war can be a just war, and so they oppose wars.

> If your enemy is hungry, give him food to eat; if he is thirsty, give him water to drink.
>
> *Proverbs 25:21*

> Turn from evil and do good; seek peace and pursue it.
>
> *Psalm 34:14*

> The Torah was given to establish peace.
>
> *Midrash*

> When someone kills your 14-year-old daughter, you want to get even and retaliate. This way is easy, but we are people not animals ... so there is also a second way. This is the way of understanding when you say, 'What can you do personally in order to prevent this hatred from affecting others?'
>
> *Rami Elhanan, an Israeli and a member of Parents' Circle, whose daughter was killed by a suicide bomber*

Questions

b) Do you think religious people should fight in wars? Give two reasons for your point of view. **(4)**

c) Choose one religion other than Christianity and explain why its followers support just wars. **(8)**

d) 'Religious people should never fight in wars.'

In your answer, you should refer to at least one religion.

  (i) Do you agree? Give reasons for your opinion. **(3)**

  (ii) Give reasons why some people may disagree with you. **(3)**

Exam Tip

d) Use the technique for answering evaluation questions from page 111. Arguments in favour of the quotation could come from the reasons why some Christians are pacifists (see Topic 8.3.5). Arguments against could come from why most Jewish people support just wars.

Summary

Jews believe in peace, but Judaism teaches that Jews must defend themselves if they are attacked, as stated in the Torah and Talmud. However, some Jews are pacifists because they think modern weapons are too destructive ever to be used.

Topic 8.3.6c Hinduism and attitudes to war

> Prepare for war with peace in thy soul. Be in peace in pleasure and pain, in gain and in loss, in victory or in the loss of a battle. In this peace there is no sin.
>
> *Bhagavad Gita 2:38*

Hindus are dedicated to peace. At the end of all their prayers they pray for peace of mind and body, for peace from natural disaster and for peace from other people.

Hindus are very tolerant of other ideas and beliefs and many of the Hindu gurus of the past 100 years have been trying to show a peaceful way through the hatred and violence which religion can bring.

However, not all Hindus are opposed to war and so there are two different attitudes to war in Hinduism.

1. Pacifism and non-violence

Some Hindus believe that violence in any form is wrong and that Hindus should not take part in wars. The reasons why they believe in non-violence are:

▶ The Hindu belief of ahimsa or non-violence is one of the moral codes of Hinduism and means that Hindus should not be violent to others.
▶ Connected with ahimsa is the belief that to take life will darken your soul and put it further back on the way to moksha; so fighting in war keeps you from liberation.
▶ India fought the only non-violent war in history when Gandhi led a war of independence against Britain in which he refused to allow any violence. This showed that it is possible to fight against oppressors without using violence.
▶ Gandhi's idea of satyagraha (truth force) showed that pacifism can work as a way of removing injustice.
▶ Modern methods of warfare are so terrible that they are bound to take innocent lives, which is against all the teachings of Hinduism.

> In non-violence, the masses have a weapon which enables a child, a woman, or even a decrepit old man to resist the mightiest government successfully.
>
> *Gandhi*

The weapon of non-violence does not need supermen or superwomen to wield it; even beings of common clay can use it and have used it before this with success.

M.K. Gandhi

2. The Hindu Just War

Perhaps the majority of Hindus believe that war is justified if fought in self-defence or to remove great injustice. India has an army that is fighting to keep Kashmir in India, and which fought to protect the Bangladeshis when they were being attacked by Pakistan. The reasons for this view are:

- In the caste system of Hinduism, the second most important caste is the warrior caste whose caste duty was to defend society by war if necessary.
- The most popular Hindu holy book, the Bhagavad Gita, says that warriors must fight in just wars and that they need not fear killing because it is only the body that is killed, the soul cannot be harmed.
- The Laws of Manu set out strict rules about war: civilians, women and children must not be harmed; anyone who surrenders, is disarmed or wounded must not be attacked; weapons must be such as to not cause unnecessary suffering (barbed, blazing or poisoned arrows are banned).
- There are many stories of battles in the Hindu Scriptures and Rama, the avatar of Vishnu, fought and killed the tyrant king Ravana.

So Hindus have a similar problem to Christians. Most probably accept the need to fight just wars, but a substantial minority is opposed to war in any form.

> Think thou also of thy duty and do not waver. There is no greater good for a warrior than to fight in a righteous war. There is war that opens up the gates of heaven, Arjuna! Happy the warrior whose fate is to fight such a war.
>
> *Bhagavad Gita 2:31–32*

Indian Hindu soldiers praying to bless their guns during the Kargil war against Pakistan, 1999.

Questions

b) Do you think religious people should fight in wars? Give two reasons for your point of view. **(4)**

c) Choose one religion other than Christianity and explain why its followers support just wars. **(8)**

d) 'Religious people should never fight in wars.'

In your answer, you should refer to at least one religion.

   (i) Do you agree? Give reasons for your opinion. **(3)**

   (ii) Give reasons why some people may disagree with you. **(3)**

Exam Tip

d) Use the technique for answering evaluation questions from page 111. Arguments in favour of the quotation could come from the reasons why some Christians are pacifists (see Topic 8.3.5). Arguments against could come from why some Hindus support just wars on this page.

Summary

All Hindus believe in peace, but there are different attitudes to war in Hinduism.

Some Hindus will not take part in any wars because they believe they should follow ahimsa (non-violence). Some Hindus think it is right to fight if attacked because this is taught in scriptures such as the Bhagavad Gita.

Topic 8.3.6d Sikhism and attitudes to war

> No one is my enemy. No one is a foreigner. With all I am at peace. God within us renders us incapable of hate and prejudice.
>
> *Guru Nanak*

> When all efforts to restore peace prove useless and no words avail, lawful is the flash of steel. It is right to draw the sword.
>
> *Guru Gobind Singh*

Painting of Guru Gobind Singh. Why might the example of Guru Gobind Singh lead Sikhs to reject pacifism?

Summary

Sikhs are not pacifists and are expected to fight to protect the oppressed and human rights. However, the war must be fought justly. Just wars must be fought by Sikhs even if there is no chance of success.

Sikhs are strongly in favour of action to promote human rights and harmony between religions and states. Sikhs are also expected to take military action against oppression.

Most Sikhs are in favour of fighting in just wars because:

▶ Sikhism has a theory of just war called Dharam Yudh (war in the defence of righteousness). The crucial difference from the just war theory in Topic 8.3.4 is that Sikhs believe that if a war is just it should be undertaken even if it cannot be won.

▶ The sixth guru, Guru Har Gobind, thought that military action would sometimes be needed to promote the cause of justice and protect the innocent from attack.

▶ The tenth guru, Guru Gobind Singh, gave the Sikhs the mission of fighting against oppression and formed the khalsa members who must always carry a Kirpan (sword), with which they are committed to 'righteously defend the fine line of the Truth'.

▶ Guru Gobind Singh made it clear that military action was to be the last resort, but emphasised that it should not be avoided if it proved necessary.

▶ It is the teaching of the Rahit Maryada that Sikhs should fight in wars which fulfil the requirements of the Dharam Yudh, and Sikhs should follow the guidance of their moral rule book.

However, some Sikhs (such as the Khudai Khidmatgar) believe that Guru Nanak was against war and taught pacifism. They also think that the nature of modern weapons means that no war can be a just war, and so they oppose wars.

Questions

b) Do you think religious people should fight in wars? Give two reasons for your point of view. **(4)**

c) Choose one religion other than Christianity and explain why its followers support just wars. **(8)**

d) 'Religious people should never fight in wars.'

In your answer, you should refer to at least one religion.

　(i)　Do you agree? Give reasons for your opinion. **(3)**

　(ii)　Give reasons why some people may disagree with you. **(3)**

Exam Tip

d) Use the technique for answering evaluation questions from page 111. Arguments in favour of the quotation could come from the reasons why some Christians are pacifists (see Topic 8.3.5). Arguments against could come from why most Sikhs support just wars on this page.

Topic 8.3.7 Christian attitudes to bullying

What is bullying?

Bullying is intimidating or frightening people who are weaker than yourself. Most people connect bullying with school where children are often picked on by groups of older or stronger children.

School bullying can include:

▶ being called names
▶ being pinched, kicked or hit
▶ having possessions taken
▶ being ignored or left out
▶ receiving abusive texts or emails
▶ being abused because of religion, ethnic origin, appearance, sexuality or disability.

Other forms of bullying can take place among adults. There is growing evidence of people being bullied at work. Such bullying is normally carried out by managers or supervisors who use their position of power and authority to frighten or humiliate workers who are under their control. Such bullying does not cause physical injury (unlike much school bullying), but can lead to stress, nervous breakdown or even suicide.

> The number of children seeking help for racist bullying increased sharply last year as campaigners claim that the heated political debate about immigration is souring race relations in the classroom. More than 1400 children and young people contacted ChildLine for counselling about racist bullying in 2013, up 69 per cent on the previous 12 months.
>
> *Emily Dugan,* The Independent, *8 January 2014*

> I'm being bullied at school because of my race and religion. They call me a terrorist because they know I'm a Muslim. I've lost my temper a few times – it really frustrates me because then I end up getting in trouble. I want the teachers to do something, but they always tell me they're too busy.
>
> *Teenage girl interviewed by* The Independent, *8 January 2014*

KEY WORDS

Bullying – intimidating / frightening people weaker than yourself

Respect – treating a person or their feelings with consideration

A school's anti-bullying campaign

Why Christians are against bullying

▶ Christianity regards using violence without a just cause as sinful, and bullying always involves using violence (whether physical or verbal) which is unjustified and so is sinful.
▶ Christianity teaches that human beings are a creation of God, made in God's image. Bullying is mistreating God's creation and so is wrong.

- Christianity teaches that it is the duty of Christians to protect the weak and innocent (for example, the Parable of the Good Samaritan). Bullying is the exact opposite of this as bullies attack and exploit the weak and innocent, so bullying must be wrong.
- Jesus taught in the Parable of the Sheep and the Goats (see page 53) that Christians should treat anyone in trouble as if they were Jesus. No Christian would bully Jesus and so they should not bully anyone.
- In a democracy, every person has human rights, including the right to be able to live free from fear. All the Christian Churches teach that Christians should protect human rights and treat people with respect, so they should not bully because bullying denies the victim's human rights.
- Bullying has harmful effects on society. The victims of bullying are likely to be prevented from achieving the careers, and therefore the contribution to society, they are capable of. The bullies are likely to go on bullying and preventing even more people making their contribution to society. Christians, however, should always try to make society better.

Why would Christians be particularly against racist bullying?

Exam Tip

b) You should already have thought about this, and you just have to give two reasons for your opinion. For example, if you think they are never bullies, you could use two reasons from why Christians should not bully. If you think they do sometimes bully, you might refer to Christian parents bullying their children to go to church and bullying their children to get confirmed.

Summary

Bullying is when stronger people pick on weak people to make their lives miserable. Bullying can lead to stress, nervous breakdown, even suicide.

Christians are against bullying because it is the duty of Christians to protect the innocent and it is sinful for Christians to use violence without a just cause.

Questions

b) Do you think Christians are ever bullies? Give two reasons for your point of view. **(4)**
c) Explain why Christians are against bullying. **(8)**
d) 'It is only human nature to bully teachers' pets.'
   In your answer, you should refer to at least one religion.
   (i) Do you agree? Give reasons for your opinion. **(3)**
   (ii) Give reasons why some people may disagree with you. **(3)**

Topic 8.3.8a Islam and attitudes to bullying

Muslims believe in a civilised society and they are against all forms of bullying because:

▶ Islamic society is based on the rule of law and mutual respect between the members of that society. Clearly, bullies have no respect for the people they bully and so have no understanding of their responsibilities as members of society.

▶ Islam regards using violence without a just cause as sinful, and bullying always involves using violence (whether physical or verbal) which is unjustified and so is sinful.

▶ Islam teaches that all Muslims are members of the ummah and should have equal treatment and respect. Any Muslim who bullies a fellow Muslim is acting against the ummah.

▶ Islam teaches that it is the duty of Muslims to protect the weak and innocent (see Surah 90:12–16). Bullying is the exact opposite of this as bullies attack and exploit the weak and innocent, so bullying must be wrong.

▶ Muhammad said in his final sermon, 'Every Muslim is a brother to every Muslim'. No one should bully their brother and so Muslims should not bully anyone.

▶ In a democracy, every person has human rights, including the right to be able to live free from fear. All law schools teach that Muslims should defend human rights and so they should not bully because bullying denies the victim's human rights.

> Let there arise out of you a band of people inviting to all that is good, enjoining what is right, and forbidding what is wrong: they are the one to attain felicity. Be not like those who are divided among themselves and fall into disputations after receiving clear signs: for them is a dreadful penalty.
>
> *Qur'an 3: 104–105*

> And what will make thee comprehend what the uphill road is. It is to free a slave, or to feed in a day of hunger an orphan nearly related, or the poor man lying in the dust.
>
> *Surah 90:12–16*

Questions

b) Do you think religious people should stop bullies from bullying people? Give two reasons for your point of view. **(4)**

c) Choose one religion other than Christianity and explain why its followers are against bullying. **(8)**

d) 'If everyone were religious, there would be no bullies.'

In your answer, you should refer to at least one religion.

    (i) Do you agree? Give reasons for your opinion. **(3)**

    (ii) Give reasons why some people may disagree with you. **(3)**

Exam Tip

c) 'Explain why' means give reasons. One way to answer this question would be to use four of the reasons on this page to explain why Muslims are against bullying. Remember to use some specialist vocabulary such as: rule of law, mutual respect, sinful, ummah, Surah, Muhammad, sermon, human rights.

Summary

Muslims are against bullying because Muslims should be responsible citizens, they should treat all Muslims as their brothers and they should protect the weak and innocent.

Topic 8.3.8b Judaism and attitudes to bullying

Jewish people believe in a civilised society and are against all forms of bullying because:

▶ Judaism is based on the rule of law and mutual respect between the members of society. Clearly, bullies have no respect for the people they bully and so have no understanding of their responsibilities as members of society.

▶ Judaism regards using violence without a just cause as sinful, and bullying always involves using violence (whether physical or verbal) which is unjustified and so is sinful.

▶ Judaism teaches that human beings are a creation of God made in God's image. Bullying is mistreating God's creation and so is wrong.

▶ Judaism teaches that it is the duty of Jewish people to protect the weak and innocent as part of loving your neighbour. Bullying is the exact opposite of this as bullies attack and exploit the weak and innocent, so bullying must be wrong.

▶ In a democracy, every person has human rights, including the right to be able to live free from fear. All different forms of Judaism teach that Jewish people should defend human rights and so they should not bully because bullying denies the victim's human rights.

Do not defraud your neighbour or rob him. Do not hold back the wages of a hired man overnight. Do not curse the deaf or put a stumbling-block in front of the blind, but fear your God. I am the LORD ... Do not go about spreading slander among your people. Do not do anything that endangers your neighbour's life. I am the LORD.

Leviticus 19:13–16

He upholds the cause of the oppressed and gives food to the hungry.

The LORD sets prisoners free,

the LORD gives sight to the blind,

the LORD lifts up those who are bowed down,

the LORD loves the righteous.

The LORD watches over the alien and sustains the fatherless and the widow, but he frustrates the ways of the wicked.

Psalm 146:7–9

Questions

b) Do you think religious people should stop bullies from bullying people? Give two reasons for your point of view. **(4)**

c) Choose one religion other than Christianity and explain why its followers are against bullying. **(8)**

d) 'If everyone were religious, there would be no bullies.'

In your answer, you should refer to at least one religion.

(i) Do you agree? Give reasons for your opinion. **(3)**

(ii) Give reasons why some people may disagree with you. **(3)**

Exam Tip

c) 'Explain why' means give reasons. One way to answer this question would be to use four of the reasons on this page to explain why Jewish people are against bullying. Remember to use some specialist vocabulary such as: rule of law, mutual respect, sinful, creation, God's image, loving your neighbour, human rights.

Summary

Jewish people are against bullying because they should love their neighbours and protect the weak and innocent who were created by God in his image.

Topic 8.3.8c Hinduism and attitudes to bullying

Hindus believe in a civilised society and are against all forms of bullying because:

▶ Hinduism is based on the rule of law and mutual respect between the members of society. Clearly, bullies have no respect for the people they bully and so have no understanding of their responsibilities as members of society.

▶ Hinduism regards using violence without a just cause as sinful because it is against the doctrine of ahimsa (non-violence) and bullying always involves using violence (whether physical or verbal) which is unjustified and so is sinful.

▶ Hindus see bullying as wrong because they believe every person has a soul, which is part of the divine essence. To mistreat that divine essence will bring bad karma, which will prevent you from gaining moksha.

▶ Many Hindus believe it is their duty to protect the weak and innocent because this brings good karma and will make it easier to gain moksha. Bullying is the exact opposite of this as bullies attack and exploit the weak and innocent, so bullying must be wrong.

▶ In a democracy, every person has human rights, including the right to be able to live free from fear. All Hindus believe they should defend human rights and so they should not bully because bullying denies the victim's human rights.

> The principle of ahimsa does not include any evil thought, any unjustified haste, any lies, hatred, ill will towards anyone.
>
> *Mahatma Gandhi*

> Manu is quite specific about the moral retribution due to action over a period of lives ... verbal actions such as lying, abuse, slander and bodily actions such as theft, violence ... and adultery, all result in a specific kind of retribution in a future life ... a sinful verbal act to rebirth as a wild animal or bird, and a sinful bodily act to rebirth as something inanimate or a plant.
>
> *Laws of Manu 12:5–10*

Questions

b) Do you think religious people should stop bullies from bullying people? Give two reasons for your point of view. **(4)**

c) Choose one religion other than Christianity and explain why its followers are against bullying. **(8)**

d) 'If everyone were religious, there would be no bullies.'

In your answer, you should refer to at least one religion.

    (i) Do you agree? Give reasons for your opinion. **(3)**

    (ii) Give reasons why some people may disagree with you. **(3)**

Exam Tip

c) 'Explain why' means give reasons. One way to answer this question would be to use four of the reasons on this page to explain why Hindus are against bullying. Remember to use some specialist vocabulary such as: rule of law, mutual respect, sinful, doctrine, ahimsa, soul, divine essence, karma, moksha, human rights.

Summary

Hindus are against bullying because it involves violence which is against belief in ahimsa. It also brings bad karma which will delay moksha. It is also denying the victim's human rights which Hindus should protect.

Topic 8.3.8d Sikhism and attitudes to bullying

Sikhs believe in a civilised society and are against all forms of bullying because:

▶ Sikhism is based on the rule of law and mutual respect between the members of society. Clearly, bullies have no respect for the people they bully and so have no understanding of their responsibilities as members of society.

▶ Sikhism regards using violence without a just cause as sinful because it is manmukh (human centred) rather than gurmukh (living by the Gurus' teachings).

▶ Bullying always involves using unjustified violence (whether physical or verbal) which is sinful.

▶ Sikhs see bullying as wrong because they believe every person has a soul which is part of the divine essence. To mistreat that divine essence will bring bad karma which will prevent you from gaining mukti.

▶ Many Sikhs believe it is their duty to protect the weak and innocent because this is gurmukh and brings good karma and will make it easier to gain mukti. Bullying is the exact opposite of this as bullies attack and exploit the weak and innocent, so bullying must be wrong.

▶ In a democracy, every person has human rights, including the right to be able to live free from fear. All Sikhs believe they should defend human rights and so they should not bully because bullying denies the victim's human rights.

> The hands of the gurmukh are blessed for they toil in the service of God and the sangat, they fetch water, grind corn, and perform any service that is required of them ... they labour to earn an honest living, and distribute part of their income for the benefit of others. Having touched the perfect guru, their hands have become holy ... Ego and pride have been lost through serving others.
>
> *Var 6:12*

Questions

b) Do you think religious people should stop bullies from bullying people? Give two reasons for your point of view. **(4)**

c) Choose one religion other than Christianity and explain why its followers are against bullying. **(8)**

d) 'If everyone were religious, there would be no bullies.'
  (i) Do you agree? Give reasons for your opinion. **(3)**
  (ii) Give reasons why some people may disagree with you. **(3)**
    In your answer, you should refer to at least one religion.

Exam Tip

c) 'Explain why' means give reasons. One way to answer this question would be to use four of the reasons on this page to explain why Sikhs are against bullying. Remember to use some specialist vocabulary such as: rule of law, mutual respect, sinful, manmukh, gurmukh, unjustified, soul, divine essence, karma, mukti, human rights.

Summary

Sikhs are against bullying because it involves unlawful violence, which is manmukh rather than gurmukh. It also brings bad karma, which will delay mukti. It is also denying the victim's human rights, which Sikhs should protect.

Topic 8.3.9 Religious conflicts within families

Although religion can be a major source of unity within families, religion can cause conflicts within families as well as between countries.

The main ways in which religion can cause conflicts within families are:

1. Children no longer wanting to take part in their parents' religion

If parents are religious and go regularly to a place of worship, they will expect their children to go with them. If their children refuse when they reach their teens, this can cause major conflict because:

▶ Religions usually tell parents that it is their duty to bring their children up in the faith and ensure they become full members of it as adults; therefore if the children no longer take part in the religion, their parents will be regarded as failures by other believers.

▶ Parents will worry that their children will become immoral without the guidance of religion.

▶ Parents will worry that their children will not be with them in the after-life because they have left the faith.

▶ Children will feel that their human right to freedom of religion (which includes the freedom not to believe) is being taken away by their parents.

> Children obey your parents in the Lord, for this is right.
>
> *Ephesians 6:1*

> Be careful of your duty to Allah and be fair to your children.
>
> *Hadith quoted by al'Bukhari*

> It is the greatest sin to quarrel with parents who have given you birth and brought you up.
>
> *Guru Granth Sahib 1200*

2. Children wanting to marry a partner from a different faith

In a multi-faith society, young people of different faiths are going to meet, fall in love and want to marry. This can raise many problems for religious parents and religious leaders because:

▶ Often there can be no religious wedding ceremony because the couple must be members of the same religion for a religious wedding ceremony to be allowed.

▶ There is the question of which religion the children of the marriage will be brought up in. Some religions insist on a child being brought up in their religion (for example, Islam and Catholic Christianity), but how can a couple decide on this?

▶ There is also the problem of what will happen after death? Will the couple have to be buried in different places according to their religion?

▶ For the parents and relatives of the couple there is often the feeling that the couple have betrayed their roots and family by falling in love with someone from a different religion.

Why might taking a family to church cause conflict?

Why might a young Muslim working in a bar cause family conflict?

Exam Tip

d) Use the technique for answering evaluation questions from page 111. Arguments in favour of the quotation could come from any of the ways in which religion causes conflicts within families. Arguments against could come from the way in which religion keeps families together, the promises religious parents make to love and care for their children, etc. (Information from Section 3.3 could be used here.)

Summary

Conflicts can occur in families if children:

- no longer wish to follow their parents' religion, but the parents want them to
- want to marry someone of a different religion
- become more religious than their parents and start criticising their parents for not following the religion strictly enough
- disagree with their parents over moral issues.

3. Children becoming more religious than their parents

Often parents are members of a religion, but not very strictly so. If their children then become strict followers of the religion it can cause major conflict as parents get angry if their children criticise them, especially when the children have religion on their side. For example:

- if the child wants to have a low-paid job as a priest (minister), imam, charity worker, or joins a religious community after their parents have spent a lot of money on their university education, the parents will often be angry; even more so if the child will have to be celibate and so deny the parents their chance of grandchildren
- if the child criticises the lifestyle of the parents, for example, Catholic parents who use contraception, Muslim parents who run off-licences and sell national lottery tickets, Hindu parents who eat beef
- if the child tries to force the parents to be more religious, for example, Baptist children expecting their parents to read the Bible every day, Jewish children expecting their parents to keep all the Shabbat rules, Sikh children trying to stop their parents from drinking alcohol.

4. Disagreements over moral issues

There can be major conflicts within a family if a family member makes a moral decision that goes against the teaching of the family's religion. For example:

- if a Catholic or a Sikh decides to divorce so they can marry someone else
- if a couple decide to live together rather than marrying even though their religion bans sex before marriage
- if a family member decides to write for a pornographic magazine, or become a striptease artist
- if a family member decides to have an abortion even though it is against their religion.

Questions

b) Do you think parents have a right to make children follow their religion? Give two reasons for your point of view. **(4)**

c) Explain why religion can cause conflict within families. **(8)**

d) 'Religion causes more trouble in families than anything else.'
   (i) Do you agree? Give reasons for your opinion. **(3)**
   (ii) Give reasons why some people may disagree with you. **(3)**

Topic 8.3.10 Christian teachings on forgiveness and reconciliation

Christians believe in forgiveness and reconciliation because:

▶ Most Christians believe that humanity had become split from God through sin, but the forgiveness of sins brought by the death of God's son, Jesus, has allowed reconciliation between God and humans. Jesus died on the cross to bring forgiveness and reconciliation.

▶ Jesus said that if people do not forgive those who have sinned against them, God will not forgive their sins.

▶ St Paul said that Christians should try to live in peace with everyone. The only way to live in peace with everyone is to try to bring about reconciliation through forgiving those who wrong you.

▶ Christianity is based on the concept of forgiveness and reconciliation. All the Churches teach that Christians should be committed to forgiveness and reconciliation when there are conflicts between families or friends. Christians believe that the power of forgiveness and love can lead to reconciliation and the ending of conflict.

However, Christians would say that if the quarrel is about a religious or moral issue and the person quarrelled with is going against Christian beliefs, then there can be no reconciliation. Christian beliefs should not be given up for either friends or family.

KEY WORDS

Forgiveness – stopping blaming someone and/or pardoning them for what they have done wrong

Reconciliation – bringing together people who were opposed to each other

Why does the crucifixion make Christians believe in forgiveness and reconciliation?

Questions

b) Do you think you should always forgive others? Give two reasons for your point of view. **(4)**

c) Explain why Christians should forgive wrongdoers. **(8)**

d) 'You can't be a good Christian if you do not always forgive others.'
In your answer, you should refer to Christianity.
   (i) Do you agree? Give reasons for your opinion. **(3)**
   (ii) Give reasons why some people may disagree with you. **(3)**

Exam Tip

b) You should already have thought about this, and you just have to give two reasons for your opinion. For example, if you think you should, you could use two reasons from why Christians should forgive others.

Summary

Christians believe they should forgive those who attack them or hurt them. They also believe they should try to settle conflicts and bring reconciliation between people. They believe this because Jesus taught forgiveness and reconciliation.

Topic 8.3.11a Islam: Teachings on forgiveness and reconciliation

Be forgiving and control yourself in the face of provocation; give justice to the person who was unfair and unjust to you; give to the one who did not help you when you were in need, and keep fellowship with the one who did not care about you.

Hadith

The conflict in the Central African Republic has become a conflict between Christians and Muslims, but there are still people of both faiths who are prepared to forgive and are seeking reconciliation. In February 2014, a lorry filled with Muslims and Christians fleeing the violence was stopped by Christian militias and the Muslims were ordered out to be shot. A Muslim mother handed her baby to a Christian woman who told the militia the baby was hers. She then found the baby's mother's brother and gave him his niece to bring up – he has taken her to Cameroon to flee the conflict.

Adapted from news stories

Muslims believe that they should be forgiving, and try to bring reconciliation, because:

◗ God is compassionate and merciful to sinners, and so Muslims should be merciful and forgiving to those who cause them offence.
◗ On the Day of Judgement God will deal with everyone as they deserve, but Muslims will be able to request his mercy. However, how can Muslims ask for God's forgiveness if they are not prepared to forgive?
◗ The Qur'an says that Muslims should forgive other people's sins against them and Muslims should obey the Qur'an as they believe it is the word of God.
◗ There are many hadith from the Prophet Muhammad about forgiving people who have offended others and bringing reconciliation to conflicts, and Muslims believe they should follow the example of the Prophet.

Nevertheless, Muslims should not forgive those who are working against Islam, or those who are denying Muslim principles.

This quotation from the Qur'an says 'In the name of God, the Merciful, the Compassionate'. Why might it make Muslims work for forgiveness and reconciliation?

Questions

b) Do you think religious people should always forgive people? Give two reasons for your point of view. **(4)**

c) Choose one religion other than Christianity and explain why its followers should forgive wrongdoers. **(8)**

d) 'You can't be religious if you don't always forgive others.'
   In your answer, you should refer to at least one religion.
   (i) Do you agree? Give reasons for your opinion. **(3)**
   (ii) Give reasons why some people may disagree with you. **(3)**

Exam Tip

c) 'Explain why' means give reasons. One way to answer this question would be to use four reasons from this page to explain why Muslims should forgive wrongdoers. Remember to use some specialist vocabulary such as: compassionate, merciful, Day of Judgement, Qur'an, sins, hadith, prophet, Muhammad, reconciliation.

Summary

Muslims try to forgive those who wrong them and try to resolve conflicts because this is the teaching of the Qur'an. Muslims are also taught to forgive if they expect God to forgive them.

Topic 8.3.11b Judaism: Teachings on forgiveness and reconciliation

Judaism teaches that Jews should forgive those who wrong them, and try to bring about reconciliation, because:

▶ In the ten days between **Rosh Hashanah** and **Yom Kippur**, Jews are expected to seek out anyone they have wronged and ask their forgiveness, so ending the conflict and becoming reconciled with them. They do this because on Yom Kippur, they are going to ask God to forgive them for all the wrongs they have done to God in the past year.

▶ Judaism teaches that God forgives those who turn to him in true repentance and the sign of true repentance is to seek forgiveness for your own sins and be prepared to forgive others their sins.

▶ The Tenakh encourages people to forgive those who wrong them and try to bring reconciliation, and Jewish people should follow the teachings of the Tenakh.

▶ The rabbis encourage Jewish people to forgive those who wrong them and become reconciled with them.

▶ The Prayer Book teaches that Jewish people should always try to forgive those who have wronged them when on their deathbed, before they ask God to forgive their sins.

However, Jewish people are not expected to forgive those who do not ask for forgiveness nor are they expected to forgive the enemies of Judaism.

> And so may it be Your will, Lord our God and God of our fathers, to have mercy on us and forgive us all our sins, grant us atonement for our iniquities, and forgive and pardon us for all transgressions.
>
> *From the prayers for Yom Kippur*

Why might the Yom Kippur service encourage Jewish people to seek reconciliation?

Questions

b) Do you think religious people should always forgive people? Give two reasons for your point of view. **(4)**

c) Choose one religion other than Christianity and explain why its followers should forgive wrongdoers. **(8)**

d) 'You can't be religious if you don't always forgive others.'

In your answer, you should refer to at least one religion.

(i) Do you agree? Give reasons for your opinion. **(3)**

(ii) Give reasons why some people may disagree with you. **(3)**

Exam Tip

c) 'Explain why' means give reasons. One way to answer this question would be to use four reasons from this page to explain why Jewish people should forgive wrongdoers. Remember to use some specialist vocabulary such as: Rosh Hashanah, Yom Kippur, repentance, sins, Tenakh, rabbis, Prayer Book, death bed.

Summary

Jews believe they should forgive those who wrong them because it is taught in the Tenakh. They also believe it is their duty to resolve conflicts as every year they have Yom Kippur when they must forgive people and resolve any personal conflicts.

Topic 8.3.11c Hinduism: Teachings on forgiveness and reconciliation

Some Hindus do not believe in forgiveness as they think that everyone suffers according to their previous lives. Whatever happens is a result of people's karma and forgiveness does not come into the matter.

However, most Hindus believe in forgiveness and reconciliation because:

> When a man sees all beings within his very self, and his self within all beings ... he has reached the seed – without body or wound, without sinews, not riddled by evil.
>
> *Isa Upanishad 6–8*

- The belief in the **gunas** means that forgiveness and reconciliation are a quality of light (sattva) whereas hatred and bitterness are part of the forces of dark (tamas) which keep the soul from moksha.
- The Upanishads teach the danger to the soul of not forgiving those who seek your forgiveness. They think it is better for one's soul to forgive those who have committed the wrong, and to bring about reconciliation of conflicts as this is more likely to lead to moksha.
- Many swamis have taught that to forgive those who have wronged a person, and to bring reconciliation to conflicts, is part of the process of liberating the soul (moksha).
- Refusing to forgive and/or be reconciled means that the soul is becoming bitter and twisted so that it will go backwards in the process of samsara rather than forwards to moksha and nirvana.

> Even if someone attacks you with abuses, insults and beatings for no reason, do not be harsh to them. Bear and endure them. Forgive and bless your tormentors.
>
> *Shiksapatri 202*

Questions

b) Do you think religious people should always forgive people? Give two reasons for your point of view. **(4)**

c) Choose one religion other than Christianity and explain why its followers should forgive wrongdoers. **(8)**

d) 'You can't be religious if you don't always forgive others.'
   In your answer, you should refer to at least one religion.

   (i) Do you agree? Give reasons for your opinion. **(3)**

   (ii) Give reasons why some people may disagree with you. **(3)**

Exam Tip

c) 'Explain why' means give reasons. One way to answer this question would be to use four reasons from this page to explain why Hindus should forgive wrongdoers. Remember to use some specialist vocabulary such as: gunas, sattva, tamas, soul, moksha, Upanishads, reconciliation, swamis, liberating, samsara, nirvana.

A swami is a religious leader honoured because he can control his senses. Why might you need to practise forgiveness and reconciliation to be a swami?

Summary

All Hindus believe they should try to bring reconciliation to conflicts to gain good karma. However, some Hindus think the law of cause and effect (karma) means no forgiveness; others believe that forgiving others is the way to moksha.

Topic 8.3.11d Sikhism: Teachings on forgiveness and reconciliation

Forgiveness and reconciliation lie at the basis of Sikhism. Sikhs believe in forgiveness and reconciliation because:

▶ The religion began because of Guru Nanak's search for reconciliation between the faiths that divided India. Reconciliation is still a fundamental goal for Sikhs when confronted with conflict.

▶ The **Adi Granth** emphasises the virtues of mercy, forgiveness, compassion and benevolence as the basis for healing and reconciliation.

▶ Paryushana Parva Mela, the Sikh festival of fasting, friendship and forgiveness, has forgiveness at its core showing that Sikhs should forgive those who wrong them.

▶ There are many examples of the Gurus showing forgiveness and seeking reconciliation and Sikhs should follow the examples of the Gurus.

▶ The holy books teach that forgiveness and reconciliation are inseparable and Sikhs should follow the teachings of the holy books.

However, there are instances where forgiveness appears to be impossible. Guru Gobind Singh has been recorded as saying when a follower's faith was questionable: 'As long as the Khalsa remain distinct and intact, I shall bless them in every way; When they detract from the prescribed path, I detest them for ever.'

Questions

b) Do you think religious people should always forgive people? Give two reasons for your point of view. **(4)**

c) Choose one religion other than Christianity and explain why its followers should forgive wrongdoers. **(8)**

d) 'You can't be religious if you don't always forgive others.'

In your answer, you should refer to at least one religion.

    (i) Do you agree? Give reasons for your opinion. **(3)**

    (ii) Give reasons why some people may disagree with you. **(3)**

Exam Tip

c) 'Explain why' means give reasons. One way to answer this question would be to use four reasons from this page to explain why Sikhs should forgive wrongdoers. Remember to use some specialist vocabulary such as: Guru Nanak, reconciliation, Adi Granth, compassion, benevolence, Paryushana Parva Mela, Gurus, reconciliation, Guru's examples, holy books.

Guru Gobind Singh was deserted by 40 Sikhs at the fifth Battle of Anandpur who had given him a disclaimer stating that he was not their Guru nor they his Sikhs. Later after a battle with the Muslim army, Guru Gobind Singh was touring the battlefield where he discovered all but one of the 40 had died in battle. It is recorded that Gobind Singh took out the disclaiming document, which he carried on his vest during all these times, and tore it up as a sign of forgiveness and reconciliation.

They who make truth their fasting, contentment their place of pilgrimage, divine knowledge and meditation their ablutions, Mercy their idol, and forgiveness their rosary, are foremost in God's favour.

Guru Granth Sahib

Summary

Sikhism believes in forgiveness and reconciliation wherever possible because this was the teaching and example of the Gurus. The Adi Granth encourages Sikhs to be merciful and forgiving; and the Paryushana Parva Mela is all about forgiving those who have wronged you.

How to answer exam questions

a) What does aggression mean? (2)

Aggression means attacking without being provoked.

b Do you think some wars are worth fighting? (4)

Yes I do because St Thomas Aquinas said that Catholics should fight in a war for a just cause, for example, if the war is fought in self-defence when another country attacks. I also think it is worth fighting in a war which is trying to remove a great injustice such as the war in Afghanistan one of whose aims is to protect the rights of women and give education to girls.

c) Explain how a religious organisation tries to promote world peace. (8)

Pax Christi is a religious organisation trying to promote world peace. It does this by organising public debates on the horrors of wars and conflicts and encouraging Catholics to support political parties opposed to war. Pax Christi also makes public statements and organises protests about war such as condemning the use of drones in Afghanistan and Pakistan, and opposing interventions in the conflicts in Syria and Democratic Republic of Congo. Pax Christi also organises and attends inter-faith conferences to help all religions work together to promote world peace. Finally, Pax Christi works for peace by working for economic justice and global recognition of human rights to remove the causes of war.

d) 'There should be no conflict in a religious family.'
   In your answer you should refer to at least one religion.

   (i)   Do you agree? Give reasons for your opinion. (3)

   (ii) Give reasons why some people may disagree
         with you. (3)

(i) I disagree with this statement because conflicts can often occur in Catholic Christian families because of religion. For example, if children no longer wish to follow their parents' religion, there can be major conflict because the parents have promised at baptism to bring them up in the faith and the parents feel betrayed if the children want to leave the faith. Conflict can also arise if the children become more religious than their parents and start criticising their parents for not going to Mass every Sunday and not going to confession. There might also be conflict between parents and children over moral issues connected with religion such as sex before marriage and the use of contraception.

(ii) I can see why some Catholics might disagree with me because Catholic Christianity says parents should love their children and children should love their parents so there should be no conflict. Also they might think that their religion brings the family closer together as they worship together and have the social life of the parish in common. There is also the fact that if the children are brought up in the same religion as their parents, they will share the same ideals and values and so will not have conflict.

Question a
High marks because it is a correct definition.

Question b
A high mark answer because an opinion is backed up by two developed reasons.

Question c
A high mark answer because it identifies a religious group dedicated to world peace and explains four ways in which Pax Christi tries to bring about world peace. It also uses specialist vocabulary such as: public debates, political parties, drones, Pakistan, Afghanistan, intervention, Syria, Democratic Republic of Congo, inter-faith conferences, economic justice, global recognition, human rights.

Question d
A high mark answer because it states the candidate's own opinion and backs it up with three clear reasons for thinking there can be conflict in a Catholic Christian family. It then gives three reasons for Catholic Christians disagreeing with their point of view.

Section

8.4

Religion: Crime and punishment

Introduction

This section of the examination specification requires you to look at issues surrounding the effects of religion on crime and punishment.

Religion and the need for law and justice

You will need to understand the effects of, and give reasons for your own opinion about:

▶ the need for law and justice
▶ theories of punishment and the arguments for and against them
▶ why justice is important for Christians
▶ why justice is important for the followers of one religion other than Christianity.

Religion and capital punishment

You will need to understand the effects of, and give reasons for your own opinion about:

▶ the nature of capital punishment and non-religious arguments about capital punishment
▶ different attitudes to capital punishment among Christians and the reasons for them
▶ different attitudes to capital punishment in one religion other than Christianity.

Religion: drugs and alcohol

You will need to understand the effects of, and give reasons for your own opinion about:

▶ laws on drugs and alcohol and the reasons for them
▶ social and health problems caused by drugs and alcohol
▶ different attitudes to drugs and alcohol in Christianity and the reasons for them
▶ attitudes to drugs and alcohol in one religion other than Christianity.

Topic 8.4.1 The need for law and justice

KEY WORDS

Crime – an act against the law

Judgement – the act of judging people and their actions

Justice – due allocation of reward and punishment, the maintenance of what is right

Law – rules made by Parliament and enforceable by the courts

Laws are rules made about how members of a society are expected to behave. In the UK, laws are either made by Parliament or by judges as a result of the decisions they reach in the cases that they hear in court (known as common law). The law is upheld by courts, who make judgements about whether laws have been broken and by whom, and the police, who ensure that all members of society obey the law.

Why do we need laws?

1. Human beings live in groups, and any group needs rules to organise the behaviour of individuals within it. Imagine what the roads would be like if there were no laws: people would be able to drive on whichever side of the road they liked; people would be able to drive at any speed they liked; there would be no traffic lights because drivers would not need to obey them. Therefore we need laws so that people know what sort of behaviour to expect from each other.
2. We need laws so that people can work and be involved in business without someone taking away all the rewards of their work. Imagine what it would be like if you worked hard for someone and then they did not pay you; or if you had a deal to sell your car to someone and they took the car without giving you the money. If there were no laws about business deals and work, modern-day society could not function as no one would bother to work.
3. We need laws to protect the weak from the strong. Imagine what life would be like if there were no laws on stealing, murder and rape. As the British philosopher Thomas Hobbes said, 'What is worst of all, (we would live in) continual fear and danger of violent death; and the life of man would be solitary, poor, nasty, brutish and short.'
4. In an advanced civilisation such as the United Kingdom's, we need laws to keep everything organised.

The British court system

```
                    Supreme Court
                    Final court
                    of appeal

   Court of appeal          Court of appeal
      (civil)                 (criminal)

    High Court                Crown Court
  Deals with claims         Judge and jury for
   over £10,000            indictable offences
  – libel, tax,
  family law, etc.
                          Magistrates Court
   County Court          Deals with committal
  Deals with small          proceedings for
  claims, straight-         Crown Courts,
  forward adoption,      less serious criminal
  divorce, custody       cases, traffic offences,
                          marital disputes,
                          public house
                          licences, etc.

    Civil Law                Criminal Law
 For settling disputes     For dealing with
 between individuals        criminal acts
```

The British court system.

How often would robberies like this happen if we had no laws?

Why does there need to be a connection between the law and justice?

St Thomas Aquinas said that an unjust law is not a proper law because:

- If a law is unjust, people will feel that it is right to break the law. If people feel it is right to break laws then the whole basis of society may disintegrate.
- If some laws are unjust, people may start to think that all laws are unjust; and if all laws are unjust then they are not fulfilling their purpose of making sure that people are rewarded for their work, the weak are protected, and so on.
- If a law is unjust, people will not obey it and will campaign against the law causing trouble in society (for example, the civil rights campaign against laws refusing equality to black people in the southern United States in the 1960s disrupted normal life there).
- If the laws do not create a just society, people will think the legal system is not working and may start a civil war (for example, Syria where some Syrian Sunni Muslims began a civil war because they thought the legal system of the Assad regime was treating them unfairly).

This means that, if laws are unjust, they will disrupt rather than unite society.

To achieve justice, the United Kingdom has a Legal Aid system that uses taxes to give free legal help to less well-off people accused of crimes.

Questions

b) Do you think we need laws? Give two reasons for your point of view. (4)

c) Explain why laws need to be just. (8)

d) 'It is always wrong to break the law.'
   In your answer, you should refer to at least one religion.
   (i) Do you agree? Give reasons for your opinion. (3)
   (ii) Give reasons why some people may disagree with you. (3)

Exam Tip

c) 'Explain why' means give reasons. One way to answer this question would be to use four reasons from this page to explain why laws need to be just. Remember to use some specialist vocabulary such as: St Thomas Aquinas, basis of society, fulfilling their purpose, civil rights campaign, just society, legal system, civil war, Syria, Sunni Muslims, Assad regime.

How does one determine when a law is just or unjust? A just law is a man-made code that squares with the moral law, or the law of God. An unjust law is a code that is out of harmony with the moral law. To put it in the terms of St Thomas Aquinas, an unjust law is a human law that is not rooted in eternal and natural law.

Dr Martin Luther King, Jr., 'Letter from a Birmingham Jail'

An unjust law is itself a species of violence. Arrest for its breach is more so. Now the law of nonviolence says that violence should be resisted not by counter-violence but by nonviolence. This I do by breaking the law and by peacefully submitting to arrest and imprisonment.

Mahatma Gandhi, Non-violence in Peace and War, 1942–49

AN UNJUST LAW IS NO LAW AT ALL!

Saint Augustine

Summary

Society needs laws for it to work properly and to protect the weak from the strong. The laws need to be just so that people will obey them and feel that they make society better.

Topic 8.4.2 Theories of punishment

KEY WORDS

Capital punishment – the death penalty for a crime or offence

Deterrence – the idea that punishments should be of such a nature that they will put people off (deter) committing crimes

Reform – the idea that punishments should try to change criminals so they will not commit crimes again

Rehabilitation – restore to normal life

Retribution – the idea that punishments should make criminals pay for what they have done wrong

Love is not always enough when you have a baby in prison. Pila Wati knows that first-hand. The social worker visits the Auckland Region Women's Corrections Facility in Wiri every week to deliver a parenting support programme to the mothers in the Mothers with Babies Unit. It is part of a three-year contract between the Department of Corrections, Family Works and Plunket. The goal is to help the mothers bond with their young ones and prepare them to reintegrate back into the community once they are released.

Auckland Now, March 2014

If a society has laws, it must also have punishments for those who break the laws. In the UK, when someone is found guilty of a crime, a judge or magistrate makes a judgement on what their punishment should be. The main aim of punishment is to try to make sure that everyone obeys the law. However, there are different theories about what is the most effective form of punishment and what it should do.

Retribution

Retribution is the theory that criminals should pay for their crime. Many people think this should be the main reason for punishment because:

▶ It makes criminals pay for their crime in proportion to the severity of the crime they have committed. In the past retributive punishments would have killed those who committed murder and taken the eyes out of those who blinded someone.

▶ It makes criminals suffer for what they have done wrong. Criminals make their victims suffer, so the criminals should also suffer.

▶ It actually punishes the criminal. The dictionary definition of punish is 'to make an offender suffer for what they have done' and this is exactly what retribution does.

Deterrence

Deterrence is the theory that the punishment should put people off committing crime. Many people think deterrence should be the main reason for punishment because the aim of punishment is to stop people from committing crimes. The idea of deterrent punishment is that punishment should be so severe no one will dare to commit crimes. For example:

▶ If someone knows they will have their hand cut off if they are caught stealing, then they will not steal, so deterrent punishment will stop theft.

▶ If people know they will be executed if they are found guilty, they will not murder.

Is prison a good way of dealing with criminals?

Reform

Reform is the theory that criminals should be taught not to commit crime again. Many people think reform should be the main reason for punishment because:

◗ They believe the only way to stop crime is to reform the criminal so that they become honest, law-abiding citizens who will not want to commit crimes again.

◗ They believe that most criminals commit crimes because of how they have been brought up and because they do not know how to live without crime.

◗ Reformative punishments often involve giving criminals education and qualifications so that they can find a proper job and no longer feel the need to be a criminal (rehabilitation of offenders).

Protection

Protection is the theory that punishment should protect society from criminals and their activities. Many people think this should be the main reason for punishment, so, for example, they might think:

◗ Capital punishment is a good punishment for murderers and terrorists because if they are dead they cannot threaten people.

◗ Long prison sentences are a good punishment for violent people or persistent burglars as they keep them out of society so that people and their property are protected.

◗ Community service can be a good punishment for hooligans and vandals because it keeps them off the streets in their leisure time.

Most forms of punishment are a mixture of theories. For example, imprisonment can deter, protect, inflict retribution and give reformation through education, training and counselling.

Is community service a more effective way of punishing and reforming offenders than prison?

Questions

b) What do you think is the best form of punishment? Give two reasons for your point of view. **(4)**

c) Explain why the law uses different types of punishment. **(8)**

d) 'It is no good trying to reform criminals.'

In your answer, you should refer to at least one religion.

(i) Do you agree? Give reasons for your opinion. **(3)**

(ii) Give reasons why some people may disagree with you. **(3)**

Exam Tip

b) You should already have thought about this, and you just have to give two reasons for your opinion. For example, if you think deterrence is, you should use two reasons for why some people think it is the best form of punishment.

Summary

The main theories of punishment are:

● retribution – that criminals should be punished for what they have done
● deterrence – that punishments should be so harsh no one would dare commit a crime
● reformation – that punishment should try to change criminals into law-abiding citizens
● protection – that punishments should protect society from criminals.

Topic 8.4.3 Why justice is important for Christians

KEY WORD

Sin – an act against the will of God

... And there is no God apart from me, a righteous God and a Saviour ...

Isaiah 45:21

Blessed are those who hunger and thirst for righteousness ...

Matthew 5:6

... Anyone who does not do what is right is not a child of God; nor is anyone who does not love his brother.

1 John 3:10

Justice has always been an important issue in Christianity because:

- The Bible says that God is just and will reward the righteous (another word for those who are just) and punish those who sin, if not in this life then in the life to come.
- The Bible says that people should be treated fairly and not cheated, and that God wants the world to be ruled justly and so they believe that Christians should be concerned about fairness.
- Jesus said that the rich should share with the poor and there are many statements in the New Testament about how Christians should treat people fairly and equally.
- The Christian Churches have made many statements about the need for Christians to work for justice and fairness in the world.
- Christian organisations in the UK have been running a campaign to stop multi-national firms operating in poor countries, hiding their profits so they don't pay taxes. Christian Aid estimates that tax dodging prevents developing countries from collecting an estimated US$160bn a year which could provide sufficient healthcare and education to lift people out of poverty.
- The World Council of Churches began a Migration and Social Justice project in 2014 to engage and challenge the churches in

When he visited a shanty town in Rio de Janeiro, Pope Francis urged people who are more economically privileged to 'never tire' of working for solidarity and social justice.

their work with migrants, including refugees, internally displaced people and victims of trafficking. As it believes the connections between xenophobia and racism and attitudes to migrants are particularly strong, the WCC is campaigning for anti-racist justice systems.

Christian Aid and Church Action on Poverty joined forces to take the campaign for tax justice on the road with The Tax Justice Bus. Over seven weeks, this campaign bus toured Britain and Ireland to spread the message that tax dodging by wealthy individuals and businesses is effectively robbing the poor.

Questions

b) Do you think Christians always behave justly? Give two reasons for your point of view. **(4)**

c) Explain why justice is important for Christians. **(8)**

d) 'If everyone was Christian, there would be no injustice.'

You should refer to Christianity in your answer.

    (i) Do you agree? Give reasons for your opinion. **(3)**

    (ii) Give reasons why some people may disagree with you. **(3)**

Exam Tip

d) Use the technique for answering evaluation questions from page 111. Arguments for could come from why justice is important for Christians. Arguments against could come from Topic 8.4.1 on the need for a connection between laws and justice to show that justice is important for non-religious people.

I would like to make an appeal to those in possession of greater resources, to public authorities and to all people of good will who are working for social justice: never tire of working for a more just world, marked by greater solidarity! No one can remain insensitive to the inequalities that persist in the world!

The culture of selfishness and individualism that often prevails in our society is not, I repeat, not what builds up and leads to a more habitable world: rather, it is the culture of solidarity that does so; the culture of solidarity means seeing others not as rivals or statistics, but brothers and sisters. And we are all brothers and sisters!

Pope Francis speaking on World Youth Day, July 2013

Summary

Christians believe justice is important because the Bible says God is a God of justice who will reward the good and punish the bad at the end of the world. The Bible and the Churches encourage Christians to work for justice by campaigning for fair treatment for the poor, etc.

Topic 8.4.4a Why justice is important for Muslims

> O ye who believe! Stand out firmly for justice, as witnesses to God, even as against yourselves or your parents, or your kin, and whether it be against rich or poor.
>
> *Surah 4:135*

> And the firmament has He raised high, and He has set up the balance of justice in order that ye may not transgress.
>
> *Surah 55:7*

Justice is important for Muslims because:

▶ The Qur'an teaches that God is a just God who will reward the good and punish the bad on the Last Day; if Muslims do not work for justice, they may be sent to hell on the Last Day.

▶ Islamic teaching on the Last Day is concerned with the need for the good to be rewarded and the evil punished which is the basis of justice.

▶ Islam teaches that it is part of their role as vice-gerents of God's creation to behave justly to other people and to ensure that the world is governed in a fair way. For Islam, the way to do this is to follow the Shari'ah. Islam has always had a system of justice based on courts with strict rules about how everyone should be treated fairly.

▶ Islam teaches that it is unjust to be involved in the charging of interest because it takes money from the poor and gives it to the rich, whereas the just thing would be to take money from the rich and give it to the poor.

▶ Islam teaches that all people should have equal rights before the law and that Muslims should work for a fairer sharing of the Earth's resources. The **pillar of zakah** and the work of groups such as Muslim Aid and Islamic Relief are all trying to bring justice into the world.

Questions

b) Do you think religious people treat everyone fairly? Give two reasons for your point of view. **(4)**

c) Choose one religion other than Christianity and explain why justice is important for the followers of that religion. **(8)**

d) 'Non-religious people don't care as much about justice as religious people do.'

   In your answer, you should refer to at least one religion.

   (i) Do you agree? Give reasons for your opinion. **(3)**

   (ii) Give reasons why some people may disagree with you. **(3)**

Exam Tip

c) 'Explain why' means give reasons. One way to answer this question would be to state that you are choosing Islam and then use four reasons from this page to explain why justice is important for Muslims. Remember to use some specialist vocabulary such as: Qur'an, Last Day, hell, Islamic teaching, vice-gerent, creation, Shari'ah, equal rights, pillar of zakah, Muslim Aid, Islamic Relief.

Summary

Muslims believe in justice because the Qur'an says that God is just, and the Shari'ah says Muslims must work for justice through zakah if they are to go to heaven on the Last Day.

Topic 8.4.4b Why justice is important for Jews

Jews believe that justice is tremendously important because:

▶ God is just, and God created the world as a place of justice and so Jews must practise justice themselves.

▶ From the earliest times, Judaism has had a system of justice and courts based on the Torah. Jews have to live their lives according to the mitzvot (laws) of the Torah and so it has always been important for the courts to operate fairly and for everyone to be treated equally by the law.

▶ The Torah says that God is a God of justice and for Jewish people the Torah is the word of God.

▶ The Tenakh says that people should be treated fairly and not cheated and there are many statements in the Responsa about how Jews should treat people fairly and equally. Most Jews believe that they should work for a fairer sharing of the Earth's resources because God's justice applies to the whole world, not simply the Jewish people. Consequently, Jews are involved in groups such as Oxfam as well as World Jewish Relief.

▶ As part of their belief in justice, Jews have been very involved in the struggle for equal rights and the change of unjust laws. Many American Jews felt it was their duty to join the civil rights movement led by the Christian Martin Luther King, which campaigned for equal rights for black Americans in the 1960s. Anatoly Scharansky, a Jewish Soviet scientist, campaigned for human rights in the USSR.

> Seek good, not evil, that you may live. Then the LORD God Almighty will be with you, just as you say he is. Hate evil, love good; maintain justice in the courts.
>
> *Amos 5:14–15*

> The best way of giving charity is not to give charity, but to take the poor into business partnerships or lend them money so that they can improve their situation without any loss of self-respect.
>
> Jewish Values, *Maimonides*

Jewish people protesting for justice in Buenos Aires in July 2013.

Questions

b) Do you think religious people treat everyone fairly? Give two reasons for your point of view. **(4)**

c) Choose one religion other than Christianity and explain why justice is important for the followers of that religion. **(8)**

d) 'Non-religious people don't care as much about justice as religious people.'

In your answer, you should refer to at least one religion.

    (i) Do you agree? Give reasons for your opinion. **(3)**

    (ii) Give reasons why some people may disagree with you. **(3)**

Exam Tip

c) 'Explain why' means give reasons. One way to answer this question would be to state that you are choosing Judaism and then use four reasons from this page to explain why justice is important for Jewish people. Remember to use some specialist vocabulary such as: Torah, mitzvot, justice system, Tenakh, Responsa, World Jewish Relief, equal rights, civil rights movement.

Summary

Jews believe in justice because the Torah says God is a God of justice and the Tenakh encourages Jewish people to work for justice by working for fair shares for the poor.

Topic 8.4.4c Why justice is important for Hindus

> Who have all the powers of their soul in harmony, and the same loving mind for all; who find joy in the good of all beings – they reach in truth my very self.
>
> *Bhagavad Gita 12:4*

> May all be happy here;
>
> May all be free from disease.
>
> May all be righteous and without suffering.
>
> *Hindu prayer*

> If you happen to be in power as the chief of state executive, then live a righteous religious life, treat your subjects like members of your family, take good care of them and make an honest attempt to consolidate morality and religion in your state.
>
> *Shikshapatri of Lord Swaminarayan*

Justice is important for Hindus because:

▶ In order to gain moksha (liberation from rebirth) Hindus must perform dharma. These are religious, social and moral duties and are based on the idea of justice – the good will be rewarded and the evil punished through the process of samsara.

▶ Most Hindus believe that to gain moksha they must try to promote justice in terms of: treating all people as equals; making sure that there is freedom of religion; making sure that everyone has equal political rights.

▶ The Hindu scriptures, especially the Bhagavad Gita, encourage Hindus to be concerned for others and to work for justice which means that Hindus should work for a fairer sharing of wealth and the Earth's resources.

▶ The Hindu belief in ahimsa (non-violence) also encourages justice because the exploitation of the poor by the rich is a form of violence and ignores the truth that society can only be happy if all the members of that society have a basic standard of living.

▶ The great Hindu leader Mahatma Gandhi based his campaign for the independence of India from British rule on the Hindu idea of justice. He also developed the idea of sarvodaya (welfare for all) from the Hindu concept of justice. Gandhi's followers since independence have tried to put these beliefs into practice by campaigning for a fairer distribution of land and equal rights for dalits (people outside the caste system) and women.

▶ Hindu gurus and swamis teach that people's souls are improved if they treat other people justly.

Questions

b) Do you think religious people treat everyone fairly? Give two reasons for your point of view. **(4)**

c) Choose one religion other than Christianity and explain why justice is important for the followers of that religion. **(8)**

d) 'Non-religious people don't care as much about justice as religious people.'

In your answer, you should refer to at least one religion.

   (i) Do you agree? Give reasons for your opinion. **(3)**

   (ii) Give reasons why some people may disagree with you. **(3)**

Summary

Justice is important for Hindus because it is the basis of beliefs in dharma and samsara. Many Hindus believe they should work for justice because this cleans their soul so they can gain moksha.

Exam Tip

c) 'Explain why' means give reasons. One way to answer this question would be to state that you are choosing Hinduism and then use four reasons from this page to explain why justice is important for Hindus. Remember to use some specialist vocabulary such as: dharma, moksha, samsara, freedom of religion, equal political rights, Bhagavad Gita, Earth's resources, ahimsa, Mahatma Gandhi, sarvodaya, equal rights, dalits, gurus, swamis.

Topic 8.4.4d Why justice is important for Sikhs

Justice is important for Sikhs because:

▶ The Guru Granth Sahib teaches that justice is an attribute of God. God is just and is the source of all justice. Sikhs believe that the justice of God is perfect. It is always and forever true.

▶ According to Sikh thought it is the right of people to get justice, and so it is the duty of Sikhs to bring God's justice into the world.

▶ Sikhs believe that human beings are imperfect and their justice is imperfect. Often it is not impartial, but weighted in favour of those in higher economic or social positions. The favoured few often escape punishment, as they have the resources or education to take advantage of loopholes or technicalities. Sikhs believe this is wrong and that Sikhs should work to bring God's justice into the world.

▶ The Rahit Maryada teaches that Sikhs should work for justice. They do this by obeying the law, working for groups which are trying to give equal rights to the poor and working for groups like Amnesty International.

▶ Sikhism teaches that while unjust people can escape the human judge, they cannot escape from the Court of God. At the end of people's lives, God will give full justice to everyone.

▶ All the Gurus worked for justice and Sikhs should follow their example.

Guru Nanak criticised corrupt judges (kazi) who take away the right to justice and sell it to the unjust rich: Kazi sits as a judge, He tells rosary and mutters God's Name. Taking bribe he usurps the right to justice (and does injustice).

Adi Granth

One can run away from man's court; but where is one to go if one runs away from the Lord?

Adi Granth

Thou hast created the Throne to Adjudicate truly.

Adi Granth

Questions

b) Do you think religious people treat everyone fairly? Give two reasons for your point of view. **(4)**

c) Choose one religion other than Christianity and explain why justice is important for the followers of that religion. **(8)**

d) 'Non-religious people don't care as much about justice as religious people.'

In your answer, you should refer to at least one religion.

    (i) Do you agree? Give reasons for your opinion. **(3)**

    (ii) Give reasons why some people may disagree with you. **(3)**

Exam Tip

c) 'Explain why' means give reasons. One way to answer this question would be to state that you are choosing Sikhism and then use four reasons from this page to explain why justice is important for Sikhs. Remember to use some specialist vocabulary such as: Guru Granth Sahib, people's rights, technicalities, favoured few, Rahit Maryada, equal rights, Amnesty International, Court of God, Gurus.

Summary

Justice is important for Sikhs because it is taught in the Guru Granth Sahib and all the Gurus worked for justice. Sikhism teaches that God is just and justice comes from God. The Rahit Maryada teaches that it is the duty of Sikhs to work for justice and remove injustice.

Topic 8.4.5 The nature of capital punishment and non-religious arguments about capital punishment

In 2013, 76 year old Ian Brady lost his battle to be transferred from the maximum-security Ashworth Psychiatric Hospital to a mainstream prison. Brady has insisted he wants to die ever since he went on hunger strike 14 years ago. Brady is currently force-fed at Ashworth and had hoped that at a normal prison he would be allowed to waste away. However, a mental health tribunal recently decided he should remain at Ashworth.

Despite the failure of his appeal, Brady maintains he still wishes to die and will refuse any life-sustaining treatment. Brady and Myra Hindley tortured and murdered five children and buried them on Saddleworth Moor in the 1960s.

Adapted from various news sources, February 2014

Capital punishment is punishment which takes away the criminal's life. This process of judicial killing is called 'execution' or 'the death penalty'. A crime which can be punished by the death penalty is called 'a capital offence'.

In the past, offences such as sheep stealing were capital offences, but gradually the number of capital offences was reduced until only murder was a capital offence. In December 1969, the United Kingdom abolished the death penalty as a form of punishment. There have been debates in Parliament since 1970 on the re-introduction of capital punishment, which have all been defeated.

Non-religious arguments in favour of capital punishment

Those who believe that murder and terrorism should be punished by the death penalty often use the following arguments:

This is the house in Gloucester where Fred West and his wife murdered at least eleven people. He hanged himself in prison whilst serving a life sentence. Does this show that life imprisonment is more of a deterrent than capital punishment?

- If people know they will lose their life if they murder someone, it will act as a deterrent and there will be fewer murders.
- Murderers and terrorists are a great threat to society, and the best way to protect society from them is to take away their lives so they cannot re-offend.
- Human life is the most important thing there is and the value of human life can only be shown by giving those who take human life the worst possible punishment, which is the death penalty.

▶ Retribution and/or compensation are major parts of punishment and the only retribution/compensation for taking a life is for the criminal's life to be taken.

Non-religious arguments against capital punishment

Those who disagree with the death penalty often use the following arguments:

▶ No court system can be sure that the correct verdict is always given. People are sometimes convicted for offences which it is later proved they did not commit. Such innocent people can be released and compensated if they have been given life imprisonment, but not if they have been executed.

▶ The statistics of countries with the death penalty and those without the death penalty show that, if anything, those countries which do not use the death penalty have a lower murder rate, showing that capital punishment does not deter.

▶ Many murderers do not expect to be caught and so do not think about the punishment.

▶ Murderers who know they are going to be killed if caught are more likely to kill more people to avoid being caught.

▶ Terrorists who are executed are hailed as martyrs, encouraging more of their followers to become terrorists.

▶ Human life is the most important thing there is, so no one has the right to take it. Executing murderers demonstrates that society does not regard human life as sacred.

▶ Murderers often regard life imprisonment as worse than the death penalty, as they try to commit suicide (for example, Harold Shipman and Ian Brady).

"MAYBE THIS WILL TEACH YOU THAT IT'S MORALLY WRONG TO KILL PEOPLE!"

www.cartoonstock.com

Questions

b) Do you think capital punishment is right? Give two reasons for your point of view. **(4)**

c) Explain why some non-religious people agree with capital punishment and why some disagree with capital punishment. **(8)**

d) 'Capital punishment is a fair punishment.'
   In your answer, you should refer to at least one religion.
   (i) Do you agree? Give reasons for your opinion. **(3)**
   (ii) Give reasons why some people may disagree with you. **(3)**

Exam Tip

b) You should already have thought about this, and you just have to give two reasons for your opinion. For example, if you think capital punishment is right, you should use two reasons for why some people agree with capital punishment.

Summary

Capital punishment is punishment which takes the life of the criminal. Some people think it is a good idea because it takes a life for a life and deters people from murdering others. Some people think it is a bad punishment because there is evidence that it does not deter and trial mistakes can lead to innocent people being killed for crimes they did not commit.

Topic 8.4.6 Different attitudes to capital punishment among Christians

The Laws of the Realm may punish Christian men with death for heinous and grievous offences.

Article 37 of the Thirty Nine Articles of the Church of England

You have heard that it was said, 'Eye for eye, and tooth for tooth.' But I tell you, Do not resist an evil person. If someone strikes you on the right cheek, turn to him the other also.

Matthew 5:38-39

But if a man hates his neighbour and lies in wait for him, assaults and kills him, and then flees to one of these cities, the elders of his town shall send for him, bring him back from the city, and hand him over to the avenger of blood to die. Show him no pity. You must purge from Israel the guilt of shedding innocent blood, so that it may go well with you.

Deuteronomy 19:11-13

There are different attitudes among Christians towards capital punishment.

Many Christians believe that capital punishment is un-Christian and can never be justified. They feel that Christians should never be involved in capital punishment and should campaign against its use. They believe this because:

◗ Christianity is based on the belief that Jesus came to save (reform) sinners. It is impossible to reform a criminal who has been executed.
◗ Jesus banned retribution when he said that an eye for an eye and a tooth for a tooth is wrong. For Christians, the law of the New Testament has replaced the law of the Old Testament which permits capital punishment.
◗ Christianity teaches that human life is sacred and that only God has the right to take life. If abortion and euthanasia are wrong, then the death penalty must be wrong.
◗ Most of the Christian Churches have condemned capital punishment, and even those which have not, such as the Roman Catholic Church, have groups of leaders which have condemned it, such as the Catholic Bishops Conference of the USA.

Such Christians would also use all the non-religious arguments against capital punishment.

10 Rillington Place, London. Timothy Evans was executed in 1950 for murders which took place here, but it was later proved that he did not commit them. Would he have been released if the murders had happened after 1970?

Some Christians believe that capital punishment can be used by Christians as the best way of preventing murder and keeping order in society. They believe this because:

▶ The Bible sets down the death penalty as the punishment for a number of crimes, so it is allowed by God.

▶ The Roman Catholic Church and the Church of England have not retracted their statements which permit the state to use capital punishment.

▶ The Christian Church itself used capital punishment in the past for the crime of heresy (holding beliefs different from official Church teachings). This means that capital punishment cannot be un-Christian.

▶ Christian thinkers such as Thomas Aquinas argued that punishment in Christianity should reform the sinner and secure peace for society. He said that the peace of society is more important than the reform of the sinner, and that Christians can therefore use capital punishment to preserve the peace of society.

A prisoner is led to her execution in Beijing immediately after being sentenced to death. Should Christians approve of this?

Such Christians would also use all the non-religious arguments in favour of capital punishment.

> The topic of capital punishment has become, in recent decades, a contentious and increasingly confusing one among Catholics. Some Catholics insist the Church has finally—and authoritatively—renounced the death penalty. Some argue further that the death penalty is no different than abortion or euthanasia, and that supporting any of these acts rends the "seamless garment" of Church teaching regarding the dignity and value of life. And not a few go so far as to say that no one deserves the death penalty, for it is cruel and unusual punishment not fit to be supported by Christians.
>
> *Catholic World Report, March 2012*

> Do not repay anyone evil for evil. Be careful to do what is right in the eyes of everybody ... Do not take revenge, my friends, but leave room for God's wrath, for it is written: 'It is mine to revenge; I will repay, says the Lord.'
>
> *Romans 12:17–19*

Questions

b) Do you think Christians should support capital punishment? Give two reasons for your point of view. **(4)**

c) Explain why some Christians agree with capital punishment and why some disagree with capital punishment. **(8)**

d) 'You can't be a good Christian and support capital punishment.' In your answer, you should refer to Christianity.

    (i) Do you agree? Give reasons for your opinion. **(3)**

    (ii) Give reasons why some people may disagree with you. **(3)**

Exam Tip

d) Use the technique for answering evaluation questions on page 111. Arguments for could come from why some Christians are against capital punishment. Arguments against could come from why some Christians support capital punishment.

Summary

Many Christians think capital punishment is wrong because of the teachings of Jesus.

Some Christians agree with capital punishment to keep order in society because it is the teaching of the Church.

Topic 8.4.7a Different attitudes to capital punishment in Islam

> Take not life – which God has made sacred – except for just cause.
>
> *Surah 17:33*

Why might some Muslim states allow execution by stoning?

Most Muslims agree with capital punishment because:

▶ It is a punishment set down by God in the Qur'an and Muslims believe the Qur'an is the word of God.
▶ Muhammad made several statements agreeing with capital punishment for murder, adultery and apostasy, and Muslims believe that Muhammad is the seal of the prophets whose words should be obeyed.
▶ Muhammad sentenced people to death for murder when he was ruler of Madinah and Muslims believe Muhammad is the final exemplar whose example should be followed.
▶ The Shari'ah says that capital punishment is the punishment for murder, adultery and apostasy, and Muslims are expected to follow the holy law of Islam.

Some Muslims do not agree with capital punishment because:

▶ They feel that capital punishment is recommended by the Qur'an, but is not compulsory.
▶ The Shari'ah says that the family of a murder victim can accept blood money from the murderer rather than requiring the death sentence.
▶ They agree with the non-religious arguments against capital punishment (see Topic 8.4.5).

Questions

b) Do you think religious people should support capital punishment? Give two reasons for your point of view. **(4)**

c) Choose one religion other than Christianity and explain why some of its followers support capital punishment. **(8)**

d) 'You can't be religious and support capital punishment.'

In your answer, you should refer to at least one religion.

   (i) Do you agree? Give reasons for your opinion. **(3)**

   (ii) Give reasons why some people may disagree with you. **(3)**

Exam Tip

c) 'Explain why' means give reasons. One way to answer this question would be to state that you are choosing Islam and then use four reasons from this page to explain why some Muslims support capital punishment. Remember to use some specialist vocabulary such as: adultery, apostasy, Shari'ah, Qur'an, Muhammad, seal of the prophets, Madinah, final exemplar, holy law of Islam.

Summary

Most Muslims agree with capital punishment because it is the punishment given for certain crimes in the Qur'an. Some Muslims do not agree with capital punishment, because it is not compulsory in the Shari'ah, and for non-religious reasons.

Topic 8.4.7b Different attitudes to capital punishment in Judaism

Most Jews believe that capital punishment is acceptable, but should be used only as a last resort and with severe restrictions. Murderers who will not pose a threat to society should not be executed as they have a potential to reform. However, those who are likely to murder again should be executed to protect society. Jews believe this because:

▶ The Torah says that capital punishment should be used for certain offences.
▶ The Talmud says that capital punishment is allowed, but only if the murderer has been warned of the consequences of their action or there are two independent witnesses to the murder.
▶ The basis of the Jewish theory of punishment is the protection of society, and so capital punishment should be used if a convicted criminal is a threat to society or if capital punishment will deter people from becoming a danger to society.

Some Jews do not believe in capital punishment because:

▶ The **Mishnah** says that a **Bet Din** that executed a person once in 70 years was a destructive Bet Din.
▶ They believe the teachings of the Torah and Tenakh need updating and do not apply to today because of the non-religious arguments against capital punishment (see Topic 8.4.5).

> If anyone takes the life of a human being, he must be put to death. Anyone who takes the life of someone's animal must make restitution – life for life.
>
> *Leviticus 24:17-18*

A Bet Din. Should a Jewish court condemn a terrorist to death?

Questions

b) Do you think religious people should support capital punishment? Give two reasons for your point of view. **(4)**

c) Choose one religion other than Christianity and explain why some of its followers support capital punishment. **(8)**

d) 'You can't be religious and support capital punishment.'

In your answer, you should refer to at least one religion.

  (i) Do you agree? Give reasons for your opinion. **(3)**

  (ii) Give reasons why some people may disagree with you. **(3)**

Exam Tip

c) 'Explain why' means give reasons. One way to answer this question would be to state that you are choosing Judaism and then use the three reasons from this page and the Leviticus quote to explain why some Jewish people support capital punishment. Remember to use some specialist vocabulary such as: Torah, offences, Talmud, Leviticus, restitution, protection, deter, convicted, criminal.

Summary

Most Jews agree with capital punishment because it is approved by the Torah, and they think it will deter criminals. Some Jews think capital punishment is wrong because of what the Mishnah says.

Topic 8.4.7c Different attitudes to capital punishment in Hinduism

Most Hindus believe that capital punishment can, and should, be used for convicted murderers. They believe that the death penalty both deters criminals and protects the order of society. They believe this because:

▶ The Vedas say that ahimsa does not apply to enemies in war or criminals, so both can be lawfully killed.

▶ The Law of Manu says that it is permitted for a Hindu to kill someone to prevent something worse happening or to maintain social order. This is taken to mean that the execution of murderers is permitted to maintain social order.

▶ The **Varaha Purana** says that a king may put a criminal to death to restore the correct dharma to society.

Such Hindus would also use the non-religious arguments in favour of capital punishment.

Some Hindus do not believe in capital punishment because:

▶ They believe execution is killing and will therefore give bad karma and delay moksha.

▶ They believe Gandhi's teaching that ahimsa means no violence to anyone, even murderers, and so they also accept the non-religious arguments against capital punishment (see Topic 8.4.5).

Questions

b) Do you think religious people should support capital punishment? Give two reasons for your point of view. **(4)**

c) Choose one religion other than Christianity and explain why some of its followers support capital punishment. **(8)**

d) 'You can't be religious and support capital punishment.'

In your answer, you should refer to at least one religion.

   (i) Do you agree? Give reasons for your opinion. **(3)**

   (ii) Give reasons why some people may disagree with you. **(3)**

Exam Tip

c) 'Explain why' means give reasons. One way to answer this question would be to state that you are choosing Hinduism and then use the three reasons from this page plus a non-religious reason to explain why some Hindus support capital punishment. Remember to use some specialist vocabulary such as: Vedas, criminals, Laws of Manu, social order, Varaha Purana, correct dharma.

Summary

Most Hindus believe capital punishment should be used for murderers because that is the teaching of the Law of Manu. Some Hindus disagree with capital punishment because of the teachings of Gandhi and non-religious arguments.

Topic 8.4.7d Different attitudes to capital punishment in Sikhism

Most Sikhs are opposed to capital punishment because:

▶ The Sikh religion lays great stress on the divine dignity of human beings. If all human beings have divine dignity, none should be executed.

▶ There is no clear instruction on capital punishment in the Guru Granth Sahib, and capital punishment is so serious that if it were allowed for Sikhs the holy book would say so.

▶ The Ten Gurus appear to have been against capital punishment and Sikhs should follow the teachings and examples of the Gurus.

▶ Executing a prisoner would be 'killing in cold blood' which is banned by Sikhism.

▶ They agree with the non-religious arguments against capital punishment (see Topic 8.4.5).

Thousands of Sikhs gathered at the Manukau Square in Auckland, New Zealand, on 25 March to protest against the death sentence awarded by an Indian court to a fellow Sikh.

Some Sikhs agree with capital punishment because there is no specific Sikh teaching on capital punishment, so it cannot be wrong and they agree with the non-religious arguments for capital punishment (see Topic 8.4.5).

Questions

b) Do you think religious people should support capital punishment? Give two reasons for your point of view. **(4)**

c) Choose one religion other than Christianity and explain why some of its followers support capital punishment. **(8)**

d) 'You can't be religious and support capital punishment.'

In your answer, you should refer to at least one religion.

   (i) Do you agree? Give reasons for your opinion. **(3)**

   (ii) Give reasons why some people may disagree with you. **(3)**

Exam Tip

c) 'Explain why' means give reasons. One way to answer this question would be to state that you are choosing Sikhism and then use the one reason from this page and three non-religious reasons from Topic 8.4.5 to explain why some Sikhs support capital punishment. Remember to use some specialist vocabulary such as: Guru Granth Sahib, Rahit Maryada, protection, re-offend, deterrent, retribution, compensation.

Summary

Most Sikhs are opposed to capital punishment because there are Sikh teachings against killing in cold blood. Some Sikhs agree with capital punishment because there are no clear instructions in the scriptures about it.

Topic 8.4.8 The laws on drugs and alcohol

Tobacco companies are using increasingly sophisticated marketing techniques to circumvent the law and promote their brands to young people, according to health experts. Cigarette advertising is banned in the EU, but wily tobacco giants are increasingly targeting young people through social networking sites such as Facebook and at major music festivals to create a 'buzz' around their products ... Several of the UK's biggest festivals have allowed tobacco firms to sell their products on site in ways that have been condemned by health experts. This weekend's Lovebox festival in east London's Victoria Park, headlined by Roxy Music, is co-sponsored by Imperial Tobacco's Rizla rolling paper, which is exempt from the ban on tobacco advertising ... 'the tobacco industry needs to recruit new young smokers as their existing customers either quit or die,' said Deborah Arnott, Chief Executive of Ash.

Jamie Doward, The Observer, 18 July 2010

In the UK there are laws on tobacco, alcohol and illegal drugs. These laws are in place to minimise the social and health problems drugs and alcohol cause. This topic looks at the laws and Topic 8.4.9 goes on to look at the reasons for them.

UK laws on tobacco

▶ It is illegal to sell tobacco products (cigarettes, cigars, roll-up tobacco and papers, etc.) to anyone under the age of eighteen.
▶ All tobacco packs must have large, hard-hitting health warnings and are not allowed to show misleading terms such as low-tar, mild and light. They must also carry shocking picture warnings on the effects of smoking.
▶ All adverts for tobacco products are banned, as is tobacco companies sponsoring events.
▶ It is against the law to smoke in all indoor public places and workplaces. It is also banned in substantially enclosed public places such as football grounds and all parts of railway stations, including open air platforms.
▶ Since 6 April 2012 it has been illegal to display tobacco products at the point of sale in large stores, such as supermarkets.
▶ You can be given a £50 on the spot litter fine for dropping a cigarette end.

UK laws on alcohol

▶ It is illegal to give an alcoholic drink to a child under five except under medical supervision in an emergency.
▶ Children under sixteen can go anywhere in a pub as long as they are supervised by an adult, but cannot have any alcoholic drinks. However, some premises may be subject to licensing conditions preventing them from entering, such as pubs which have experienced problems with underage drinking.
▶ Young people aged sixteen or seventeen can drink beer, wine or cider with a meal, if it is bought by an adult and they are accompanied by an adult. It is illegal for this age group to drink spirits in pubs even with a meal.
▶ It is against the law for anyone under eighteen to buy alcohol in a pub, off-licence, supermarket, or other outlet, or for anyone to buy alcohol for someone under eighteen to consume in a pub without a meal or in a public place.
▶ Some towns and cities have local by-laws banning drinking alcohol in public.

Do you think adverts like these will stop people smoking?

UK laws on illegal drugs

The different kinds of illegal drugs are divided into three different categories or classes. These classes (A, B and C) carry different levels of penalty for possession and dealing.

Class	Example	Penalty for possession	Penalty for dealing
A	Ecstasy, LSD, heroin, cocaine, crack, magic mushrooms, amphetamines (if prepared for injection)	Seven years in prison or an unlimited fine (or both)	Up to life in prison
B	Amphetamines, Cannabis, Methylphenidate (Ritalin), Pholcodine	Up to five years in prison or an unlimited fine (or both)	Up to fourteen years in prison
C	Tranquilisers, some painkillers, Gamma hydroxybutyrate (GHB), Ketamine	Up to two years in prison or an unlimited fine (or both)	Up to fourteen years in prison

Class A, B and C drugs are termed as controlled substances under the Misuse of Drugs Act 1971, which states that it is an offence to:

▶ possess a controlled substance unlawfully
▶ possess a controlled substance with intent
▶ supply or offer to supply a controlled drug (even where no charge is made for the drug)
▶ allow premises you occupy or manage to be used for the purpose of drug taking.

To enforce this law the police have special powers to stop, detain and search people under the 'reasonable suspicion' that they are in possession of a controlled drug.

Mike Barton, Durham's Chief Constable and one of Britain's most senior police officers, has suggested that Class A drugs should be decriminalised. He claimed that giving addicts access to drugs via the NHS would stop them having to access drugs via criminal gangs, thereby reducing the power and influence of these gangs. Mr Barton compared the effects of outlawing Class A drugs to the effects of Prohibition in the USA in the 1920s when he said, 'The Mob's sinister rise to prominence in the US was pretty much funded through its supply of a prohibited drug, alcohol. That's arguably what we are doing in the UK.'

Adapted from various news sources, September 2013

Questions

b) Do you think the laws on drugs and alcohol are fair? Give two reasons for your point of view. **(4)**

c) Explain why it is a good idea to have nothing to do with Class A drugs. **(8)**

d) 'The laws on alcohol and tobacco should be the same as those on Class A drugs.'
   In your answer, you should refer to at least one religion.
   (i) Do you agree? Give reasons for your opinion. **(3)**
   (ii) Give reasons why some people may disagree with you. **(3)**
   (You need information from Topic 8.4.9 to answer this question.)

Exam Tip

b) You should already have thought about this, and you just have to give two reasons for your opinion. For example, if you think they are not fair, you should refer to two laws and say what you think is wrong with each one.

Summary

The law bans smoking in public and workplaces and says tobacco products cannot be sold to under-eighteens. Alcohol cannot be sold to under-eighteens, or drunk by under-fives. All classified drugs are illegal. Class A drugs (such as heroin and cocaine) have the most severe penalties.

Topic 8.4.9 Social and health problems caused by drugs and alcohol

KEY WORDS

Addiction – a recurring compulsion to engage in an activity regardless of its bad effects

Responsibility – being responsible for one's actions

What was once seen by many in developing countries as the disease of industrialised nations is now a worldwide trend. Alcohol alone contributed to 27 per cent of all deaths involving 15 to 29-year-olds in economically developed countries in 2002, and illicit drugs a further four per cent.

The Lancet, *27 March 2007*

Drugs and alcohol are controlled by law because it is assumed that people have a **responsibility** to control anti-social behaviour (which drugs and alcohol can encourage).

Health problems caused by tobacco

- Smoking increases the risk of at least 50 medical conditions including dementia and digestive problems.
- Some conditions that can be caused by smoking are: various cancers, coronary heart disease, stroke, chronic bronchitis and emphysema.
- In men, smoking can also cause impotence as it limits the blood supply to the penis. It can also affect men's fertility.
- If women smoke during pregnancy their baby is likely to have a lower birth weight, be weaker and not develop normally.
- Smoking during pregnancy also increases the chances of complications during pregnancy and labour, including the risk of premature birth and stillbirth.

Health problems caused by alcohol

Your liver and body can usually cope with drinking a small amount of alcohol. However, if you drink heavily you have an increased risk of developing:

- serious liver problems
- some stomach disorders
- mental health problems
- sexual difficulties such as impotence
- heart disease
- some cancers
- obesity (alcohol has many calories)
- alcohol dependence (addiction).

Drinking alcohol is also associated with a much increased risk of accidents. About one in seven road deaths is caused by drink driving.

What are the potential effects from these women's binge drinking?

Health problems caused by drugs

- The physical health of users can be damaged by the toxic effects of a drug, dependence, or the way it is used (such as infection with a dirty needle).
- Many deaths of drug users are caused by bacterial or viral infections, liver or cardiovascular diseases or intentional self-harm.
- Heavy users often have psychiatric illnesses, although it may be difficult to establish which came first.

Social problems caused by drugs and alcohol

Tobacco

The social problems caused by tobacco use mainly relate to the families of smokers who are caused great upset by watching their loved ones die slowly from diseases that could have been prevented if they had never smoked.

Alcohol

Alcohol causes many social problems as can be seen in any UK town centre on Friday and Saturday evenings when binge drinkers often make them no-go areas for anyone else.

However, research shows that alcohol is also responsible for numerous crimes and fatalities:

- 41 per cent of all deaths from falls, 30 per cent of drowning deaths, 25 per cent of boating deaths, and 45–55 per cent of fire fatalities involve alcohol consumption
- 55–75 per cent of murder victims and 40 per cent of rape offenders had been drinking at the time of the incident
- 50 per cent of those who commit sex abuse crimes also abuse alcohol.

Illegal drugs

The main social problems caused by drug abuse are connected with the fact that drugs are illegal and so all drug dealers are criminals. This leads to violence between different criminal gangs operating the transport and supply of drugs. Another major problem is that the heavy cost of maintaining a heroin or cocaine habit forces users into a life of crime. An addict may need upwards of £50 a day to fund their addiction, an amount of money they have no hope of finding legally. Although no drug consistently produces violence, some users become violent under a drug's influence.

Nevertheless, statistics show that the use of illegal drugs is falling. In 1998, 12.1 per cent of adults admitted to using illegal drugs in the past year, but this had fallen to 10.5 per cent in 2006, and 8.2% in 2013.

- Alcohol is 45 per cent more affordable than it was in 1980.
- Average alcohol consumption has gradually fallen in many OECD countries between 1980 and 2009 with an average overall decrease of 9 per cent. The UK however, has seen an increase of over 9 per cent in these three decades.
- There were 1.2 million alcohol-related hospital admissions in England in the year 2011/12, a 135 per cent increase since 2002/03.
- Over 36 children or young people per day are admitted to hospital in England for alcohol-related conditions.

Source: Alcohol Concern

Questions

b) Do you think using drugs always hurts people? Give two reasons for your point of view. **(4)**

c) Explain why some people think alcohol is the worst drug. **(8)**

d) 'Using drugs doesn't harm anyone.'
   (i) Do you agree? Give reasons for your opinion. **(3)**
   (ii) Give reasons why some people may disagree with you. **(3)**

Exam Tip

d) Use the technique for answering evaluation questions on page 111. Arguments for could come from the effects of small amounts of drugs and/or alcohol. Arguments against could come from the health and social effects of drug abuse.

Summary

Smoking can cause many bad health effects and deaths which cause problems for families, employers, etc. Alcohol causes many health problems such as liver disease and alcoholism. It also causes major social problems as people behave violently and irrationally when drunk. Drug abuse can cause addiction and death. It also causes criminal gang problems and stealing to fund the habit.

Topic 8.4.10 Different attitudes to drugs and alcohol in Christianity

> Do you not know that your body is a temple of the Holy Spirit, who is in you, whom you have received from God? You are not your own; you were bought at a price. Therefore honour God with your body.
>
> *1 Corinthians 6:19–20*

> The drinking of alcohol, but not drunkenness, is affirmed in scripture. The Church of England does not then advocate total abstinence herself, but calls for moderate drinking and points to the effects of drunkenness in marital violence and crime.
>
> *From* What the Churches Say, *third edition*

All Christians are against illegal drug usage because:

▶ It is against the law for good reasons, and Christians should obey the law as long as it is just.

▶ St Paul taught in 1 Corinthians 6:19–20 that a Christian's body is a temple of the Holy Spirit which should not be abused, and taking drugs is abusing God's temple.

▶ Taking drugs has mental effects which make it difficult to worship God properly or follow the Christian way of life.

▶ All the Christian Churches teach that the use of illegal drugs is wrong: 'The General Synod (of the Church of England), in a recent debate, deplored the destructive effects of drugs on individuals and communities' (from *What the Churches Say*, third edition).

There are two different attitudes to tobacco and alcohol among Christians.

Most Christians believe that the correct approach to alcohol and tobacco is moderation because:

▶ The first miracle that Jesus performed was at the wedding feast in Cana where he changed water into wine (John 2:1–11), so he must have approved of drinking alcohol.

▶ St Paul said that Christians could drink in moderation: 'Stop drinking only water, and use a little wine because of your stomach ...' (1 Timothy 5:23)

▶ Jesus drank wine during his life and even at his death. 'A jar of wine vinegar was there, so they soaked a sponge in it, put the sponge on a stalk of the hyssop plant, and lifted it to Jesus' lips. When he had received the drink, Jesus said, "It is finished." With that, he bowed his head and gave up his spirit.' (John 19:29–30)

▶ Jesus used bread and wine at his Last Supper and told his disciples to continue the tradition: 'This cup is the new covenant in my blood; do this, whenever you drink it, in remembrance of me.' (Jesus' words at the Last Supper according to St Paul in 1 Corinthians 11.)

▶ Most Churches use alcoholic wine in their communion services, so Christians must be able to drink wine in moderation.

▶ Moderation is the teaching of the Catholic Church in the Catechism: 'The virtue of temperance disposes us to avoid every kind of excess: the abuse of food, alcohol, tobacco or medicine.' (Catechism of the Catholic Church 2290)

Some Christians (especially Pentecostals, members of the Salvation Army and many Methodists) believe in total abstinence. This means they do not drink alcoholic beverages, and they do not smoke because:

▶ These Christians believe that taking tobacco or alcohol is abusing God's temple just as much as taking drugs.

- There are passages in the Bible warning against drunkenness which they consider sufficient reason for advocating complete abstinence from the use of alcohol, tobacco, or narcotics. For example, Noah's drunkenness brought shame to his family (Genesis 9:20–27), Lot's drunkenness resulted in an incestuous relationship with his two daughters (Genesis 19:30–38).
- The Bible also teaches that consumption of alcohol impairs judgement, inflames passions and invites violence (Leviticus 10:8–11; Proverbs 20:1, 23:29–35, 31:4–5).
- They are also concerned about the social and health problems connected with the use of tobacco and alcohol, and feel that Christians should set an example of a good and healthy lifestyle by abstaining from them.
- Many of these Christians are involved in working with alcoholics and know how much it helps in social situations if they are supported by others who refuse to have alcoholic drinks (recovering alcoholics cannot have even the smallest amount of alcohol).

> To argue for any level of 'moderate use' of alcohol, narcotics, or tobacco is to be insensitive to the weight of scripture and the present perils of our society. Christians realise the pressing need for a pure testimony before our world. As the apostle Paul said, 'I urge you … in view of God's mercy, to offer your bodies as living sacrifices, holy and pleasing to God – this is your spiritual act of worship. Do not conform any longer to the pattern of this world, but be transformed by the renewing of your mind. Then you will be able to test and approve what God's will is – his good, pleasing and perfect will.' (Romans 12:1, 2).
>
> *Statement from the official website of the Holiness Churches and Assemblies of God (Pentecostals)*

Questions

b) Do you think Christians should drink alcohol? Give two reasons for your point of view. **(4)**

c) Explain why some Christians drink alcohol, but others do not. **(8)**

d) 'You can still be a good Christian and drink alcohol.'

In your answer, you should refer to Christianity.

    (i) Do you agree? Give reasons for your opinion. **(3)**

    (ii) Give reasons why some people may disagree with you. **(3)**

Exam Tip

c) 'Explain why' means give reasons. One way to answer this question would be to use two reasons from the opposite page to explain why most Christians allow the drinking of alcohol in moderation and two reasons from this page to explain why some Christians believe in total abstinence. Remember to use some specialist vocabulary such as: Jesus, wedding at Cana, St Paul, moderation, Last Supper, new covenant, Pentecostals, Methodist, Bible, Noah, Lot, judgement.

Summary

All Christians are against drugs because they are illegal and abuse the body which is God's temple. Most Christians accept the use of alcohol and tobacco in moderation because this is the teaching of the Church. Jesus drank wine and wine is used for communion in many churches. Some Christians believe they should not touch wine or tobacco because of their harmful social and health effects and because the Bible shows concern for the harmful effects of alcohol.

Topic 8.4.11a Attitudes to drugs and alcohol in Islam

> O ye who believe! Intoxicants and gambling, dedication of stones and divination by arrows are an abomination, of Satan's handiwork; eschew such abominations that ye may prosper. Satan's plan is to excite enmity and hatred between you with intoxicants and gambling, and hinder you from the remembrance of God, and from prayer: Will ye not abstain?
>
> *Surah 5: 93–94*

Should Muslims protest about the use of alcohol in non-Muslim societies?

Islam teaches that alcohol and drugs are prohibited for Muslims (haram) because:

▶ The Qur'an says in Surah 5:93–94 that intoxicants are a means by which Satan tries to keep people from God and from saying their prayers and so Muslims should abstain from them.
▶ The Prophet Muhammad said that every intoxicant (anything which clouds the mind or changes perception and reasoning) is khamr and every khamr is forbidden to Muslims.
▶ Islam forbids its followers from committing suicide, and Muslim lawyers equate taking drugs or alcohol as a form of suicide because you are harming your body.
▶ Muslim lawyers take Muhammad's statement 'Do not harm yourselves or others' to mean that alcohol and all illegal drugs are forbidden because they all harm the body.
▶ Muhammad said on several occasions that not only must Muslims not drink alcohol, they must have nothing to do with the production or sale of alcohol.

Tobacco is regarded as haram by some Muslims because it harms the body, but Muslim lawyers have declared that tobacco is makruh (not haram but extremely disliked) because it is not specifically mentioned by either the Qur'an or Muhammad.

Questions

b) Do you think religious people should run shops selling alcohol? Give two reasons for your point of view. **(4)**

c) Explain the attitudes to alcohol consumption in one religion other than Christianity. **(8)**

d) 'You can't be religious and sell alcohol and tobacco.'

In your answer, you should refer to at least one religion.

   (i) Do you agree? Give reasons for your opinion. **(3)**

   (ii) Give reasons why some people may disagree with you. **(3)**

Exam Tip

c) When there are different views on an issue depending on the religion you choose, you may get a question phrased in this way. 'Explaining an attitude' just means giving the reasons why a religion has this attitude. To answer this question you should say you are answering on Islam and then use four reasons from this page to explain why Islam does not allow the drinking of alcohol. Remember to use some specialist vocabulary such as: Qur'an, Surah, Prophet Muhammad, Satan, khamr, intoxicants, Muslim lawyers.

Summary

Islam forbids the use of drugs or alcohol because they are banned in the Qur'an and in the hadith of the Prophet and they cause much harm.

Tobacco is disapproved of, but not banned.

Topic 8.4.11b Attitudes to drugs and alcohol in Judaism

All Jewish people are against the use of illegal drugs because:

▶ The Torah teaches that a youth who steals meat and wine from his father and gobbles it down should be put to death because he is addicted to physical pleasures, and will do anything to support his habit, even rob and kill. The same is true of drugs, and so drugs are banned in Judaism.

▶ Using drugs leads to a lack of the concentration needed to pray, fulfil mitzvot and learn the Torah properly.

▶ Parents are usually distressed by a child's drug usage, so using drugs stops children from honouring their parents.

▶ The Torah says, 'You shall be holy' which the rabbis take to mean that Jewish people should not take drugs.

Since the discoveries of the effects of smoking on health, Jewish people are advised not to smoke because the mitzvah to be holy means not to do things which harm the health of your body.

Most Jewish people believe that the correct approach to alcohol is moderation because:

▶ The Tenakh speaks in praise of wine as a substance that 'gladdens the human heart', and Judaism ordains special blessings to be recited prior to and following its consumption, just as it does for bread.

▶ The use of wine is required in such ritual practices as Kiddush (blessing of the wine at Shabbat and festivals).

▶ Drunkenness is condemned in the Tenakh and anyone under the influence of alcohol may not perform religious, legal or political functions and is forbidden to pray until sober.

▶ The command of the Torah to be holy means that Jewish people must be moderate in their use of alcohol.

Exam Tip

c) When there are different views on an issue depending on the religion you choose, you may get a question phrased in this way. 'Explaining an attitude' just means giving the reasons why a religion has this attitude. To answer this question you should say you are answering on Judaism and then use four reasons from this page to explain why Judaism allows the drinking of alcohol. Remember to use some specialist vocabulary such as: Torah, Tenakh, ordains, blessings, Kiddush, Shabbat, religious functions, commands.

Questions

b) Do you think religious people should run shops selling alcohol? Give two reasons for your point of view. **(4)**

c) Explain the attitudes to alcohol consumption in one religion other than Christianity. **(8)**

d) 'You can't be religious and sell alcohol and tobacco.'
   In your answer, you should refer to at least one religion.
   (i) Do you agree? Give reasons for your opinion. **(3)**
   (ii) Give reasons why some people may disagree with you. **(3)**

Summary

Judaism is against the use of drugs because they lead to addiction and prevent the keeping of the mitzvot. It is also against smoking because Jewish people should not harm their bodies. It allows the use of alcohol in moderation because the Tenakh praises wine, and wine plays a central part in Jewish rituals such as Kiddush.

Topic 8.4.11c Attitudes to drugs and alcohol in Hinduism

Exam Tip

c) When there are different views on an issue depending on the religion you choose, you may get a question phrased in this way. 'Explaining an attitude' just means giving the reasons why a religion has this attitude. To answer this question you should say you are answering on Hinduism and then use two reasons from this page to explain why some Hindus do not allow the drinking of alcohol and two reasons to explain why some Hindus allow the drinking of alcohol in moderation. Remember to use some specialist vocabulary such as: smriti scriptures, sins, Krishna, incarnation, Vishnu, dharma, moksha, monastic order, tantric, ritual, sacramental, communing, Goddess Burga, Devi-mahatmyam.

Some Hindus do not allow drugs, tobacco or alcohol because:

- The **smriti scriptures** classify the drinking of wine as one of the Five Great Sins.
- It is said that Brahma, the Creator, and Krishna, an incarnation of Vishnu, cursed wine because of its harmful effects.
- The use of drugs, tobacco or alcohol may lead people away from God, and make it difficult to fulfil one's dharma. As this will make moksha impossible, they should be avoided.
- Many Hindu monastic orders take a vow to refrain from alcohol, drugs and tobacco as they believe they cloud the soul.

In the Hindu **tantric tradition** drugs, tobacco and alcohol are allowed in moderation because:

- There are tantric rituals to remove the curses on wine so that it can be drunk sacramentally.
- A slight degree of intoxication and the joy that one can experience from that is used as an aid to the remembrance of the joy of communing with God.
- Feminine aspects of God are sometimes depicted as enjoying the intoxication of wine, as does the Goddess Durga in the Devi-mahatmyam (Hymn on the Greatness of the Goddess).

However, the tantric tradition condemns drunkenness as it may lead to the absence of the remembrance of God.

Summary

Some Hindus do not allow the use of drugs, tobacco or alcohol because of the teachings of the scriptures and the danger that they may make it impossible to gain moksha.

Other Hindus allow them in moderation because they help in remembering God, and some goddesses are shown drinking wine.

Questions

b) Do you think religious people should run shops selling alcohol? Give two reasons for your point of view. **(4)**

c) Explain the attitudes to alcohol consumption in one religion other than Christianity. **(8)**

d) 'You can't be religious and sell alcohol and tobacco.'

In your answer, you should refer to at least one religion.

   (i) Do you agree? Give reasons for your opinion. **(3)**

   (ii) Give reasons why some people may disagree with you. **(3)**

Topic 8.4.11d Attitudes to drugs and alcohol in Sikhism

Sikhism does not allow the use of alcohol, drugs or tobacco because:

- When a Sikh becomes a member of the Khalsa, one of the rules they have to agree to is never to use tobacco or other drugs.
- The Guru Granth Sahib says that Sikhs should avoid wine and marijuana, and Sikhs should follow its teachings as they believe it is their living Guru.
- Guru Nanak said that his followers should avoid all intoxicants, and Sikhs should follow the advice of the first Guru and founder of Sikhism.
- Sikhs are taught to shun all that harms the body or the mind. This means that all intoxicants – tobacco, alcohol or any mind-altering 'recreational' drugs – are forbidden because they harm both the body and the mind.
- The aim of Sikhism is to move from being manmukh to becoming gurmukh, but the use of alcohol, drugs and tobacco drives a person away from the spiritual realities of life (gurmukh) and give birth to mental, moral, social, legal, and physical deterioration (manmukh).

> Those who do not use intoxicants are true; they dwell in the court of the Lord.
>
> *Guru Nanak, Siree Raag, 15*

Questions

b) Do you think religious people should run shops selling alcohol? Give two reasons for your point of view. **(4)**

c) Explain the attitudes to alcohol consumption in one religion other than Christianity. **(8)**

d) 'You can't be religious and sell alcohol and tobacco.'

In your answer, you should refer to at least one religion.

    (i) Do you agree? Give reasons for your opinion. **(3)**

    (ii) Give reasons why some people may disagree with you. **(3)**

Exam Tip

c) When there are different views on an issue depending on the religion you choose, you may get a question phrased in this way. 'Explaining an attitude' just means giving the reasons why a religion has this attitude. To answer this question you should say you are answering on Sikhism and then use four reasons from this page to explain why Sikhism does not allow the drinking of alcohol. Remember to use some specialist vocabulary such: as Khalsa, Guru Granth Sahib, living Guru, Guru Nanak, intoxicants, mind-altering, manmukh, gurmukh.

Summary

Sikhs are taught not to use alcohol, drugs or tobacco because it is the teaching of Guru Nanak and the Guru Granth Sahib, and one of the rules of the Khalsa.

How to answer exam questions

a) What does judgement mean? (2)

Judgement is the act of judging people and their actions.

b) Do you think laws help society? Give two reasons for your point of view. (4)

Yes I do because we need laws so that people can work and be involved in business without someone taking away all the rewards of their work. Imagine what it would be like if you worked hard for someone and then they did not pay you; or if you had a deal to sell your bike to someone and they took the bike without giving you the money. We also need laws to protect the weak from the strong. Imagine what life would be like if there were no laws on stealing, murder and rape. As Thomas Hobbes said, life without laws would be 'nasty, brutish and short'.

c) Choose one religion other than Christianity and explain its attitude to alcohol. (8)

I am choosing Islam as my religion. Islam does not allow the use of alcohol at all because the Qur'an says in Surah 5 that intoxicants are a means by which Satan tries to keep people from God and from saying their prayers and so Muslims should abstain from them. The Prophet Muhammad said that every intoxicant (anything which clouds the mind or changes perception and reasoning) is khamr and every khamr is forbidden to Muslims. Islam forbids its followers from committing suicide, and Muslim lawyers equate taking drugs or alcohol as a form of suicide because you are harming your body. Muhammad said on several occasions that not only must Muslims not drink alcohol, they must have nothing to do with the production or sale of alcohol and Muslims must follow his example because they believe he is the perfect exemplar.

d) 'Capital punishment is a sin.'

In your answer you should refer to at least one religion.

    (i)   Do you agree? Give reasons for your opinion. (3)

    (ii)   Give reasons why some people may disagree with you. (3)

(i) I agree because I am a Christian and Christianity teaches that human life is sacred and that only God has the right to take life. If abortion and euthanasia are sinful, then the death penalty must be a sin. Also, Christianity is based on the belief that Jesus came to save or reform sinners. It is impossible to reform a criminal who has been executed, and denying people access to reform has to be a sin for Christians. Jesus himself made retribution a sin when he said that an eye for an eye and a tooth for a tooth is wrong. For Christians, the law of the New Testament has replaced the law of the Old Testament which permits capital punishment.

(ii) Muslims might disagree with me because capital punishment is a punishment set down by God in the Qur'an and Muslims believe the Qur'an is the word of God. Also the Prophet Muhammad made several statements agreeing with capital punishment for murder, adultery and apostasy and Muslims believe that Muhammad is the seal of the prophets whose words should be obeyed. Finally, Muhammad sentenced people to death for murder when he was ruler of Madinah and Muslims believe Muhammad is the final exemplar whose example should be followed.

Question a

High marks because it is a correct definition.

Question b

A high mark answer because an opinion is backed up by two developed reasons.

Question c

A high mark answer because it explains four clear reasons why Muslims must have nothing to do with alcohol. There is also a good use of specialist vocabulary such as Qur'an, Surah, Satan, prayers, Prophet Muhammad, khamr, Muslim lawyers, perfect exemplar.

Question d

A high mark answer because it states the candidate's own opinion and backs it up with three clear reasons for thinking capital punishment is a sin. It then gives three reasons for Muslims disagreeing with their point of view so all the reasoning is religious.

Glossary

Unit 3 Key words

Abortion The removal of a foetus from the womb before it can survive

Adultery A sexual act between a married person and someone other than their marriage partner

Agnosticism Not being sure whether or not God exists

Assisted suicide Providing a seriously ill person with the means to commit suicide

Atheism Believing that God does not exist

Civil partnership A legal ceremony giving a homosexual couple the same legal rights as a husband and wife

Cohabitation Living together without being married

Community cohesion A common vision and shared sense of belonging for all groups in society

Contraception Intentionally preventing conception from occurring

Conversion When your life is changed by giving yourself to God

Discrimination Treating people less favourably because of their ethnicity/gender/colour/sexuality/age/class

Ethnic minority A member of an ethnic group (race) which is much smaller than the majority group

Euthanasia The painless killing of someone dying from a painful disease

Faithfulness Staying with your marriage partner and having sex only with them

Free will The idea that human beings are free to make their own choices

Homosexuality Sexual attraction to a same sex partner

Immortality of the soul The idea that the soul lives on after the death of the body

Interfaith marriage Marriage where the husband and wife are from different religions

Miracle Something which seems to break a law of science and makes you think only God could have done it

Moral evil Actions done by humans which cause suffering

Multi-ethnic society Many different races and cultures living together in one society

Multi-faith society Many different religions living together in one society

Natural evil Things which cause suffering, but have nothing to do with humans

Near-death experience When someone about to die has an out-of-body or religious experience

Non-voluntary euthanasia Ending someone's life painlessly when they are unable to ask, but you have good reason for thinking they would want you to do so

Nuclear family Mother, father and children living as a unit

Numinous The feeling of the presence of something greater than you

Omni-benevolent The belief that God is all-good

Omnipotent The belief that God is all-powerful

Omniscient The belief that God knows everything that has happened and everything that is going to happen

Paranormal Unexplained things which are thought to have spiritual causes, for example, ghosts, mediums

Prayer An attempt to contact God, usually through words

Prejudice Believing some people are inferior or superior without even knowing them

Pre-marital sex Sex before marriage

Procreation Making a new life

Promiscuity Having sex with a number of partners without commitment

Quality of life The idea that life must have some benefits for it to be worth living

Racial harmony Different races/colours living together happily

Racism The belief that some races are superior to others

Re-constituted family Where two sets of children (stepbrothers and stepsisters) become one family when their divorced parents marry each other

Reincarnation The belief that, after death, souls are reborn in a new body

Religious freedom The right to practise your religion and change your religion

Religious pluralism Accepting all religions as having an equal right to co-exist

Re-marriage Marrying again after being divorced from a previous marriage

Resurrection The belief that, after death, the body stays in the grave until the end of the world, when it is raised

Sanctity of life The belief that life is holy and belongs to God

Sexism Discriminating against people because of their gender (being male or female)

Voluntary euthanasia Ending life painlessly when someone in great pain asks for death

Unit 8 Key words

Addiction A recurring compulsion to engage in an activity regardless of its bad effects

Aggression Attacking without being provoked

Artificial insemination Injecting semen into the uterus by artificial means

Bible The holy book of Christians

Bullying Intimidating/frightening people weaker than yourself

Capital punishment The death penalty for a crime or offence

Church The community of Christians (with a small c, it means a Christian place of worship)

Conflict resolution Bringing a fight or struggle to a peaceful conclusion

Conscience An inner feeling of the rightness or wrongness of an action

Conservation Protecting and preserving natural resources and the environment

Creation The act of creating the universe, or the universe that has been created

Crime An act against the law

Decalogue The Ten Commandments

Democratic processes The ways in which all citizens can take part in government (usually through elections)

Deterrence The idea that punishments should be of such a nature that they will put people off (deter) committing crimes

Electoral processes The ways in which voting is organised

Embryo A fertilised egg in the first eight weeks after conception

Environment The surroundings in which plants and animals live and on which they depend to live

Exploitation Taking advantage of a weaker group

Forgiveness The act of stopping blaming someone and/or pardoning them for what they have done wrong

Global warming The increase in the temperature of the Earth's atmosphere (thought to be caused by the greenhouse effect)

Golden Rule The teaching of Jesus that you should treat others as you would like them to treat you

Human rights The rights and freedoms to which everyone is entitled

Infertility Not being able to have children

In-vitro fertilisation (IVF) The method of fertilising a human egg in a test tube

Judgement The act of judging people and their actions

Just war A war that is fought for the right reasons and in a right way

Justice Due allocation of reward and punishment, the maintenance of what is right

Law Rules made by Parliament and enforceable by the courts

Natural resources Naturally occurring materials, such as oil and fertile land, which can be used by humans

Organ donation Giving organs to be used in transplant surgery

Pacifism The belief that all disputes should be settled by peaceful means

Political party A group which tries to be elected into power on its policies (for example, Labour, Conservative)

Pressure group A group formed to influence government policy on a particular issue

Reconciliation Bringing together people who were opposed to each other

Reform The idea that punishments should try to change criminals so they will not commit crimes again

Rehabilitation Restore to normal life

Respect Treating a person or their feelings with consideration

Responsibility Being responsible for one's actions

Retribution The idea that punishments should make criminals pay for what they have done wrong

Sin An act against the will of God

Situation ethics The idea that Christians should base moral decisions on what is the most loving thing to do

Social change The way in which society has changed and is changing (and also the possibilities for future change)

Stewardship Looking after something so it can be passed on to the next generation

Surrogacy An arrangement whereby a woman bears a child on behalf of another woman, or where an egg is donated, and fertilised by the man through IVF and then implanted into the woman's uterus

The United Nations An international body set up to promote world peace and co-operation

Weapons of mass destruction Weapons which can destroy large areas and numbers of people

World peace The ending of war throughout the whole world (the basic aim of the United Nations)

General terms

Acid rain Rain which is made more acidic by pollutants such as coal smoke

Bigamy Marrying a person while still married to someone else

Cash crops Crops that LEDC countries can sell to gain foreign currency, for example, coffee and cotton

Charter A legally binding statement of rights or functions (for example, the EU Charter of Fundamental Rights)

Colonialism Originally meaning strong countries ruling weak countries by making them colonies. Now it means rich countries treating poor countries as if they were colonies

Community service A form of punishment where criminals have to perform unpaid work instead of going to prison

DNA Deoxyribonucleic acid: the enzyme which carries the genetic information for life

EDC Economically developing countries (for example, Mexico)

Equality The state in which everyone has equal rights regardless of gender/race/class

Ethnicity Having the characteristics of a certain race culture

Extended family Children, parents and grandparents/aunts/uncles living as a unit or very near to each other

Genocide The mass extermination of human beings usually of a certain ethnic group

Homophobia A hatred or fear of homosexuals

Human Genome Project The international project begun in 1988 to map the entire sequence of genes making up the human genome

Ideological A system of ideas on which political systems are based

Inclusivism Believing that while only Christianity has the whole truth, non-Christian religions are searching for God and have some truth

LEDCs Less economically developed countries, which are very poor (for example, Bangladesh, Mali, etc.)

MEDC More economically developed countries (for example, USA)

Nationalism A strong feeling of belief in the rightness of one's native country

Stem cells The master cells of the human body. They can divide to produce copies of themselves and many other types of cell. Stem cells taken from embryos that are just a few days old can turn into any of the 300 different types of cell that make up the adult body

Christian terms

Anglican Churches Churches that are in communion with the Church of England

Annulment A declaration by the Church that a marriage was never a true marriage and so the partners are free to marry

Apostle One who was sent out by Jesus to preach his gospel (often used only for the twelve apostles)

Baptism The Christian rite of initiation involving purification by water. It is one of the sacraments of the Church

Bishops Priests specially chosen by the Pope who are responsible for all the churches in a diocese

Born again An Evangelical Protestant phrase for personal conversion to Christianity

Brethren The name given to a variety of Christian groups with strict beliefs about what jobs can be held by Christians and how Christians should behave (for example, no cinema, dancing, etc.)

Cardinal A specially chosen bishop who advises the Pope and elects new popes

Catechism Official teaching of the Roman Catholic Church

Catholic Universal or worldwide (the Church reaches out to all people)

Children's liturgy A celebration and explanation of the readings in Mass especially for children

Christ The Messiah or Anointed One

Confession Admitting to, and repenting of, one's sins. It is a major part of the Sacrament of Reconciliation, sometimes used to describe the sacrament itself

Confirmation The sacrament admitting a baptised person to full participation in the Church

Covenant An agreement between God and his people

Creed Statement of Christian beliefs

Disciple A follower of Jesus

Easter The festival celebrating the resurrection of Jesus

Evangelical Protestants Protestants who emphasise the sole authority of the Bible and the need to be born-again

First communion The first time a person receives the sacrament of the Eucharist

Holy Spirit The third person of the Christian Trinity

Homily A talk by the celebrant or other minister on how to apply the scripture readings in daily life

Immaculate Conception The Catholic belief that God preserved the Virgin Mary from original sin from the moment she was conceived

Liberal Protestant Members of the Protestant Churches who interpret the Bible and Christian beliefs in the light of reason and the modern world

Magisterium The Pope and bishops being guided by the Holy Spirit to interpret the Bible and tradition for Roman Catholics today

Mass The name given to the Eucharistic liturgy of the Catholic Church

Mixed faith marriage See 'interfaith marriage'

New Testament The second half of the Bible including the Gospels, and letters (epistles)

Nonconformist Churches Protestant Christians separated from the Church of England

Old Testament The first half of the Bible including holy writings of the Jewish people and their history as the chosen people

Parish A local church community

Pentecost The festival celebrating the gift of the Holy Spirit

Pentecostal A Christian belonging to those Churches which emphasise the gifts given to the Apostles at Pentecost

Pope The head of the Roman Catholic Church

Priests Specially called chosen people who are ordained to be ministers of the word and the sacraments

Protestant Those Christians who reject the authority of the Pope and bishops and accept only the authority of the Bible

Purgatory A place where Catholics believe souls go after death to be purified.

Sabbath Day The seventh day of the week (Saturday)

Sacrament An outward sign through which invisible grace is given to a person by Jesus

Sermon on the Mount Jesus' description of Christian living

St Paul The first Christian missionary and the last Apostle appointed. St Paul wrote many of the New Testament letters

Vatican The governing body of the Catholic Church and or the residence of the Pope in the Vatican City

Vows Solemn promises made to God

Hindu terms

Ahimsa The principle of non-violence

Ashrama A stage of Hindu life. There are four ashramas: student, householder, the forest dweller and the life-renouncer

Avatar The descent of a god/goddess to Earth

Caste The idea that people are born into a particular part of society according to their deeds in their last life

Dharma Religious duty

Gunas The qualities of goodness, passion and ignorance

Guru A spiritual teacher

Householder stage The ashrama of married life and bringing up a family

Karma Actions: Hindus believe that every action has an effect on the soul

Laws of Manu A Hindu holy book saying how Hindus should behave

Moksha The belief in liberation from samsara or rebirth

Nirvana The state after moksha about which Hindus have differing ideas

Samsara The process of reincarnation

Smriti scriptures The Vedas and Upanishads regarded as authoritative by many Hindus

Swami A religious leader honoured because he/she can control his/her senses

Tantric tradition An unorthodox form of Hinduism concerned with acquiring spiritual power and liberation by discovering one's own divinity

Varaha Purana One of eighteen Puranas (stories based on the Vedas)

Vedas The earliest and most important Hindu holy book

Jewish terms

Bet Din A Jewish court of law

Holocaust The ordeal suffered by European Jews (and other groups) between 1933 and 1945 when 6 million Jews were exterminated by the Nazis

Messianic Age A period of global peace and prosperity that will come at the end of the world when the Messiah arrives/returns

Mishnah The oral law as written by Rabbi Judah the Prince in about 200CE

Mitzvot/Mizvah The commandments a Jew must follow

Orthodox Jews Jews who follow all the Mitzvot and believe the Torah can never be adapted

Reform Jews Those Jews who think the Torah needs interpreting in light of the modern world

Responsa A collection of replies by rabbis to difficult questions

Rosh Hashanah Jewish New Year

Talmud Collection of Mishnah and other writings on Jewish law

Tenakh The 24 book of the Jewish Bible

Torah The five books of Moses which contain God's law and are the first part of the Tenakh

Yom Kippur The Day of Atonement (the solemn day of fasting)

Muslim terms

Apostasy Giving up or denying your religious faith

Day of Judgement/Last Day The day at the end of the world when it is believed God will judge people

Fatwa A legal opinion or ruling issued by an Islamic lawyer

Khalifah Steward or successor

Pillar of zakah One of the five pillars of Islam which commands Muslims to pay a tax for the poor

Qur'an The holy book of Islam believed by Muslims to have been written by God

Shari'ah Islamic law based on the Qur'an and the Sunnah of the Prophet

Ummah The worldwide Muslim community

Sikh terms

Adi Granth The first collection of Sikh scripture. Another name for the Guru Granth Sahib

Gurmukh God centred, one who lives by the Guru's teaching

Guru A spiritual teacher

Guru Granth Sahib The Sikh holy book

Khalsa The community of the pure/the Sikh community

Manmukh Self-centred, human centred, the opposite of gurmukh

Mukti Spiritual liberation

Rahit Maryada The Sikh code of conduct

Sewa Voluntary service

Index

Acknowledgements

Photo credits

p.1 © Heritage Image Partnership Ltd/ Alamy; **p.2** © Art Directors & TRIP/Alamy; **p.3** © M.T.M. Images/Alamy; **p.5** t © akg-images, b © incamerastock/Alamy; **p.7** l © Caro/Alamy, r © Zvonimir Atletic/Alamy; **p.8** © Li Mingfang/ Landov/Press Association Images; **p.11** l © Jill Watton, r X-ray © NASA [http://www.nasa.gov/]/ CXC/M. Markevitch et al. Optical & Lensing Map: NASA [http://www.nasa.gov/]/STScI [http:// www.stsci.ed...] Magellan/U.Arizona/D. Clowe et al.; **p.12** © Mona Schweizer/CERN; **p13** © Mark Higgins/Alamy; **p.16** © Maurizio Gambarini/DPA/ Press Association Images; **p.17** © NTSB via Getty Images; **p.18** © Gene Blevins/Reuters/Corbis; **p.19** © Sipa Press/REX; **p.20** © Image Source/ Alamy; **p.21** t © Aly Song/Reuters/Corbis, b © Clive Postlethwaite/REX; **p.22** © Pictorial Press Ltd/ Alamy; **p.23** © AP/Press Association Images; **p.24** © Samir Bor/Anadolu Agency/Getty Images; **p.26** © The Photolibrary Wales/Alamy; **p.29** tr © Victor Watton, c © Peter Morrison/AP/Press Association Images; **p.32** © BSIP/UIG (via Getty Images); **p.33** t © Picture Perfect/REX, b © UPI; **p.35** © Robert Stone; **p.36** © Luke Sharratt/NYT/Redux/eyevine; **p.37** © Lee Marriner/AP/Press Association Images; **p.40** © Dave Hunt/AAP Image; **p.41** © Steffen Schmidt/AP/Press Association Images; **p.43** © Claire Paxton & Jacqui Farrow/Science Photo Library; **p.45** l © AP Photo/Hussein Malla/Press Association Images, r © Albert Gonzalez Farran/ Demotix/Corbis; **p.47** © ITV/REX; **p.48** © Snap Stills/REX; **p.49** © Maher Attar/Sygma/Corbis; **p.50** © IHH/Anadolu Agency/Getty Images; **p.51** t © Steve Stock/Alamy, b © Igor Dutina (Fotolia); **p.55** © Victor Watton; **p.57** © Victor Watton; **p.58** © See Li/Demotix/Corbis; **p.60** © Robert Stone; **p.63** © Norbert Schaefer/Corbis; **p.65** © Art Directors & TRIP/Alamy; **p.66** © Godong/ Robert Harding/REX; **p.68** © Mark J. Terrill/AP/ Press Association Images; **p.69** © C. Lyttle/Corbis; **p.70** © Dr Cecilia Pyper and Jane Knight, Fertility UK 2009; **p.73** © BSIP/UIG/Getty Images; **p.74** © Azure Films/Isle of Mann Film Commission/ Keeping Mum Productions/Tusk Productions/ Ronald Grant Archive; **p.75** © Lime Pictures; **p.77** © Victor Watton; **p.78** © Jaguar Landrover; **p.79** © US National Archives/Alamy; **p.81** © Michael Debets/Alamy; **p.83** © Reuters/Corbis; **p.84** © Peter Marshall/Demotix/Demotix/Press Association Images; **p.85** © REX; **p.87** © Dylan Martinez/Reuters/Corbis; **p.88** © Todd Gipstein/ Corbis; **p.89** © Stephen Bisgrove/Alamy; **p.90** © Mazur/catholicnews.org.uk; **p.91** © Society of Saint Columban for Foreign Missions; **p.93** l © Alphatucana (Fotolia), r © Robert Harding Picture Library Ltd/Alamy; **p.94** © Jeffrey L. Rotman/Corbis; **p.95** © Sipa Press/REX; **p.97** © Victor Watton; **p.98** © Michael J. Doolittle/ The Image Works/TopFoto; **p.99** © ABACA/ Press Association Images; **p.100** © CSG CIC Glasgow Museums and Libraries Collections; **p.103** © Everett Collection/REX; **p.105** l © PA Archive/ Press Association Images, r © Neneo/Alamy; **p.106** © Johnny Green/PA Archive/Press Association Images; **p.108** © Johnny Green/PA Archive/Press Association Images; **p.109** © Osservatore Romano/ Reuters/Corbis; **p.110** © marco iacobucci/ Alamy Live News; **p.114** © Sarah L. Voisin/The Washington Post/Getty Images; **p.115** © Startraks Photo/REX; **p.116** © Dan Dennison/Getty Images; **p.118** © Signe Wilkinson/cartoonistgroup.com; **p.120** © PA Wire/PA Archive/Press Association Images; **p.123** © Victor Watton; **p.125** © Newcastle University (photo: Neil Wasp); **p.126** © Andrzej (Fotolia); **p.127** © Gary Varvel/Creators; **p.129** l © Victor Watton, r © Allpix/Splash News/ Corbis; **p.131** t © nidpor/Stockimo/Alamy, b © Jim West/Alamy; **p.133** © FLPA/Alamy; **p.134** © AP/Press Association Images; **p.135** © Peter Noyce GBR/Alamy; **p.136** © Victor Watton; **p.137** © Victor Watton; **p.138** © Nils Jorgensen/REX; **p.140** © Victor Watton; **p.142** © Photofusion Picture Library/Alamy; **p.143** © David McGlynn/ COEJL/JCPA; **p.144** © Stapleton Collection/Corbis; **p.145** © Diptendu Dutta/AFP/Getty Images; **p.147** © EcoSikh; **p.148** © Darren Baker (Fotolia); **p.150** © Alex Macnaughton/REX; **p.151** © Startraks Photo/REX; **p.152** © Stephanie Maze/Corbis ; **p.153** © MBI/Alamy; **p.156** © AP/Press Association Images; **p.157** © Alvey & Towers Picture Library/ Alamy; **p.159** © Reuters/Corbis; **p.160** © Augustin Ochsenreiter/AP/Press Association Images; **p.161** © Chabad (www.chabad.org/1578725); **p.165** l © chrisdorney (Fotolia), r © Manuel Willequet/Alamy; **p.166** © Niu Xiaolei/Landov/ Press Association Images; **p.167** © Toussaint Kluiters/AP/Press Association Images; **p.168** © Marc Hofer/AP/Press Association Images; **p.170** © Jerome Delay/AP/Press Association Images; **p.171** © Schalk van Zuydam/AP/Press Association Images; **p.173** © Pete Riches/Demotix/ Corbis; **p.174** © Pool/Anwar Hussein Collection/ WireImage/Getty Images; **p.175** © Kenny Ferguson/ Alamy; **p.176** © Richard Milnes/Demotix/Corbis; **p.179** © Narinder Nanu/AFP/Getty Images; **p.180** © Dinodia Photos/Alamy; **p.181** © dalekhelen/ Alamy, **p.182** © Bubbles Photolibrary/Alamy, **p.187** © BasheeraDesigns (Fotolia); **p.188** © STR/ Reuters/Corbis; **p.189** © Igor Stevanovic (Fotolia); **p.190** © World Religions/Christine Osbourne; **p.191** © Ted Spiegel/Corbis; **p.192** © Tiziana and Gianni Baldizzone/Corbis; **p.195** © Jeff Gynane (Fotolia); **p.196** © UPPA/Photoshot; **p.198** © Paul Faith/PA Wire/Press Association Images; **p.199** © Kevork Djansezian/Getty Images; **p.200** © Victor R. Caivano/AP/Press Association Images; **p.203** © Hugo Villalobos/AFP/Getty Images; **p.206** © David White/Alamy; **p.207** © Harley Schwadron/Cartoonstock (www.cartoonstock.com); **p.208** © PA Archive/PA Photos; **p.209** © AFP/ Getty Images; **p.210** © Stephanie Pilick/AFP/Getty Images; **p.211** © Brian Hendler/Getty Images; **p.213** © Indian Newslink ; **p.214** © Richard Hickson/Demotix/ Press Association Images; **p.216** © Jonathan Hordle/REX ; **p.220** © Demotix/Press Association Images

Acknowledgements

Denise Cush, Carol Miles, Margaret Stylianides, extracts from *Christians in Britain Today*, (Hodder Arnold, 1991); extracts from *The Catechism of the Catholic Church* © The Vatican, (Continuum, 2000); Alister Hardy Trust, 'The Spiritual Nature of Man', (Oxford University Press, 1979); John Betjeman, extract from 'In Westminster Abbey', John Betjeman's *Collected Poems* (John Murray Press), reproduced by permission of the publisher; extract from *St Louis Catholic Examiner*, 3 July 2009; The Society of Authors, on behalf of the Bernard Shaw Estate; Bible quotations from *The Holy Bible*, New International Version Anglicised © 1979, 1984, 2011 by Biblica, (Hodder & Stoughton, 2011); scriptures from *The Holy Bible*, New International Version © 1973, 1978, 1984, 2011 by Biblica, used by permission of Zondervan; Pearson Education Ltd., Edexcel examination questions, Q2 from June 2013 Religious Studies Unit 3; extract from *The Tribune of India*, 2003; Office for National Statistics, Table: Number of abortions carried out in England and Wales, 1971–2012, © Crown copyright; General Medical Council, extracts from Advice to doctors from Personal Beliefs and Medical Practice, 2008; extracts from *What the Churches Say*, 3rd edition (Christian Education Movement, 2000); extracts from The Independent © The Independent, www.independent.co.uk, 2013; Pearson Education Ltd, Edexcel examination questions, Q4(a) and (b), Q3(c) and (d), June 2013 Unit 3; Catholic Bishops Conference in England and Wales; Church of England, House of Bishops Pastoral Guidance on Same Sex Marriage, 15 February 2014; Pearson Education Ltd, Edexcel examination questions, Q6(a) and (b), Q5(c) and (d), June 2013 Unit 3; UK Census 2001, employment data © Crown copyright; Office for National Statistics, © Crown copyright; UK Census 2011, data on different religions living in England and Wales © Crown copyright; extract from the *Catholic Herald*, 23 October 2013; United States Conference of Catholic Bishops www.usccb.org; extract from *The Times*, 'Faith in community spirit', Dr J. Romain, 31 March 2004; extract from *The Times*, 'Twelve years ago, Mary and Daniel fell in love with each other', Dr J. Romain, 7 September 2002; www.catholicnews.org.uk, Guidance on Community Cohesion, 14 February 2008; extract from the *Catholic Herald*, 2 August 2013; Pearson Education Ltd, Edexcel examination questions, Q8, June 2013 Unit 3; *The Church Times*; extracts from the *Catholic Herald*, 17 March 2014; Pearson Education Ltd, Edexcel examination questions, Q2 from June 2012 Religious Studies Unit 8; extracts from *The Guardian* © Guardian News and Media Ltd, 2009, 2010, 2013, 2014; extracts from *The Holy Qur'an: English Translation, Commentary and Notes with Full Arabic Text*, translated by Abdullah Ali Usuf, (IPCI, 2001); © www.greenmuslims. org; Pearson Education, Piara Singh Sambhi: quotes from *Guru Granth Sahib (Discovering Sacred Texts)*, (Heinemann Library, 1994), reprinted by permission of the publisher; © www.ecosikh. org; Pearson Education Ltd, Edexcel examination questions, Q4(a), Q3(b), (c) and (d), June 2012 Unit 8; extracts from *The Times*, 9 October 2004; extracts from *Cambridge News*, 26 March 2014; © The Independent, www.independent.co.uk, 'Racist bullying: Far-right agenda on immigration being taken into classrooms', Emily Dugan, 8 January 2014; Pearson Education Ltd, Edexcel examination questions, Q5, June 2012 Unit 8; Manukau Courier; © Copyright Libreria Editrice Vaticana; *The Lancet* online, 'Interventions to reduce harm associated with adolescent substance use', 27 March 2007, http://www.thelancet.com/ series/adolescent-health; Pearson Education Ltd, Edexcel examination questions, Q7(a), Q8(b) and (d), June 2012 Unit 8 [question (c) was written by the author of this book and is not an Edexcel examination question]